DOCUMENTS OF UTOPIA

Nonfictions is dedicated to expanding and deepening
the range of contemporary documentary studies.
It aims to engage in the theoretical conversation
about documentaries, open new areas of scholarship,
and recover lost or marginalised histories.

Other titles in the **Nonfictions** series:

Direct Cinema: Observational Documentary and the Politics of the Sixties
by Dave Saunders

Projecting Migration: Transcultural Documentary Practice
edited by Alan Grossman and Aine O'Brien

The Image and the Witness: Trauma, Memory and Visual Culture
edited by Frances Guerin and Roger Hallas

Films of Fact: A History of Science in Documentary Films and Television
by Timothy Boon

Building Bridges: The Cinema of Jean Rouch
edited by Joram ten Brink

Vision On: Film, Television and the Arts in Britain
by John Wyver

Chavez: The Revolution Will Not Be Televised – A Case Study of Politics and the Media
by Rod Stoneman

Documentary Display: Re-Viewing Nonfiction Film and Video
by Keith Beattie

The Personal Camera: Subjective Cinema and the Essay Film
by Laura Rascaroli

The Cinema of Me: The Self and Subjectivity in First Person Documentary
by Alisa Lebow

Killer Images: Documentary Film, Memory and the Performance of Violence
edited by Joram ten Brink and Joshua Oppenheimer

Documenting Cityscapes: Urban Change in Contemporary Non-Fiction Film
by Iván Villarmea Álvarez.

DOCUMENTS OF UTOPIA

THE POLITICS OF EXPERIMENTAL DOCUMENTARY

PAOLO **MAGAGNOLI**

WALLFLOWER PRESS
LONDON & NEW YORK

A Wallflower Press Book
Published by
Columbia University Press
Publishers Since 1893
New York • Chichester, West Sussex
cup.columbia.edu

Copyright © Columbia University Press 2015
All rights reserved.
Wallflower Press® is a registered trademark of Columbia University Press

Cover image:
Bubble House (1999)
(Courtesy Tacita Dean and Marian Goodman Galley, New York)

A complete CIP record is available from the Library of Congress

ISBN 978-0-231-17270-7 (cloth)
ISBN 978-0-231-17271-4 (pbk.)
ISBN 978-0-231-85077-3 (e-book)

CONTENTS

	Acknowledgments	vii
	Introduction – Nostalgia: Pathalogical and Critical	1
1	RUINS OF UTOPIA	23
2	REINVENTING PROPAGANDA FILMS	53
3	ARCHIVES OF COMMODITIES	87
4	DIGITAL UTOPIA IN THE POST-INTERNET AGE	123
	Epligue – Utopia Now	161
	Bibliography	165
	Index	179

ACKNOWLEDGMENTS

This book would have remained a utopian project itself were it not for the support and guidance of numerous individuals over many years. I have a lot of people to thank, and wholeheartedly so, although limitations of space prevent me from being as specific as I would like. My first debt is to TJ Demos, a remarkable teacher and writer who ignited my interest in contemporary art and the conjunction of art and politics, encouraged me to pursue this subject and offered tremendous inspiration, insight and assistance along the way. I am also grateful to Tamar Garb and Briony Fer, whose strength and enthusiasm have been an inspiration for me throughout all my years as a research student at University College London (UCL). I thank Amna Malik of the Slade School of Fine Art at UCL for offering me some constructive criticism on chapter one.

I would also like to thank the faculty members of the Department of History of Art at UCL, where a significant part of this research was developed: Diana Dethloff, Natasha Eaton, Mechthild Fend, Charles Ford, Sarah James, Petra-Lange Berndt, Maria H. Loh, Rose Marie San Juan, Stephanie Schwartz, Frederic Schwartz and Alison Wright. Aspects of this book were presented during the course of its preparation at a diverse range of lectures, symposia and conferences, and it always came away better as a result. I am grateful to all of those who have invited me to present my drafts and to all the audiences and participants at these events. A section of chapter three was presented in a panel on art and obsolescence organised by Richard Taws and Katie Scott at the 2011 Association of Art Historians (AAH) Conference. Chapter four benefitted from my participation as a speaker in the conference 'The Versatile Image: Photography in the Era of Web 2.0', which was held at the University of Sunderland in June 2011 and organised by Alexandra Moschovi and Carol McKay. Also, I would like to convey my gratitude to Margaret Iversen for providing unpublished materials on Zoe Leonard and Tacita Dean.

I also owe a debt of gratitude to the artists whose work is the subject of the book: Anri Sala, Joachim Koester, Hito Steyerl, Ilya and Emilia Kabakov, Zoe Leonard, Rachel Harrison, Richard Vijen, Alison Craighead and Jon Thomson have all been tremendously patient and collaborative over the years of my research. The staff of numerous galleries have been crucial to the research for this project, and I would like to recognise some of them here: Florence Marqueyrol of Galerie Noisy-Le-Sec, Paris; Marie-Laure Gilles at Galerie Chantal Crousel, Paris; Catherine Belloy at Marian Goodman Gallery, New York; Linda Yun at Greene Naftali Gallery, New York; Janice Guy at Murray Guy, New York; Claus Robenhagen at Nicolai Wallner Gallery, Copenhagen; Margherita Molinari at Sprovieri Galley, London; and Annis Fitzhugh and Britta Funck at Dundee Contemporary Arts. I would like to thank Alexandra Lody, Elizabeth Robertson and Julia Crompton, who have painstakingly read every word, correcting my grammatical mistakes and suggesting graceful alternatives to my awkward phrasing. A special thanks goes to Jean Charles-Leyris at the Archive National du Monde du Travail in Roubaix for his help in reconstructing the history of Jean-Luc Moulène's *objets de grève*.

For friendship, collaboration, conversation and advice of various kinds, in various places and over different periods of time, many thanks are also due to Antonio Costa, Paul Wilson, Peter McNeil, Malcolm Turvey, Richard Dyer, Melissa Gronlund, Andrew Fisher, Alisa Lebow, Matilde Nardelli, Irene Montero Sabin, Denise Frimer, Milena Tomic, Teresa Kittler, Cadence Kinsey, Tom Morgan Evans, Sergio Martins and Margit Neuhold. Many thanks also to my students in London and Sydney, with whom I regularly tested part of this book, for their caring and engaged responses.

My editor, Yoram Allon, at Wallflower Press has been wonderfully supportive since day one and I will always be grateful for his wisdom, experience and wit as this project has progressed. I would also like to thank all the team at Wallflower Press for their efficiency in expertly steering the book to publication.

This book has evolved over a number of years. Part of chapter three appeared as 'Moulène, Rancière and 24 Objets de Grève: Productive Ambivalence or Reifying Opacity?' in *Philosophy of Photography*, vol. 3, no. 1 (2012). A section of the final chapter was published as 'Capitalism as Creative Destruction: The Representation of the Economic Crisis in Hito Steyerl's *In Free Fall*' in *Third Text*, vol. 27, no. 6 (2013). I am grateful to the publishers and editors of these articles for their permission to reproduce material here.

Finally, thanks to my family and in particular to my partner, Benedetta Brevini, for her continued, unswerving, often undeserved support. Much more importantly, she makes my life better every day. This work is dedicated to her.

INTRODUCTION
Nostalgia: Pathological and Critical

Nostalgic memories are histories of the future. Even before I begin to explain that sentence, some readers may feel a nagging concern, for the very term 'nostalgia' is usually understood as the opposite of a positive future or utopia: while utopia is the projection of a better world into the future, nostalgia is a longing for something far away or long ago. Yet there are strong affinities between these two impulses. Like utopia, nostalgia conjures up the image of a society in which the problems that beset our current condition are transcended or resolved; and like utopia, nostalgia may have a critical dimension, as it originates from a feeling of discontent towards the society one lives in. As Linda Hutcheon points out, 'nostalgic and utopian impulses share a common rejection of the here and now'.[1]

Yet this sentiment has not fared well in art history and theory. This book was born out of my discomfort in the presence of an idea about nostalgia and memory circulating in art criticism. This is the image of this sentiment as inherently conservative and ideological. Benjamin Buchloh's famous dismissal of the work of the German painters Georg Baselitz and Anselm Kiefer exemplifies this negative image of nostalgia.[2] Referring to their imitation of motifs and pictorial techniques drawn from 1920s Germany, Buchloh argued that Baselitz's and Kiefer's paintings are utterly anachronistic for the time in which they were produced (the 1970s) and that their nostalgic impulse betrayed 'a desire for cultural legitimation' and 'served the politics of a rigid conservativism'.[3] Nostalgia also appears as an inherently regressive sentiment in the writings of post-structuralist theorists like Susan Stewart. For her, nostalgia is an escapist fantasy, a social disease that expresses an impossible desire for authenticity and pure origins. 'Nostalgia, like any form of narrative, is always ideological,' Stewart remarked, 'the past it seeks has never existed except as narrative, and hence, always absent, that past continually threatens to reproduce itself as a felt lack.'[4]

The pathologisation of nostalgia is rooted in the history of the term itself. The word has two Greek roots: *nostos*, meaning 'return home', and *algia*, meaning 'longing'.[5] It was coined in 1688 by Johannes Hofer (1669–1752), a Swiss student of medicine at the University of Basil, who introduced the term in his medical dissertation. For Hofer, nostalgia was 'the sad mood originating from the desire for the return to one's native land', and, according to him, its often-fatal symptoms were 'continued sadness, meditation only on the Fatherland, disturbed sleep either wakeful or continuous, hunger, thirst, senses diminished, and cares or even palpitations of the heart, frequent sighs, also stupidity of the mind'.[6] Fast-forward from 1688 to the present, and within the fields of art history and critical theory this sentiment is still referred to metaphorically as a disease. The work of many contemporary artists who excavate and nostalgically valorise the past has been dismissed as a pathological and even dangerous escapist fantasy (a point to which I will return shortly). The image of nostalgia as amnesiac and reactionary has not faded away. Indeed, it keeps circulating in art history and theory, as demonstrated by the reception of the 'historiographic turn' in contemporary art. Emerging in the early years of the twenty-first century and comprising a large number of artists of various provenance – from Gerard Byrne to Tacita Dean, from Felix Gmelin to Joachim Koester, from Goshka Macuga to Deimantas Narkevicius – this diverse tendency is characterised by a marked interest in archival research and the exploration of the mechanics of historical representation. For some critics, this work demands critical attention, as it reveals contemporary art's complicity with the status quo. These artists' retreat to the past, writes curator Dieter Roelstraete, 'is potentially *reactionary*'.[7] Roelstraete reiterates some of the common accusations made against nostalgia: contemporary artists' turn to the past lacks critical edge and is nothing but a subtle strategy to invest art works with legitimacy; it is escapist in that it does not address the gloomy political present, inaugurated by 11 September 2001 and the Bush era; it is the symptom of a crisis of collective memory in that it perpetuates an antiquarian approach to history which, according to Roelstraete, pervades commercial culture.

A catastrophic rhetoric has been deployed against nostalgia as historians have presented these artistic practices as the evidence of a sense of social failure. This rhetoric of crisis is indicative of a certain difficulty in getting to grips with the concept and phenomenon of nostalgia. This difficulty certainly owes something to the elusive and proteiform nature of this sentiment; but it also stems from the postmodernist denigration of the term and its association with political conservativism and the idea – widespread in the 1980s and 1990s – that a manifest longing for the past is indicative of a 'crisis' in cultural memory.

NOSTALGIA AS THE END OF MEMORY: A POSTMODERNIST FANTASY?

As the story of Johannes Hofer suggests, the image of nostalgia as a pathological impulse harks back to the beginning of modern history; and yet, in cultural criticism the term acquired general currency in the period between the 1970s and 1980s, that is to say, at the time when theories of the postmodern became popular. In this period, Western countries witnessed an unprecedented boom in the development of the heritage industries, museums and archives, and historical films became a fashionable and much exploited genre. In art history, the most energetically discussed artistic strategy of that moment was appropriation, in which an artist takes the images of another as his or her own. The examples of this aesthetic were numerous: in a 1977 installation entitled *Hitler Asleep in His Mercedes*, Troy Brauntuch re-appropriated an image from 1934 of Hitler's back, enlarged it, displayed it next to a detail, and framed it with two images of stadium lights which themselves were enlarged past the point of recognition; in 1981 artist Sherry Levine photographed reproductions of Walker Evans's famous pictures of sharecroppers in the American Midwest. For most art historians, appropriation highlights the inability to recapture the past. According to them, the recycling of past visual motifs and contents was a distinctive trait of the postmodern, which was theorised as a feeling of a general loss of historicity and the exhaustion of the creative and utopian forces animating modernity.[8] Thus, when Douglas Crimp described Troy Brauntuch's rephotography strategies, he pointed out that the photographs in Brauntuch's works did not 'divulge anything of the history they are meant to illustrate'. If anything, the work suggested 'our distance from the history that produced these images'.[9]

In the same period, negative evaluations of nostalgia were developed by intellectuals from both the political Left and the political Right.[10] For those on the Left, nostalgic culture was a complement to bourgeois ideology: it symbolised the final commodification of culture, a widespread complacency, and the disappearance of revolutionary and utopian desires; for those on the Right, it was the symptom of the ossification of traditions, a reaction to the 'chaos' produced by increasing social fragmentation and anomie. For both the Left and the Right, nostalgia acted as a screen for fundamental anxieties about incipient political trends: for the former, the cause for anxiety was the downfall of the working-class movement and the rise of neoliberalism; for the latter, it was the emergence of multiculturalism due to the process of decolonisation and growing immigration. In what follows, I will consider two very different and extremely influential indictments of nostalgia which were written over the same historical period: the first is Pierre Nora's *Lieux de Memoire* (1984–1992), which I take as symptomatic of a certain right-wing conservativism; the second is Frederic Jameson's *Postmodernism, or, The Cultural Logic of Late Capitalism* (1991), which can be viewed as a no less problematic Marxist version of the nostalgia critique. Nora's and Jameson's theories are more nuanced than how they might appear from this brief summary and perhaps do not hold the same apocalyptic tone characteristic of the discourse of several philosophers and historians writing at the end of the twentieth century.[11] Nevertheless, they too evoke the idea of nostalgia as the first and foremost symptom of the decline of Western civilisation. I will begin by isolating the central claims made by both authors, before moving on to their difficulties and ambiguities.

Les Lieux de Mémoire is a collection of essays written by Nora and his collaborators that classifies a broad range of memorial practices and sites or 'locations of memory' (*lieux de mémoire*) – from monuments to novels, from paintings to popular songs – related to the production of French identity. Nora's magnum opus is based on a negative teleology of history which divides it into three periods: the premodern, the modern and the postmodern. Importantly, Nora depicts the premodern epoch as a time in which memory was real, immediate and spontaneous and did not need *lieux de mémoire*, while he describes the postmodern age as one in which memory is increasingly reified and reduced to empty signifiers.

More specifically, Nora's thesis builds upon the observation that the number and scale of the locations of memory have grown disproportionately. According to him, institutions like museums and popular festivals only serve to produce an ersatz or second-grade memory and, ultimately, the proliferation of retro-fashions and nostalgic culture is evidence that traditions are no longer experienced as organic to everyday experience. 'The less memory is experienced from the inside,' he warned, 'the more it exists through its exterior scaffolding and outward signs'.[12] For Nora, the proliferation of *lieux de mémoire* is thus a pathological symptom, the proof of a profound social amnesia. In other words, although memory seems omnipresent in postmodern culture, memory is dead. Hence, as he famously declared, 'memory is constantly on our lips because it no longer exists'.[13] Nora's lament about the end of memory provides a useful bridge to the second theorist to be considered in this overview – Fredric Jameson, a man who also vehemently condemned postmodernism as a culture of amnesia. Like Nora, Jameson tried to provide an explanatory model for the *fin-de-siècle* hypertrophy of memory. It was indeed the great success of period movies such as Stanley Kubrick's *Barry Lyndon* (1975) that prompted his celebrated critique of postmodernism.[14]

Indeed, Jameson theorised nostalgia as a fundamental trait of the postmodern era. For him, costume, or historical, films are 'nostalgia films', which appeal to the spectator's infantile desires for regression and reduce the past to a 'fashion plate' or a 'glossy image'. More importantly, the significant success of these cinematic productions expressed the incapacity of the late capitalist subject to grasp its present as part of a broader historical process. While Jameson does not conceive the present as straightforwardly amnesiac, he criticises the hyper-proliferation of historical representations under conditions of late capitalistic production: these convey the past as a series of disconnected, quasi-hallucinatory experiences that never offer any sense that the future might be different from the present as the present was from the past. According to Jameson, under postmodernity the subject 'has lost its capacity to organize its past and future into coherent experience' and nostalgia is 'a terrible indictment of consumer capitalism itself – or, at the very least, an alarming pathological symptom of a society that has become incapable of dealing with time and history'.[15] Significantly, Jameson's theory of nostalgia influenced a generation of film historians; consider, for instance, Phil Powrie's or Andrew Higson's acerbic analysis of the 1980s English and French 'heritage film', which are both heavily indebted to Jameson's discussion of nostalgia in cinema.[16] 'The heritage films', Higson wrote, 'work as pastiches, each period of the national past reduced through a process of reiteration to an effortlessly reproducible, and attractively consumable, connotative style.'[17] According to this critic, the genre was the expression of a dangerous shift towards a traditional conservative pastoral Englishness: 'the postmodernism of these films', Higson concluded, 'is actually an anti-modernism that clothes itself in all the trappings of classical art'.[18]

The problems with Nora's and Jameson's arguments are numerous. Firstly, their claims about the end of memory are often highly speculative and operate at a very abstract level. In fact, the proliferation of memory culture, which both Nora and Jameson vehemently criticise, can be held as evidence of an increased historical consciousness: that is, it demonstrates that since the late twentieth century the past has become more accessible to us than it was in previous epochs. Secondly, Nora's and Jameson's end-of-memory thesis rests on the dubious assumption that the premodern age was a time when experience was unmediated and purer and that modern or postmodern media technologies destroy memory. Yet this assumption is historically disputable: in fact, scholars have demonstrated how a variety of memory aids and techniques exteriorising memory have existed since the antiquity and the middle ages, and, following philosopher Bernard Stiegler, we might argue that the exteriorisation of memory through technology is intrinsic to the logic and function of memory.[19]

Thirdly and perhaps more importantly, end-of-memory arguments implicitly and perhaps involuntarily risk valorising a kind of traditional and static society whereby cultural memory functions as a means for the reproduction of hierarchical and patriarchal social structures. This point is clearly exemplified by Nora's

Les Lieux de Mémoire. Written in the 1970s and 1980s – that is to say, in a period when the French state was being threatened by internal decolonisation, increased political authority of neglected minorities and the erosion of the centralising powers of the state – Nora's end-of-memory thesis is informed by a deep conservativism: indeed, his endeavour to exhaustively catalogue the nation's *lieux de mémoire* reveals the historian's melancholy for the vanishing of an ethnically homogenous and imperialist France. However, as Bill Schwarz has remarked, 'what looks like a calamity from Nora's location, at the apex of the French cultural system where many privileges accrue, may elsewhere be welcomed'.[20]

Jameson's theory may also be accused of romanticising modernity. Jameson describes modernity as a period where experience and memory were authentic and unmediated and contrasts it to the postmodern, dismissively defined as a time of utter amnesia and incessant repetition. For him, the modern is an age where innovation was still possible while the postmodern is a period in which culture has exhausted all creative forces: or, to use Jameson's words, the postmodern is 'a world in which stylistic innovation is no longer possible … all that is left is to imitate dead styles', and one of the essential messages of postmodern art is 'the failure of the new'.[21] Jameson's Marxist critique tends to excessively valorise modernist art, with which he is more familiar, over contemporary art. Jameson's bias against the postmodern manifests itself more clearly in his discussion of experimental video, a genre that, in the 1980s, was characterised by strategies such as appropriation and quotation. Here Jameson defines video art as quintessentially postmodern and compares it with film, as the privileged form of modernism. 'If anything like critical distance is still possible in film,' Jameson writes, 'it is surely bound up with memory itself. But memory seems to play no role in television, commercial or otherwise (or, I am tempted to say, in postmodernism generally).'[22] Jameson's hostility towards video, as Nicholas Zurbrugg remarked, is the sign of profound conservatism. 'Trapped behind the 1930s–1950s "time-wall",' Zurbrugg pointed out, 'Jameson compulsively contrasts the apparent inauthenticity of the "now" with the authenticity of Modernism's "then".'[23] Incapable of accepting imitation and appropriation as creative strategies, Jameson ends up by discarding them *tout court*; that is to say, he ultimately denies the possibility that nostalgia can hold some critical potential.

Jameson's indictment of nostalgia can be better understood if seen within the context of the 1980s and the rise of neo-conservative governments such as those of Ronald Reagan and Margaret Thatcher. Indeed, both conservative leaders used nostalgic appeals to the 'glorious' pasts of their nations in their political propaganda.[24] 'Victorian values serve Mrs Thatcher as an imprimatur for scuttling the Welfare State,' claimed David Lowenthal, 'but [her nostalgia] is primitive capitalism masquerading as Whig History.'[25] The privatisation and expansion of the heritage industry fostered by the administrations of both Reagan and Thatcher further reinforced the reduction of nostalgia with conservative traditions, kitsch and reactionary politics. Therefore, seen within the politics of memory of the 1980s, Jameson's definition of nostalgia as a fundamental trait of late capitalist culture is not surprising.

Both Nora's and Jameson's theories are also problematic in their claim that amnesia is a fundamentally postmodern phenomenon. Indeed, they are oblivious of the fact that similar end-of-memory arguments were made a long time before the rise of postmodernism, in the 1920s and 1930s at the height of Modernism. These arguments can be found in Georg Lukács's and Siegfried Kracauer's critiques of modernism.[26] Lukács argued that, after the revolution of 1848, bourgeois art and literature signalled a significant loss of historical consciousness, as the possibility of a proletarian revolution had become more and more imminent. The connections of the past with the present were cut in European historical novels, which gradually became a dead antiquarian genre, specialising in more or less decadent representations of a remote past with no living connection to contemporary existence, but functioning rather as a rejection and escape from it. According to Lukács, the historical fiction of the late nineteenth century had ceased to be a form which offered a better understanding of the social conflicts of the present. Rather, historical novels had turned into a futile exercise in nostalgia or a pure display of literary skills. Surprisingly, Lukács's description of the erosion of historical consciousness in late nineteenth-century French literature recalls Jameson's notion of postmodern amnesia:

> [In the literature of post-1848] the past appears, more so even than the present, as a gigantic iridescent chaos. Nothing is really objectively and organically connected with the objective character of the present; and for this reason a freely roaming subjectivity can fasten where and how it likes. And since history has been deprived of its real inner greatness – the dialectic of contradictory development, which has been abstracted intellectually – all that remains for the artists of this period is a pictorial and decorative grandeur.[27]

Jameson's theory also reiterates ideas about the relation between new reproductive media and memory which were already circulating in the early twentieth century. His scathing attack on video, defined as the epitome of the contemporary waning of historicity, brings to mind Siegfried Kracauer's indictment of photography and the illustrated magazine. Kracauer criticised the overwhelming 'blizzard of photographs' circulating in the popular culture of Weimar Germany as the symptom of a widespread memory crisis. As he remarked, 'never before has an age been so informed about itself, if being informed means having an image of objects that resembles them in a photographic sense', and yet, 'never before has a period known so little about itself'.[28]

If subjected to careful historical analysis, the idea of a loss of memory emerges less as a fact, and rather more as a fantasy, rooted in the history of both modernism and postmodernism. Against this fantasy, I would argue, *pace* Nora and Jameson, that nostalgia is not necessarily symptomatic of a crisis of memory or history and that we need to disentangle it from powerful and apocalyptic narratives of amnesia. Only through careful sifting of concrete evidence, working close to the ground, can the larger claims of nostalgia's systemic forgetting be assessed. More specifically, we do need to make the effort to distinguish between those cultural practices that dwell on the past in order to reinforce current dominant political, social and economic conventions and those that, instead, evoke the past to challenge these conventions. In other words, to admit the possibility of a critical nostalgia means to acknowledge that, in some instances, this sentiment can be the expression of a memory of a repressed desire for the future.

NOSTALGIA, OR UTOPIA IN DISGUISE

Is the crisis of history discussed by Jameson and Nora real or imaginary? And are artists' evocation of the past always and necessarily a form of escapism? This book follows a different and, in my view, more productive approach to these questions, which is to consider the denigration of nostalgia as indicative of art theory's inability to relinquish rooted ideas about time and historical development. More specifically, I would argue that art historians such as Roelstraete and Buchloh seem to be unable to abandon modernist philosophies of progress, for which the affective investment in the past which is a distinguishing characteristic of nostalgia is fundamentally an aberration, a politically reprehensible and empirically untenable act. These modernist philosophies date back to Kant, Hegel and Marx. According to them history was a continuous movement towards greater freedom and reason and, consequently, nostalgia could not be anything but an irrational and mystifying impulse; more specifically, for Marx, the past corresponded to a more oppressive form of the organisation of society and therefore nostalgia was politically conservative and hindered the pursuit of the proletarian cause. 'The social revolution of the nineteenth century', he wrote, 'cannot draw its poetry from the past, it can draw that only from the future.'[29] Embraced by art historians, this particular notion of revolutionary change inevitably transforms any nostalgic impulse into a profoundly anti-utopian and conservative trend. Roelstraete also defines the contemporary historiographic tendency in this way, declaring that by focusing on a relentless excavation of the past, the historiographic tendency 'effectively closes [itself] off from other, possibly more pressing obligations, namely that of imagining the future, of imagining the world otherwise ("differently").'[30]

Indeed, it is not coincidental that in the 1980s, simultaneously with the rise of memory in culture, dramatic warnings and lamentations about the end of utopianism were often raised. The decline of socialism, symbolised by the collapse of the Soviet Union, was held as the final evidence for the crisis of utopia as well as one crucial condition that made it possible for the new memorial discourses to arise. Charles Maier was one of the first historians to link the hypertrophy of memory with the discourse on the end of utopia. For Maier, while the late nineteenth century was filled with visions and hope for a better future, the late twentieth century seemed to be energised less by the future than by the past. Maier remarked that in an age of failing expectations, 'the surfeit of memory is a sign not of historical confidence but a retreat from transformative politics'.[31] Following Mayer, critics of the recent historiographic turn could argue that contemporary artists' obsessions with the past are simply further evidence of the crisis of utopianism which emerged in the last decades of the twentieth century.

What if, however, the emergence of nostalgia in contemporary art is the sign of the *return* of utopianism rather than the symptom of its waning? This is the provocative argument proposed by Andreas Huyssen in his essay 'Memories of Utopia' (1995). Huyssen suggested an alternative reading of the *fin-de-siècle* 'memory boom', pointing at the difficulties of drawing a clear boundary between nostalgia and utopia.[32] He argued that, instead of taking nostalgia as the symptom of the crisis of Western culture and the waning of utopia, we should consider it as the sign of the revitalisation of utopian desire. According to him, memory is a Janus-faced entity which looks both to the past and to the future. 'Nostalgia', he remarked, 'is not the opposite of utopia, but, as a form of memory, always implicated, even productive in it.'[33] Nostalgia can contain a critical element, as it 'is always also a longing for another place'.[34] Huyssen also pointed out that the surfeit of memory practices should be understood more as a projection of utopian energies onto the past than as the symptom of their exhaustion or atrophy.[35]

My argument is that nostalgia is not always the expression of a conservative politics but may in fact be seen to respond to a diversity of desires and political needs: in other words, along with a conservative, reactionary nostalgia, there can be a critical and progressive one, which can be 'a resource and strategy central to the struggles of all subaltern cultural and social groups'.[36] The past can provide positive models of resistance to the status quo and show possibilities which are still valid in the present. In other words, as a longing for another place, nostalgia contains a utopian impulse; that is to say, it reveals a desire for an alternative, better world. Moreover, the dismissal of nostalgia as inherently conservative neglects the crucial fact that memory and utopia are not so paradoxical and antithetical as they would seem. Utopian visions are not always located in the future. Images of lost paradise and golden ages populate several utopian narratives.[37] Secondly, as theorist Ruth Levitas has observed, even those representations that seem to break more radically with the past cannot simply forget it: even these, in order to be intelligible, deploy materials and sources that are inevitably borrowed from our shared collective memories. 'If the Not Yet has the otherness of the Novum,' writes Levitas, 'representations of future utopias are always simultaneously dependent on existing cultural resources.'[38] Likewise, Jameson admits that visions of an absolutely new and different world are ultimately impossible, since all representation and language is in some way historical and inherited from the past. 'Even our wildest imaginings', Jameson remarked in his book *Archaeologies of the Future* (2007), 'are all collages of experience, constructs made up of bits and pieces of the here and now.'[39]

The question here is not whether the nostalgic impulse in contemporary art is necessarily a regrettable or a progressive historical development. Rather, the question is whether the very characterisation of nostalgia as escapist and pathological ignores and then discourages the possibility that this affective attachment to the past could lead, in some instances, to critical knowledge about the present and the desire to transform it. My argument possesses significant affinities with previous research in art history that has attempted to defend the recent turn to history and memory in contemporary art. Christine Ross, Mark Godfrey and Hal Foster have each tried to redeem contemporary archival art from the accusation of nostalgia, addressing its partially submerged utopian dimension. Ross, for example, argues that artists strive to 'potentialize' modernist remains 'as forms of resistance to and redeployment of modern life';[40] commenting on the work of Matthew Buckingham, Godfrey similarly contends that 'the artist is a historian who can open up new ways of thinking about the future';[41] and Foster claims that archival art can turn 'belatedness into becomingness' and '"excavation sites" into "construction sites"' and can 'transform the no-place of the archive into the no-place of a utopia'.[42] However, these authors avoid using the term 'nostalgia' as a means of defending the artists they champion and thus reveal the persistence of the bias against this concept.

What is more, Ross, Godfrey and Foster do not elaborate on the ways in which the history and theory of utopianism is addressed in many of the works of contemporary artists. In fact, a significant number of the works that constitute this tendency nostalgically revisit unrealised utopian dreams of the past or explore the utopian potential of past digital technologies and discarded mass culture. This book is devoted to them. The imbrication of utopia and nostalgia is particularly evident in these works: the return to the past is, in fact, clearly an attempt to recuperate an alternative vision of the present and a hopeful vision of progress. The nostalgia of contemporary artists could be seen as a compensatory fantasy, that is to say, as an attempt to take refuge in the certainties of previous ideologies and aesthetic movements in a time when 'anything goes' and everything looks precarious. This is the tentative reading of the current nostalgia for modernism proposed by art historian Claire Bishop. As she succinctly put it:

> The nostalgia is not for pure ('socialist') Modernism but for the sense of purpose and clarity of vision that accompanied its forms. Today, for the average person in what used to be called the first world, the future is no longer equated with a hopeful modern vision of progress (if indeed it ever were), but a seething pit of anxiety about short-term work contracts, unaffordable healthcare, and a lifetime of debt repayments (mortgages, student loans, credit cards). To an extent, aesthetic uncertainty is part and parcel of this greater precarity – hence the comforts of returning to a time when forms were the vehicle of ideological convictions, attached to a party position one could gladly subscribe to.[43]

Yet, *contra* Bishop, I would argue that some of contemporary artists' nostalgic returns to the past can be more than a defeatist escape into a comforting vision of the past. As Ernst Bloch pointed out in his magnum opus *The Principle of Hope*, even the most compensatory of utopian/nostalgic fantasies has some critical function insofar as it expresses the experience of 'something's missing' in the actuality of the present political and cultural landscape. The crucial challenge for contemporary artists today is to make explicit the critical element of their nostalgia and to inspire the pursuit of a world transformed.

To claim that nostalgia expresses a utopian impulse does not automatically legitimise the works of artists who return to the past: indeed, the term 'utopia' can be used to refer to a large variety of texts that can serve very different political projects –including visions of alternative societies in which trade union activity is treated as subversive and soaring income gaps, extreme individualism, and gender and social discrimination are the norm. In other words, as there is nothing inherently reactionary in a vision of the past that elevates it as a model for the future, there is nothing inherently progressive in a vision of the future that claims to radically break with the past. In fact, it is only by attending to the specificities of each work that it is possible to evaluate whether nostalgia, like utopia, is progressive or reactionary, critical or ideological, generative or sterile. If it becomes clear that for contemporary artists nostalgia is, ultimately, the expression of a longing for another world, we need to identify the specific content and function of this longing, its ethical and political significance and, equally, its possible limitations. I agree with Ross, Godfrey and Foster that excavations of the past might reveal a utopian impulse; however, their contributions overlook the fact that the very concept of utopia is one fraught with contradictions and ambiguities. As a philosophical and sociological concept, which has informed several political projects in the past, and as a literary genre, utopia itself has a long and troubled history.[44] This volume pays particular attention to the philosophical and critical debate on the desirability and ramifications of utopianism and thus significantly departs from previous analysis of the turn to historical representation and memory in contemporary art.

This book defines utopia as 'the desire for a different, better way of being', following a philosophical tradition in utopian studies that originates in the work of Ernst Bloch and has been further elaborated in the writings of Levitas and Jameson.[45] However broad this definition is, it has the advantage of showing how the idea of utopia can be found in a wide range of materials and texts, including social pamphlets but also fairy tales, art works, mass culture and other objects which are not necessarily meant to be taken as capable of materialisation. It also implies the rejection of the existence of anything like a universal and eternal idea of utopia, since, as Levitas pointed out, 'needs are differently perceived by different observers' and since 'needs actually do vary between societies'.[46] The form and function of the utopian impulse varies historically, and utopianism is not an inherently progressive and emancipatory cultural construct. Indeed, as Levitas compellingly argues, the neoconservative image of a free market that dominated Western society throughout the past thirty years can be defined as utopian, to the extent that it also expresses a desire for a different way of being. Consequently, to define the works of contemporary artists as utopian does not tell us much about their cultural politics: indeed, we need to look at the kind of image of the desired 'good life' that can be evinced from each practice, before evaluating its critical and progressive function.

HISTORICISING UTOPIA

Utopia is a contested concept, which has been used in different ways by different social commentators throughout history, and it has not always carried positive connotations.[47] For some critics, there is a significant anti-utopian veneer even in Marxist thought, insofar as Marxism discarded the idea of transcendence and neglected subjective factors such as desire that are considered to be constitutive features of the concept of utopia. For the critic E. P. Thompson, Marxism and utopia are dialectically opposed: while the former concerns knowledge, the latter concerns desire, and 'one may not assimilate desire to knowledge'.[48] Indeed, in

Western literature and philosophy texts that consider the notion of utopia problematic and even politically dangerous have a long tradition. Anti-utopia can be found already in the eighteenth- and nineteenth-century satirical literature, which ridiculed the utopian spirit and exposed previous utopian works and intellectual traditions as impractical (e.g. Dostoevsky's *Notes from the Underground*, [1864] and Aldous Huxley's *Brave New World* [1932]); it is also represented by those fictional texts that show the disastrous consequences of attempts to implement utopian visions (e.g. Edmund Burke's *Reflections on the Revolution in France*, [1790] and Karl Popper's two-volume *The Open Society and Its Enemies* [1945]). But anti-utopianism also can be situated in those writings that suggest that existing reality is, in substance, already utopian (e.g. David Hilton Wheeler's *Our Industrial Utopia and Its Unhappy Citizens* [1895]).[49] One of the most recent and notorious texts in this genre is Francis Fukuyama's essay 'The End of History?' (1989). Writing at the time of the collapse of the Soviet Union and the end of the Cold War, the political scientist proclaimed that humanity had reached 'the end point of mankind's ideological evolution and the universalization of Western liberal democracy as the final form of human government'.[50] Fukuyama's statements have been rightly considered as part of the anti-utopian tradition, since the celebration of liberal democracy as the ultimate and perfect stage of human political 'evolution' implicitly thwarts and pre-empts any forms of critical practice that aim to overcome the limitations of global capitalism by imagining an alternative.

But utopianism was under attack long before Fukuyama's famous pronouncements. Since the end of World War II, utopia has been vehemently contested and rejected from both Right and Left and identified with the authoritarian politics and ideologies of Stalinism and Fascism. Anti-utopianists equate utopia with those plans that aspire to freeze society into a perfect and static configuration which not only is impossible to achieve but has dangerous social ramifications. Utopia, they say, is paradise for some but hell for others. Violence, terror, conformism and the repression of subaltern minorities are seen as the inevitable outcomes of the attempt to implement utopian political plans. Lyman Tower Sargeant effectively described this catastrophic image of utopia:

> [...] utopians behave as follows: First, they develop a plan, a blueprint for the future. Second, they attempt to put the plan into operation and find it does not work because other people are unwilling to accept it, it is too rational for human nature, or it is out of touch with current realities. Third, knowing they are right, the utopians do not reject the plan, but reject reality. They attempt to adapt people to the plan rather than the plan to the people. Fourth, such action inevitably leads to violence, to the movement from an attempt to

encourage people to adapt the plan to forcing them to change to fit the plan. Fifth, in the end, the plan or utopia fails, and a new one is tried. Utopia is thus the ultimate tragedy of human existence, constantly holding out the hope of a good life and repeatedly failing to achieve it.[51]

The Right's hostility to utopia owes to its tendency to conflate the concept with socialism and communism. But challenges to utopia have also come from the Left. Indeed, a critical anti-utopianism has been the dominant trend in post-1968 Left social thought. Philosophers such as Jacques Derrida, Michel Foucault, Étienne Balibar, Jacques Rancière, Gilles Deleuze, Félix Guattari and Toni Negri have treated the idea of utopia with suspicion: again, utopia has been associated with a pernicious desire for order, uniformity and transcendence.[52] Importantly, at the same time that they contest utopianism's claims to totality, critics on the Left do not reject the need to question the current social order and continue to advocate for radical social change. However, they seem to forget that utopian thought and visions are an inevitable first step and prerequisite for *any* transformative, emancipatory political project. As I hope my analysis will make clear, the films and video installations discussed in this book must be situated within this fraught post-1968 revision and critique of utopia. They reflect some of the ambivalent attitude and scepticism that have characterised thought on utopia over the past fifty years. On the one hand, the documentary films and videos of contemporary artists tend to reanimate the desire called utopia; on the other, they warily avoid too strong, systematic and normative claims, as if to suggest that utopia is not a truly desirable condition. Their works emphasise provisionality and reflexivity over content and prescription. As a consequence, the somehow elusive quality of their utopia may weaken the force of their interventions and constitute one of the main problematic aspects of the tendency (see epilogue).[53]

***

This volume is structured thematically. More precisely, each chapter examines the work of three artists in regard to a clearly articulated question, issue or problem. This structure offers the potential to identify and explore larger trends and positions rather than merely present a collection of monographic chapters. The artists examined in this study are mid-career international artists who mainly work with photo-based media (film, video, photography) and who have been widely exhibited in the global art world. The selection of artists and works is by no means exhaustive, and I am deeply aware that other practices could have been explored, and that different geographical and cultural contexts could have been examined (in fact, the artists discussed here are based in Western countries such as the UK, the USA, Denmark, France and Germany). Yet exclusions and

selective choices are inevitable when the subject is as complex and vast a cultural trend as the one addressed here.

Chapter one, 'Ruins of Utopia', considers the films of contemporary artists Tacita Dean, Matthew Buckingham and Joachim Koester. Their works portray abandoned and rundown architectural spaces where failed utopian projects were once based. The shorthand I propose for discussing these artists' films is Foucault's notion of heterotopia. Like Foucault's heterotopias, Dean's, Buckingham's and Koester's ruins appear less as clear blueprints for a future society than fluid and real spaces that mirror some of the utopian desires of the societies in which they are located. Importantly, the concept of heterotopia allows us to detect the latent anti-utopianism buried under the surface of these seductive films. These projects convey the notion that a utopian alternative to our present world is possible and should be sought after; yet they also represent utopia as an always impossible model which will never be achieved and which may reflect society's inadmissible desires for authority and order. The ambivalence of these artists' experimental films thus lies in their implicit scepticism about utopianism – a scepticism that is also expressed by Foucault's theory of heterotopia. While they do not uphold the desirability of the current social order or reject the prospects of radical social change, Dean, Buckingham and Koester seem to be wary of utopianism's claims to totality and thus share some of the postmodern doubts about utopianism.

In chapter two, 'Reinventing Propaganda Films', I take a look at the films of Anri Sala, Hito Steyerl, and Ilya and Emilia Kabakov. The works can be linked to the cultural phenomenon of *Ostalgie* ('nostalgia for the East'), a German word that emerged in the early 1990s to describe a collective mourning for the communist past and a longing for the hopes for progress of the Soviet period. These artists appropriate propaganda and popular films from the period of the Yugoslavian, Albanian and Russian communist regimes. Importantly, these archival materials are not presented as blatant lies and examples of how mass media can manipulate audiences and produce false historical consciousness; rather, they are used as a means by which to access the utopian desires of communism and trigger memories of the past – memories that can be relevant in the present and have transformative political value. Blurring the line between documentary and fiction, these works problematise the dualism of fantasy and reality, fact and fiction, and ideology and utopia. I read these films through the lenses of the philosophy of Ernst Bloch and in particular his distinction between 'abstract' and 'concrete' utopia. Bloch's 'open' ontology considers utopia as an essential element of the real and, consequently, proposes a more nuanced approach to the relation of utopia to reality; but Bloch's ontology, like the blurring of fact and fiction of the films at issue here, is not immune from contradictions and problems. Indeed, distinctions between 'ideology' and 'utopia' – which are inevitably grounded on normative or prescriptive evaluations – are required in order to make utopia a political project involving a commitment to actual social transformation. While in Steyerl's documentary this distinction appears clearer, in Sala's and Kabakov's films it is more ambiguous and veiled.

Chapter three, 'Archives of Commodities', discusses three photographic series by the American artists Zoe Leonard and Rachel Harrison and the French artist Jean-Luc Moulène. Depicting kitsch and low-budget goods and market stalls, their projects share a fascination with disappearing and obsolete commodities which challenges traditional Marxist approaches to consumer culture. Since Adorno's famous analysis of the culture industry, Marxist critical theory has considered the commodity as the locus of a profound collective memory disturbance. Instead of demystifying commodity culture as an orthodox Marxist approach would demand, Moulène, Harrison and Leonard nostalgically record and glorify it. Through their photographic series, these artists articulate a provocative dialectical approach to commodity culture that attempts to recover some positive utopian elements inherent in capitalism. This approach, I argue, is not very far from a Marxist philosophy of utopia. As Terry Eagleton has remarked, authentic Marxism does not project the future in some distant and fanciful world or some 'metaphysical outer space'; rather, the alternative to capitalism has to spring forth from the system's immanent contradictions. Leonard's, Moulène's and Rachel Harrison's projects seem to address these contradictions. They eschew the representation of utopia as radical and absolute transcendence and suggest that we could find the way to alternative social formations in the fissures and cracks within capitalism; and yet, these documentary projects seem to collapse the notion – fundamental to utopia – that utopia is the desire for difference, or the desire to desire in a different way from what society endorses.

Like other pervasive technologies, media – be they new or obsolescent media – tend to elicit utopian or dystopian fantasies. In the mid-1990s, in vernacular discourse as well as in certain science fiction and digital art, the Internet was portrayed as an alternative space: a realm that offered a thrilling escape from an oppressive everyday perceived as utterly dystopian. Now, 25 years since it went public, the web seems to have betrayed many of the promises that were connected with its development. The medium appears to be increasingly subservient to corporate and military interests; it looks less and less like a tool for the free circulation of information and the empowering of individuals and more like a gigantic shopping mall, a narcissistic platform and an instrument of surveillance: from a thing in the world to escape into, the technology has turned into the world one sought to escape from. In Chapter four, 'Digital Utopia in the Post-Internet Age', I examine the representation of the Internet in some recent film installations by Richard Vijgen, Jon Thomson and Alison Craighead, and Hito Steyerl.

Appropriating or mimicking the low-tech aesthetic of early websites, Vijgen, Thomson and Craighead appeal to a widespread nostalgia for the do-it-yourself aesthetics of 1990s Internet; while Steyerl refuses this approach, she nevertheless invests the Internet with a latent revolutionary force. The chapter considers the digital utopia expressed by these artistic practices in relation to the critique of Internet romanticism proposed by critics Thomas Streeter and Richard Barbrook. According to them, the celebration of cyber-culture, personal computers and information networks, which originated in the romantic discourse of the counterculture and played a crucial part in promoting the development of the Internet, was complicit with the rugged individualism of neoliberal and conservative ideology on the rise during the 1970s and 1980s. The chapter asks whether one of the risks of the works of contemporary artists is the support of this particular brand of Internet romanticism and whether there is a kind of digital utopia that can be mobilised to promote collectivity instead of unbridled individualism and capitalist values.

The artists under examination in this book emphasise the role of the imaginary in fostering political and technological change. Their nostalgic and utopian impulse demands critical attention nonetheless because it shows that we should not undervalue the all-too-human need for fantastic visions, especially in a context in which the political Right is building its power on fantastic threats (from the fear of terrorism to the spectre of communism and the welfare state) and, equally, on dangerous utopian visions (from the image of the free, unregulated market as the land of opportunity to the post-Thatcherite myth of the Big Society). In the reign of 'capitalist realism', argues Mark Fisher, it is more and more difficult to imagine a coherent alternative to the dominant socio-political system; for this critic, capitalist realism suggests that, today, 'it's easier to imagine the end of the world than the end of capitalism'.[54] And yet, in spite of this, the imagination of difference is essential to all political movements that strive to produce significant social change. As Jameson pointed out:

> it is difficult enough to imagine any radical political programme today without the conception of systemic otherness, of an alternate society, which only the idea of utopia seems to keep alive, however feebly. This clearly does not mean that, even if we succeed in reviving utopia itself, the outlines of a new and effective practical politics for the era of globalization will at once become visible; but only that we will never come to one without it.[55]

Contemporary artists' nostalgia for utopia is welcome when it offers an historical analysis of utopian visions – and of the conditions that produce them – and when it exercises our imaginations, breathing new life into transformative politics.

NOTES

1. Linda Hutcheon, 'Irony, Nostalgia, and the Postmodern,' in Raymond Vervliet and Annemarie Estor, eds, *Methods for the Study of Literature as Cultural Memory* (Amsterdam: Rodopi, 2000), p. 204.
2. Benjamin Buchloh, 'Figures of Authority, Ciphers of Regression: Notes on the Return of Representation in European Painting', *October*, no. 16 (Spring 1981), pp. 39–68.
3. *Ibid.*, p. 60.
4. Susan Stewart, *On Longing: Narratives of the Miniature, the Gigantic, the Souvenir, the Collection* (Durham, NC: Duke University Press, 1993), p. 23.
5. For a history of nostalgia, see Jean Starobinsky, 'The Idea of Nostalgia', *Diogenes*, vol. 14, no. 54 (1966), pp. 81–103; Georg Rosen, 'Nostalgia: A Forgotten Psychological Disorder', *Clio Medica*, vol. 10, no. 1 (1975), pp. 29–51; Edward S. Casey, 'The World of Nostalgia', *Man and World*, vol. 20, no. 4 (1987), pp. 361–84.
6. Johannes Hofer, 'Medical Dissertation on Nostalgia (1688)', *Bulletin of the History of Medicine*, vol. 2 (1934), pp. 381, 386.
7. Dieter Roelstraete, 'The Way of the Shovel: On the Archaeological Imaginary in Art', *e-flux*, no. 3 (2009), np. See also the sequel to this article, Dieter Roelstraete, 'After the Historiographic Turn: Current Findings', *e-flux*, no. 6 (2009), np.
8. In art history the sense that art has exhausted its possibilities emerged from the works of Hans Belting and Arthur Danto. See Hans Belting, *The End of the History of Art?*, trans. Christopher S. Wood (Chicago: University of Chicago Press, 1987); Arthur Danto, *After the End of Art: Contemporary Art and the Pale of History* (Princeton: Princeton University Press, 1997).
9. Douglas Crimp, 'Pictures', *October*, no. 8 (Spring 1979), p. 85.
10. Feminist critics were no less harsh than Marxists in their repudiation of nostalgia. In the mid-1990s, Linda Hutcheon claimed that feminism 'has no tendency toward nostalgia, no illusion of a golden age in the present', and that nostalgia was indeed a defensive male response to the changes in culture brought about by the rise of feminism. Hutcheon, 'Irony, Nostalgia, and the Postmodern', p. 205.
11. One could think of the writings of Jean Baudrillard as a further example of the late twentieth century end-of-memory and end-of-utopia discourse. See Jean Baudrillard, *The Illusion of the End* (Cambridge: Polity Press, 1994).
12. Piere Nora, 'Between Memory and History: Les Lieux de Memoire', *Representations*, 26, *Special Issue: Memory and Counter-Memory* (1989), p. 13.
13. Pierre Nora, 'General Introduction: Between Memory and History', in Pierre Nora, ed., *Realms of Memory: The Construction of the French Past*, vol. 1 (New York: Columbia University Press, 1996), p. 1. See also P. Nora, ed., *Rethinking France: Les Lieux de Mémoire*, vol. 1–4 (Chicago: University of Chicago Press, 2006).
14. Fredric Jameson, *Postmodernism, or, The Cultural Logic of Late Capitalism* (London: Verso, 1991).
15. Fredric Jameson, 'Postmodernism and Consumer Society', in *The Cultural Turn: Selected Writings on the Postmodern* (London: Verso, 1998), pp. 9–10.
16. Phil Powrie, *French Cinema in the 1980s: Nostalgia and the Crisis of Masculinity* (Oxford: Oxford University Press, 1997); Andrew Higson, 'Re-presenting the National Past: Nostalgia and Pastiche in the Heritage Films', in Lester D. Friedman, ed., *British*

Cinema and Thatcherism: Fires Were Started (London: University College London, 1993), pp. 91–109.
17 Higson, 'Re-presenting the National Past', p. 95.
18 *Ibid.*
19 See Mary Carruthers, 'How to Make a Composition: Memory Craft in Antiquity and in the Middle Ages', in Bill Schwarz and Susannah Radstone, eds, *Memory: Histories, Theories, Debates* (New York: Fordham University Press, 2010), pp. 15–29. To think of media devices as 'false memory' means to reiterate Plato's dualism between *hypomnesis* (the technical exteriorisation of memory) and *anamnesis* (the embodied act of remembering), which is one of the reasons for Western philosophy's antipathy to the theme of technics. Indeed, this binary opposition must be unravelled and, Stiegler suggests, 'mnemo-technologies' should be considered as an essential dimension of being human. See Bernard Stiegler, *Technics and Time: The Fault of Epimetheus* (Stanford: Stanford University Press, 1998).
20 Bill Schwarz, 'Memory, Temporality, Modernity: *Les Lieux de Mémoire*', in Bill Schwarz and Susannah Radstone, eds, *Memory: Histories, Theories, Debates* (New York: Fordham University Press, 2010), p. 57.
21 Fredric Jameson, 'Postmodernism and Consumer Society', pp. 115, 116.
22 Fredric Jameson, 'Video: Surrealism without the Unconscious', in *Postmodernism, or, The Cultural Logic of Late Capitalism* (London: Verso, 1991), p. 70.
23 Nicholas Zurbrugg, 'Jameson's Complaint: Video-Art and the Intertextual "Time-Wall"', *Screen*, vol. 32, no. 1 (1991), p. 30.
24 For a critique of the rise of the heritage industry in Britain and its political implications, see Patrick Wright, *On Living in an Old Country: The National Past in Contemporary Britain* (London: Verso, 1985) and Robert Hewison, *The Heritage Industry: Britain in a Climate of Decline* (London: Methuen, 1987). For an investigation into Ronald Reagan's political use of nostalgia, see James Combs, *The Reagan Range: The Nostalgic Myth of American Politics* (Bowling Green, OH: Bowling Green State University Popular Press, 1993).
25 David Lowenthal, 'Nostalgia Tells It Like It Wasn't', in Christopher Shaw and Malcolm Chase, eds, *The Imagined Past: History and Nostalgia* (Manchester: Manchester University Press, 1989), p. 30.
26 For an overview of nineteenth-century philosophical and literary reflections on modernity's 'memory crisis', see Richard Terdiman, *Present Past: Modernity and the Memory Crisis* (Ithaca, NY: Cornell University Press, 1993).
27 Georg Lukács, *The Historical Novel* (Lincoln, NE: University of Nebraska Press, 1983), p. 182.
28 Siegfried Kracauer, 'Photography', in *The Mass Ornament* (Cambridge: Harvard University Press, 1995), p. 58.
29 Karl Marx, 'The Eighteenth Brumaire of Louis Bonaparte', in Robert C. Tucker, ed., *The Marx-Engels Reader* (New York: W. W. Norton, 1978), p. 597.
30 Dieter Roelstraete, 'The Way of the Shovel', np.
31 Charles Maier, 'A Surfeit of Memory? Reflections on History, Melancholy and Denial', *History and Memory*, vol. 5, no. 2 (1993), p. 136.
32 Andreas Huyssen, 'Memories of Utopia', in *Twilight Memories: Marking Time in a Culture of Amnesia* (New York: Routledge, 1995), pp. 85–101.

33 *Ibid.*, p. 88.
34 Andreas Huyssen, 'Nostalgia for Ruins', *Grey Room*, no. 23 (2006), p. 7.
35 In its attempt to re-evaluate nostalgia, my study follows in the steps of a broad revisionist literature on this tendency that has emerged primarily in the field of literary studies. I am referring not only to Huyssen work on cultural memory but also to Svetlana Boym. In her often cited book *The Future of Nostalgia*, Boym invites readers to view nostalgia as a diverse and nuanced approach to the past that may include 'restorative' but also 'reflective' elements. More importantly, she has pointed out that 'longing and critical thinking are not opposed to one another, as affective memories do not absolve one from compassion, judgment or critical reflection', *The Future of Nostalgia* (New York: Basic Books, 2001), p. 50. Of course, there have also been attempts to revise and contest the knee-jerk dismissal of nostalgia in the field of film studies. To my knowledge, the most relevant are Pam Cook, *Screening the Past: Memory and Nostalgia in Cinema* (London: Routledge, 2004), and Alisa Lebow, 'Strategic Sentimentality: Nostalgia and the Work of Eleanor Antin', *Camera Obscura*, vol. 22, no. 3 (2007), pp. 129–67.
36 Stuart Tannock, 'Nostalgia Critique', *Cultural Studies*, vol. 9, no. 3 (1995), p. 459.
37 For an accessible account of the importance of memory in representations of utopia, see Gregory Claeys, *Searching for Utopia: The History of an Idea* (London: Thames & Hudson, 2011).
38 Ruth Levitas, 'The Archive of the Feet: Memory, Place and Utopia', in Michael J. Griffin and Tom Moylan, eds, *Exploring the Utopian Impulse: Essays on Utopian Thought and Practice* (Oxford: Peter Lang, 2007), p. 20.
39 Fredric Jameson, *Archaeologies of the Future: The Desire Called Utopia and Other Science Fictions* (London: Verso, 2007), p. xiii.
40 Christine Ross, *The Past Is the Present, It's the Future Too: The Temporal Turn in Contemporary Art* (London: Bloomsbury Academic, 2014), p. 40.
41 Mark Godfrey, 'The Artist as Historian', *October*, no. 120 (2007), p. 171.
42 Hal Foster, 'An Archival Impulse', *October*, no. 110 (2004), p. 22.
43 Claire Bishop, 'Monumental Bling', *Still Searching: An On-Line Discourse on Photography*, 24 September 2013; http://blog.fotomuseum.ch/2013/09/2-monumental-bling/ (accessed 12 November 2013).
44 For a concise and accessible survey of the utopia as a literary genre and a philosophical concept, see Fatima Viera, 'The Concept of Utopia', in Gregory Claeys, ed., *The Cambridge Companion to Utopian Literature* (Cambridge: Cambridge University Press, 2010), pp. 3–27.
45 See Ruth Levitas, *The Concept of Utopia* (London: Philip Allan, 1990), p. 181. See also Fredric Jameson, *Archaeologies of the Future: The Desire Called Utopia and Other Science Fictions* (London: Verso, 2007).
46 Ruth Levitas, *The Concept of Utopia*, p. 213.
47 For an overview of the use of the term 'utopia' in social theory, see Ruth Levitas, *The Concept of Utopia*.
48 Edward P. Thompson, *William Morris: Romantic to Revolutionary* (London: Merlin, 1977), p. 807.
49 For an extremely clear and informative taxonomy of anti-utopias and dystopias in fiction and non-fiction, see Antonis Balasopoulos, 'Anti-Utopia and Dystopia:

Rethinking the Generic Field', in Vassilis Vlastaras, ed., *Utopia Project Archive, 2006– 2010* (Athens: School of Fine Arts, 2011), pp. 59–67.
50 Francis Fukuyama, 'The End of History?', *The National Interest*, no. 16 (Summer 1989), p. 3. See also Fukuyama, *The End of History and the Last Man* (New York: Free Press, 1992).
51 Lyman Tower Sargent, 'The Problem of the Flawed Utopia: A Note on the Costs of Eutopia', in Raffaella Baccolini and Tom Moylan, eds, *Dark Horizons: Science Fiction and the Dystopian Imagination* (New York: Routledge, 2003), p. 226.
52 For Rancière and Balibar's anti-utopianism, see their interview in Molly Nesbit, Hans-Ulrich Obrist and Rirkrit Tiravanija, 'What is a Station?', in Francesco Bonami, ed., *Dreams and Conflicts: The Dictatorship of the Viewer* (Venice: La Biennale di Venezia, 2003); see also Michel Foucault, 'Of Other Spaces', in Michiel Dehaene and Lieven De Cauter, eds, *Heterotopia and the City: Public Space in a Postcivil Society* (New York: Routledge, 2008); Gilles Deleuze and Félix Guattari, *Kafka: Toward a Minor Literature* (Minneapolis: University of Minnesota Press, 1986); Jacques Derrida, 'Not Utopia, the Im-possible', in *Paper Machine* (Palo Alto: Stanford University Press, 2005), pp. 121–35; Antonio Negri, *Insurgencies: Constituent Power and the Modern State* (Minneapolis: University of Minnesota Press, 1999).
53 For a critique of the emphasis on provisionality and reflexivity in contemporary, postmodern utopianism, see Ruth Levitas, 'For Utopia: The (Limits of the) Utopian Function in Late Capitalist Society', *Critical Review of International Social and Political Philosophy*, vol. 3, nos. 2–3, pp. 25–43.
54 Mark Fisher, *Capitalist Realism: Is There No Alternative?* (Winchester: Zero Books, 2009), p. 2.
55 Frederic Jameson, 'The Politics of Utopia', *New Left Review*, no. 25 (2004), p. 36.

CHAPTER ONE
Ruins of Utopia

Is there any space, whether conceptual or practical, for thinking about utopia after the disasters of the twentieth century – a century that has given us two world wars, the military application of technology, the rise of totalitarian regimes, the Holocaust and the failure of the communist revolution? British-born, Berlin-based artist Tacita Dean's *Bubble House* (1999) both poses and represents one response to this question. Shot in pristine 16mm, this seven-minute-long film explores the eccentric form of a dilapidated and unfinished construction that the artist found on the coast of Cayman Brac, a Caribbean island. Named 'Bubble House' for its strange oval shape, the ruin suggests simultaneously the breakdown of the utopian impulse in the twentieth century and its stubborn persistence in spite of its disastrous history. The derelict building was begun in the 1960s and never completed; it now lies abandoned in the middle of the jungle. Like many of Dean's films, *Bubble House* has no characters and a minimal narrative; the film opens with a panoramic shot taken from the nearby road, from which we can see the house in the far background, hidden behind the overgrown scrub. Dark emerald greens and greyish whites are the most recurring colours of the film's cinematography, while the sound is composed of the noise of heavy rain, gusting winds, violent thunderstorms and the crying of birds. The film then cuts to a closer view of the construction. The roof protrudes noticeably on one side of the building, where an enormous aperture opens the space of the house to the exterior. Finally, the camera moves into the interior, where skeletons of staircases and walls are shot against the glaring light of one of the windows. Strong beams of light penetrate the otherwise dark interior while the vivid sound of the storm and the ocean reverberates in the empty structure. After lingering on the

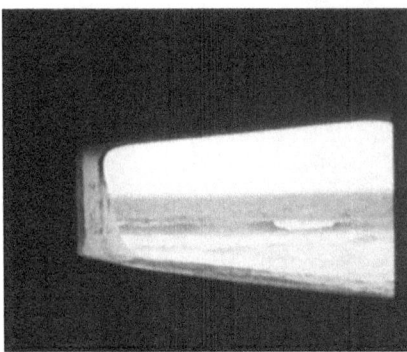

Figs. 1, 2, 3.
Tacita Dean, *Bubble House*, 1999, 16mm colour, sound, 7 minutes
(Courtesy Tacita Dean and Marian Goodman Gallery, New York)

interior for considerable time, the film ends with two other views of the building in its surroundings.

Dean is less interested in uncovering the historical record regarding the run-down house than in transforming it into a mesmerisingly enchanted place. Reminiscent of 1960s structural cinema, Dean's camerawork is enthralling: one of the longest shots in the film portrays the ocean as seen through one of the ruin's imposing windows; waves are constantly rolling and dissolving into the sea to create a hypnotic flux and, at certain moments, the ocean seems to almost enter the interior of the building.[1] The consequent visual and acoustic effects produce an epiphanic experience, as the house appears extraordinarily animated. The site significantly differs from the rest of the island. As the artist has remarked, Cayman Brac was an 'absolutely unbearable, very claustrophobic, moneyed [place]',[2] rife with the 'neat housing' and the air-conditioned resorts of the 'ideal holiday location', a 'tax heaven and a paradise for the rich'.[3] Unlike the sealed, wealthy and polished architecture of elsewhere, the ruin is open to the exterior through gigantic rectangular windows, but it also appears as a self-enclosed, protective space, which might evoke the form of the maternal womb. With its enormous frontal opening, the Bubble House also recalls the shape of

Thomas More's famous imaginary island of Utopia. In his well-known book of the same title, More described the imaginary and perfect land as a sort of crescent with its tips divided by a strait, creating a vast circular standing pool.[4] Like More's Utopia, the boundaries of the Bubble House are porous to the outside yet entirely controlled from within.

An aesthetics of ruins is a trademark of Dean's practice. Destitute architectural constructions, discarded films and outmoded technologies are the subjects of many of her projects. Dean has declared to be interested in 'places of disrepair' and in 'things which do not sit very easily in their own time'.[5] She has filmed the rotting remains of the *Teignmouth Electron*, a trimaran used by a daring British sailor who died during a solo race across the world (*Teignmouth Electron*, 1999); an outmoded and discarded sound receiver in the south of England devised during World War I (*Sound Mirrors*, 1999); and a government building opened in 1976 in former East Berlin serving as the seat of the German Democratic Republic parliament (*Palast*, 2004). These forlorn objects never fulfilled the promise of security, happiness and emancipation that they were supposed to deliver: beached on the scrub of a Caribbean island, the *Teignmouth Electron* is the symbol of the optimism of the 1960s – 'a time of exploration, of moon travel and experimentation, of pushing the limits of human experience' – but also a reminder of the tragic death of the boat's owner;[6] the futuristic sound mirrors turned out to be a very flawed technology, unable to guarantee the security of the southern England coast, and were therefore abandoned; the Palace of the Republic in East Berlin became a monument to repression and surveillance, the evidence of how quickly the communist utopia turned into dystopia. Yet Dean's beautiful camerawork transforms these places into sites of difference, flux and becoming.

Importantly, Dean was far from alone in exploring the ruins of failed utopian projects. Between 1998 and 2008 artists gave us experimental documentary films and photo-essays devoted to abandoned radical communes, tragic heroic journeys to the North Pole, the splendid past of industrialism in Detroit or the Soviet Union, modernist architecture by Le Corbusier or Jean Prouvé, and a number of works about unsuccessful nineteenth-century experiments with cinematic technologies. Contemporary artists' fascination for ruins is hardly new: an aesthetics of ruins dominated late neoclassicism and early romanticism (e.g. in the etchings of Giovan Battista Piranesi), and, although in a much more deconstructive and ironic mode, this fascination was also significantly manifest in the 1960s land art (e.g. the sculptural work of Robert Smithson).[7] Yet an aesthetic of ruins with a distinctive character of its own is again pervasive – enough so as to be considered a tendency in its own right. If the figure of the ruin is a trope of 'the reflexivity of a culture that interrogates its own becoming', what does this recent obsession with the sites of failed utopian projects tell us about our current condition?[8] Contemporary artists' fascination for ruins interests me because it is so powerfully and uniquely appropriate to our historical moment – which is to say, powerfully and uniquely troubling.

We could view this desire to revisit failed utopian projects in the past as symptomatic of the exhaustion of the utopian impulse after the disasters of the twentieth century. The century has generated a plethora of dystopian literature and cinema, from Aldous Huxley's *Brave New World* and George Orwell's *Nineteen Eighty-Four* to Ridley Scott's *Blade Runner* (1982) and the Wachowskis' *Matrix* trilogy (1999, 2003, 2003). Likewise, the past decade has offered plenty of inspiration for the production of apocalyptic scenarios: opening with the collapse of the Twin Towers in New York, continual wars in Afghanistan, Iraq and elsewhere in the Middle East, macro-economic crises and the acceleration of global warming, the twenty-first century presents sufficient warnings against unbridled optimism. The times of utopia, we might conclude, are long gone, and artists' interest in ruins melancholically laments the loss of the idea of the future as a hopeful modern vision of progress. In light of this crisis, the recent 'nostalgia for utopia' may appear distinctly untimely insofar as we might most readily conceive ourselves as being situated in a historical period marked by a post-utopian outlook. But the crisis of utopia is also philosophical. Because of its complicity with fascism, Nazism and Stalinism, over the past fifty years the concept of utopia itself has been vehemently attacked by thinkers of different provenance. For Martin Jay, Judith Shklar, Étienne Balibar and Gianni Vattimo – to mention just a few prominent theorists – utopia expresses the dangerous desire for a perfect, controlled and pure society; it is also the residue of a classic metaphysical tradition that betrays an elitist longing for order and purity. As Martin Jay once wrote, utopia is 'a sure-fire recipe for totalitarian domination'.[9] For Francois Lyotard, the classical utopia in the tradition of Thomas More is a 'grand narrative' and therefore naturally under suspicion of totalitarianism; likewise, for Gianni Vattimo the utopia of progress at the centre of the philosophy of the Enlightenment is a dangerous 'will to system', a 'mix of social discipline, repression, calculative objectivization and the technological application of science'.[10] In light of this trenchant critique, should we assess contemporary artists' tendency to revisit utopian dreams of the past as symptomatic of a reactionary desire for order and conformity?

I would say 'no'. In fact, through the appropriation of modern ruins, most contemporary artists construct utopia as the image of flux, becoming and disruption of pre-existing structures and codified meanings. Rather than belonging to a crepuscular and romantic world of death and loss, contemporary photographers' and filmmakers' ruins are often framed as sites that anticipate the becoming of new orderings and forms. Geographer Tim Edensor has well described the utopian impulse underpinning this aesthetic of ruins. 'While ruins always constitute an allegorical embodiment of a past,' he has remarked, 'they also gesture towards the present and the future as temporal frames [and] help to conjure up critiques of present arrangements and potential futures.'[11] It is precisely the challenge of reinventing the seemingly exhausted legacy of utopian thought that contemporary photographers and filmmakers take up.

However, these artists' ruins are invested with extraordinary ambiguity and even ambivalence, as they can be read as both dystopian and utopian. On the one hand, these artistic projects convey the notion that an alternative to our present world is possible and should be sought after; on the other, they also represent utopia as a non-place or a fiction, that is, as an always impossible model which will never be achieved due to society's inherent inability to overcome its own authoritarian tendencies and contradictions. As we will see, their belief in the necessity of imagining alternative modes of living is accompanied by a dormant scepticism about societies' potential to realise utopian blueprints and transcend the present.

Also animated by a latent scepticism about utopian thought is Michel Foucault's notion of heterotopia. First introduced in *The Order of Things* in 1966, then re-elaborated in a lecture for architects in 1967 and finally published as a text in 1984, this concept expresses many of the doubts and anxieties characterising thought on utopia in the aftermath of World War II.[12] Reading contemporary artists' fascination for ruins through the shorthand of Foucault's heterotopia, I would argue, enables us to capture the inherent ambivalence and limitations of recent experimental documentary practices.

Foucault's scepticism about utopia stemmed from his distrust of any metaphysical or orthodox system of knowledge. For him, any discussion of imaginary perfect societies deflected attention from the here and now; utopian thought entails a prescriptive vision of the future based on a set of fixed ideal norms: positing truth as something fixed once and for all, utopian thought may lead to authoritarianism and the repression of dissent. 'For a rather long period, people have asked me to tell them what will happen and give them a program for the future', the philosopher declared; 'we know very well that, even with the best intentions, those programs become a tool, an instrument of oppression. Rousseau, a lover of freedom, was used in the French Revolution to build up a model of social oppression. Marx would be horrified by Stalinism and Leninism.'[13] Foucault's suspicion of utopia also emerges in his 1967 lecture at the Circle d'Études Architecturales (Circle of Architectural Studies) in Paris, wherein he deployed the term 'heterotopia'. While utopias are purely metaphysical and imaginary spaces, heterotopias are real 'emplacements'. Heterotopias are far from perfect sites: indeed, many of the examples provided by Foucault – prisons, missionary colonies, brothels, cemeteries, touristic resorts – cannot be said to represent ideals of happiness and freedom. Nevertheless, heterotopias are interesting in that they interrupt the apparent continuity and normality of everyday space. Etymologically, the word denotes the contraction of 'hetero' (another or different) and 'topos' (place), suggesting that heterotopias contain certain elements of alterity that distinguish them from the other remaining spaces.

> There are also, and this probably in all culture, in all civilization, real places, effective places, places that are written into the institution of society itself, and that are a sort of counter-emplacements, a sort of effectively realized utopias in which the real emplacements, all the other real emplacements that can be found within culture, are simultaneously represented, contested and inverted; a kind of places that are outside all places, even though they are actually localizable. Since these places are absolutely other than all the emplacements that they reflect, and of which they speak, I shall call them, by way of contrast to utopias, heterotopias.[14]

What made heterotopias a relevant object of study, for Foucault, was their imbrication with the everyday. Heterotopias are not radically other than the spaces of ordinary life: that is, they are not sites of the complete erasure of the normative. But neither are they absolutely negative and nightmarish historical configurations. Foucault concluded his lecture with an evocative and adventurous image of a sixteenth-century boat crossing the ocean to explore new territories. 'The ship is the heterotopia *par excellence*', he concluded. 'In civilizations without boats, dreams dry up, espionage replaces adventure, and the police the pirates.'[15] With this poetic image, Foucault suggested that heterotopias, although real, somehow encapsulate the dreams and desires of a society. In other words, heterotopias may harbour humanity's attempt to transcend strict social relations and disciplinary structures.

Reading through Foucault's text, the initial opposition between heterotopias and utopias becomes increasingly blurred. Lying at the intersection of the real and the imaginary, they retain some of the positive elements of utopian dreams, being places and spaces where certain of the norms of ordinary life are under suspension. Owing to their attachment to utopia, heterotopias are charged with the full ambiguity, even undecidability, of whether to attribute them 'utopic' or 'dystopic' qualities. This ambiguity is certainly one of the causes of the different and sometimes contradictory readings generated by Foucault's concept. Since it entered architectural and urban theory in the late 1960s, the term 'heterotopia' has been a source of inspiration in urban and architectural theory, but also one of confusion. Critics have argued that the notion is ill-defined and that the different examples discussed by Foucault turn heterotopia into an all-too-encompassing concept.[16] The inherent ambiguity of this notion is probably one of the reasons for its success and its different interpretations: some have viewed heterotopias as absolutely marginal spaces of resistance and emancipation, whereas others – stressing Foucault's anti-humanism – have applied the term to describe the illusory quality of inclusion provided by gated communities and other semi-private forms of urban space. Rather than siding with one or another interpretation, here I would like to preserve the ambiguity of Foucault's concept. Paradoxically, I would argue, it is the undefined quality of the concept that turns heterotopias into spaces from which a critique of society's structures can be possibly advanced. One of the functions of heterotopias is, indeed, to mirror society. Foucault explains:

> The last trait of heterotopias is that they have, in relation to the rest of space, a function. The latter unfolds between two extreme poles. Either their role is to create a space of illusion that exposes all real space, all the emplacements in the interior of which human life is enclosed and partitioned, as even more illusory. Perhaps that is the role played for a long time by those famous brothels of which we are now deprived. Or else, on the contrary, creating another space, another real space, as perfect, as meticulous, as well arranged as ours is disorderly, ill construed and sketchy.[17]

Heterotopias, then, are less unique and stable entities, defined once and for all, than a relational concept which may contain a critical element. Their heuristic value lies in the ways they reflect back on the society they belong too; although different from other spaces, heterotopias also mirror them in an excessive and perhaps grotesque manner. As Foucault scholar James Faubion has pointed out, 'heterotopias are extreme – in their exaggerations of scale, but also in their reductions, their miniaturizations and diminutions, their fussily disciplinary attention to every last detail'.[18] As 'distorting mirrors', heterotopias can offer a space for critical thinking from which to reflect on and contest dominant power structures. Foucault's notion helps us to articulate the model of nostalgia emerging from the works of contemporary filmmakers. Like Foucault's heterotopias, the ruins filmed by Dean and others lie at the intersection of distinct categories: the imaginary and the real, the banal and the extraordinary, the different and the homogenous, and the ordered and the disordered. By approaching contemporary filmmakers' and photographers' works through Foucault's concept, I hope to point at the critical dimension of their nostalgia for ruins. In this chapter, I will extend my analysis to films by Matthew Buckingham and Joachim Koester, two artists who have explored the history of nineteenth- and twentieth-century utopianism through photographic and filmic projects that depict derelict buildings and abandoned urban spaces. Like Dean, Buckingham and Koester represent these forlorn spaces not to proclaim the end of utopia but to reclaim the urgency of utopian thinking today. Like Dean, they capitalise on the polysemic nature and semantic instability of ruins, which are invested with utopian and transformative energies very much oriented toward the future. What are the advantages and, equally, the risks of their politics of nostalgia, and how can we define its significance?

***

Like in Dean's work, a sense of re-enchantment animates the filmic and photographic essays of New York-based artist Joachim Koester. A significant number of Koester's works examine the history of past utopias through the representation of ruined edifices. In *Row Housing* (1999), for example, Koester has documented the remains of architect Ralph Erskine's utopian city of Resolute, one of Canada's northernmost communities and the site of another failed social experiment of the 1970s. Koester has defined his practice as a form of 'ghost hunting'.[19] In fact, several of his works appear as attempts at reanimating forgotten memories through the representation of abandoned spaces, discarded documents and other objects. Overall, three main formal devices and motifs have emerged throughout Koester's practice. As we will see, these devices have often been associated with nostalgia.

The first device is the imitation of past works of art. Koester often remakes previous films or photographs or directly appropriates them. The cinema of Jean-Luc Godard is quoted in early projects such as *Weekend* (1993) and *Anna Karina* (2001), while seminal works of photoconceptualism are remade in *histories* (2003–05) and *Occupied Plot, Abandoned Futures* (2007).[20] Importantly, Koester's appropriation strategies differ from those of postmodern photographers such as Richard Prince or Sherrie Levine. More than articulating a critique of representation, authenticity or authorship, Koester's imitation functions as a strategy to conjure up the past and to fictionalise the present.

A second device frequently deployed by Koester is re-enactment. Through actors and dancers, Koester has re-enacted old folkloristic practices from the south of Italy and Central America (*Tarantism* [2007] and *To navigate, in a genuine way, in the unknown necessitates an attitude of daring, but not one of recklessness* [2009]). I would also consider as a special sort of re-enactment those films in which the artist has resurrected various documentary and indexical materials such as drawings and photographs by turning them into short and abstract animation films (as in *Message from Andrée* [2005] and *My Frontier Is An Endless Wall of Point* [2007]). Again, these re-enactments do not have a parodic intent but should be viewed as ritualistic performances through which

Fig. 4. Joachim Koester, installation view, *One + One + One*, S.M.A.K., Ghent, 2012, double video projection, 5 & 6 minutes (Courtesy Joachim Koester and Galleri Nicolai Wallner)

the past is conjured up.

A third recurring motif in Koester's work is the representation of architectural ruins. For example, Koester has photographed deteriorated modern condominiums in Kaliningrad, Russia (*The Kant Walks* [2005]), abandoned developments from the communist era in Romania (*From the Travel of Jonathan Harker* [2003]) and the run-down barracks of the free city of Christiania in the outskirts of Copenhagen (*Day for Night Christiania* [1996]). Importantly, Koester depicts these ruins in a way that often enhances their ghost-like quality. He films or photographs them in the absence of people, or deploys lighting and colour effects that evoke a dreamy, uncanny atmosphere. For instance, in his Christiania project, Koester used the cinematic 'day for night' effect, a filter used by Hollywood filmmakers in the 1960s to turn daytime scenes into nocturnal ones. This effect significantly re-enchants the drab space of the Danish hippie community.

In *Morning of the Magicians* (2005) and *One + One + One* (2006), Koester travelled to Cefalù, Sicily, in order to explore Aleister Crowley's now decrepit Abbey of Thelema, a modest farmer's house in the outskirts of the Sicilian town. Founded in the 1920s, the abbey was supposed to become the home of a new society of freed men, but a series of unfortunate events forced Crowley and his followers to abandon the project and leave the Abbey, which now appears in a state of abandon. Crowley moved from London to Cefalù in 1920 to found the utopian

Fig. 5. Joachim Koester, *Morning of the Magicians*, 2005, C-print, 47.5 × 60.3 cm. (Courtesy Joachim Koester and Galleri Nicolai Wallner, Copenhagen)

community named 'Thelema' after François Rabelais' classic novel *Gargantua* (1534). In the novel Rabelais describes 'Theleme' (from the Greek, meaning 'will') as an ideal society free from rules and constraints.[21] Once in Cefalù, which, in the 1920s, was a very small fishing town near Palermo, Crowley rented a one-storey house on the outskirts of the village with thick plaster walls and a tiled roof. The house was named the Abbey of Thelema and Crowley and his disciples redecorated the walls, the doors and even the shutters of the house with pictures depicting unbridled sex scenes in a colourful style reminiscent of Paul Gauguin, an artist held by Crowley as a 'precursor-saint of Thelema'.[22] These fantastic paintings sustained and stimulated the trance-like experiences of Crowley and his followers, provoked by the heavy consumption of cocaine, heroin and opium. According to filmmaker Kenneth Anger, who visited the Abbey in the 1950s to produce a film documentary, some of these images were deliberately obscene.[23] In 1923, after the death from enteritis of one of Crowley's followers brought public attention to the commune, the London popular press published violently defamatory articles about him, denouncing Thelema as a site of human sacrifice and vice. Not long afterwards Crowley's community was forced to leave by order of the fascist government of Benito Mussolini and the Italian authorities carefully covered the frescos with a coat of whitewash.

One + One + One and *Morning of the Magicians* both show various examples of footage of Crowley's house and its surroundings. *One + One + One* is a black-and-white double screen projection that follows the movements of a mysterious young woman in 1960s casual attire. The woman wanders across Thelema and at some point is depicted playing drums in the garden. This mysterious character as well as the title of the film are allusions to 1960s counterculture and its subversive radical spirit: *One Plus One* was Jean-Luc Godard's experimental documentary about the making of the Rolling Stone's song 'Sympathy for the Devil'. Shot shortly after the political uprising of May 1968 in France, the documentary celebrated the revolutionary and transgressive power of rock, taking the Rolling Stones as the symbol of the nonconformity, creativity, waywardness, antiestablishment bravado, rampant sexuality and drug experimentation of the 1960s countercultural movement.

Morning of the Magicians is a series of ten photographs depicting the Abbey's interior, its garden and its surroundings as they appear today. Although the frescoes are barely discernible and the house appears in an absolute state of abandon,

Fig. 6. Joachim Koester, *Morning of the Magicians*, 2005, C-print, 47.5 × 60.3 cm. (Courtesy Joachim Koester and Galleri Nicolai Wallner, Copenhagen)

Fig. 7. Joachim Koester, *Morning of the Magicians*, 2005, C-print, 47.5 × 60.3 cm. (Courtesy Joachim Koester and Galleri Nicolai Wallner, Copenhagen)

the interior walls still show some traces of Crowley's erotic paintings. For example, Crowley's signature, a phallic symbol encased in a hexagram, is still clearly visible on the top of one of the room's walls; below, at almost floor level, a human figure, lying horizontally, looks to be engaged in a sexual act with a monstrous animal. In another photograph, a phrase belonging to Crowley's original paintings can still be read. Written in electric blue over an orange stripe horizontally crossing the wall, the phrase reads: 'Stab your demonic smile into my brain, soak me in cognac, cunt and cocaine.'

As Koester's photographs show, sex played a crucial role in Crowley's theories of magic and mysticism. Drawing on syncretic combinations of Egyptian, Hindu, Buddhist and Celtic mythologies, Crowley identified sex as the route to knowledge and liberation. Significantly, as cultural historian Hugh Urban has pointed out, for Crowley sexual magic was not simply a hedonistic practice but an act of transgressing social taboos which promoted a radical liberation of the self. 'Through explicit acts of transgression, homoerotic intercourse, and masturbation,' Urban writes, 'Crowley sought a radical form of liberation on all levels – sexual, social, and political alike.'[24] Born in 1875 into a Protestant family, Crowley 'deliberately set out to overturn what he saw as the oppressive, hypocritical attitudes of Victorian England'.[25]

For his radical subversion of religious and sexual taboos, Crowley was later appropriated by countercultural movements of the 1950s and 1960s, and today he survives in numerous newly published books, as well as in the myriad of websites that still circulate his writings and ideas. Koester's *Morning of the Magicians* could be viewed as a further example of such nostalgic revivalism. Yet his work differs from this contemporary literature in that it does not romantically celebrate Crowley's persona, nor take his demonic mythology at face value. Rather, Koester shuns specific references to Crowley's decadent writings and rather emphasises all the contradictions that characterised his life and work. In the crucial text that accompanies his photographic installation, he notes that, instead of leading to a liberated self, the philosophy of absolute transgression promoted by Crowley left him and his disciples with 'a heroin habit as an unwanted souvenir'.[26] In addition, the artist mentions Crowley's despotic and patriarchal nature: 'With Crowley as a drugged, benevolent dictator at his best,' writes Koester, 'and a gruesome, perverted manipulator at his worst, the days at the Abbey could be harsh.'[27]

Importantly, Koester's project is driven by two opposite impulses: on the one hand, the artist constructs the remains of Crowley's commune as a place of enchantment, otherness and transgression; on the other, he shows Thelema as part of contemporary urban space. The tendency to fictionalise Thelema is exemplified by a series of representational strategies which belong to the register of the fantastic. For example, the artist photographs the thicket of the garden in such a way that the house turns into a faint shadow, a marvellous apparition hiding behind the bushes. Also, in Koester's work the windows of the house appear as either overexposed or underexposed, a fact that increases the sense of mystery of the otherwise squalid and banal place. In its tendency to turn entropy into a transcendental mythical entity, Koester's work redeploys certain key tropes of conceptual art. In particular, the artist's representation of Thelema recalls Smithson's slide show *Hotel Palenque* (1972). In the slide lecture he gave about the collapsing Mexican hotel to architecture students at the University of Utah, Smithson described the hotel as an irrational and fantastic place. Significantly, the artist repeatedly linked ancient Mayan mythology to the convoluted structure of the hotel. 'Palenque actually used to be called the city of the snake', Smithson said at the beginning of the lecture; 'there were people there who worshipped the snake and, in a sense, the hotel was built in a kind of intertwining snaking way.'[28] Smithson continue to describe the Mexican hotel as an example of anti-architecture caught within entropic forces; his slides showed staircases which did not lead anywhere, dry swimming pools, incomplete walls and floors whose functionality was utterly unclear. Like Smithson's Mexican hotel, Koester's Thelema appears as a labyrinthine space with multiple facades and hallways. In Koester's photographs, the frescoed walls are never continuous, as doors and windows appear in the margins of the frame alluding to a space beyond. Also, just as Smithson conferred upon the contemporary Mexican ruin a mythical and archaic dimension, Koester's narrative often hints at an irrational presence embedded in the Abbey. Koester writes that once he entered the garden of the house, he felt as if 'the sediments, pieces of leftover narratives and ideas from the individuals that once passed through the Abbey had formed knots, as tangled as the bushes and trees that were now taking over, creating a kind of sleeping presence'.[29]

Yet unlike Smithson's *Hotel Palenque* – and Tacita Dean's *Bubble House* – Koester's project does not turn the figure of the ruin into a merely imaginary space, outside of time. Instead, *Morning of the Magicians* draws attention to the contemporary geographical and social context of Crowley's house. The artist photographs the Abbey within the sprawling suburban landscape of the Sicilian town as it appears today and thus demonstrates that Thelema is a concrete reality and not an eternal, mythical entity. The ruin looks threatened by the claustrophobic uniformity of its surroundings. Once in Cefalù, the artist writes, 'I started to doubt whether the house still existed'; 'instead of vacant lots I found my way blocked by the barrier of a gated community, or newly built condos with BMWs and Porsches crowding the parking lots.'[30] In Koester's photographs, Thelema appears to be overwhelmed by the suburban architecture of the Italian city: newly-built housing, a gigantic empty stadium, and serpentine concrete roads obstruct the view of the house, and we have to carefully scan this chaotic landscape in order to locate the Abbey. In another photograph, Koester depicts the ruin from a road above. With its caved-in roof, Thelema looks like a hole in the centre of Cefalù.

Also indicative of the uncertain 'ontological' status of the ruin is the artist's use of colour. Some of the pictures are in black-and-white and some are in colour, without any apparent motivation. Traditionally associated with the pedagogical discourse of documentary, black-and-white photography may connote sobriety, detachment and gritty realism. The colour photographs, however, disrupt the detached tone of black-and-white images, attaching an emotional and subjective charge to the representation. In the film version of the project, *One + One + One*, Koester manipulated the colour of the cinematography through solarisation. The inversion of the colour tones and the shift from black-and-white to colour places the ruin at the intersection of past and present, reality and fantasy, the normal and the other.

The hybridity of Thelema recalls Foucault's concept of heterotopia. Like Foucault's heterotopic spaces, Crowley's commune is charged with the full ambiguity of whether to attribute it 'utopic' or 'dystopic' qualities. Simultaneously dreamlike and abjectly real, both hippie utopia and case study in decay and redevelopment, Thelema is an aporetic space: on the one hand, the house looks like a haunted place carrying the transgressive and subversive spirit of Crowley and 1960s youth culture; on the other, the ruin is not a faraway island and its proximity with the rather banal and everyday architecture of its neighbourhood turns it into a faint shadow of utopia. In Koester's panoramic photographs the Abbey looks strangely similar to the banality and ordinary appearance of its surroundings. Thelema emerges for what it actually was: not an exotic imposing palace but a poor and humble Sicilian farmhouse.

For its ambivalence Koester's ruin recalls Foucault's definition of heterotopias as 'a space of illusion that exposes all real space, all the emplacements in the interior of which human life is enclosed, as even more illusory'.[31] Thelema shows how the normality of its bourgeois surrounding is just a façade, a superficial appearance of order which lacks any real substance. It discloses the self-deluding fantasy that sustains our 'normality', and the fiction that is our reality. Conversely, there is something grotesque and pathetic in the hyperbolic and mystical language of transgression and subversion conveyed by Crowley's frescoes. The ruin's crumbling and unassuming walls hint at the transgressive spirit of Crowley's beliefs but also at his trickery. A con artist and a guru – Koester's project suggests – Crowley built his superior wisdom on an illusion. Like Foucault's heterotopias, Koester's Thelema is a stage where the transgressive desires of modern societies are played out; at the same time, by foregrounding its ephemerality and precariousness, the artist reveals how Crowley's commune never completely achieved the illusions of perfect sexual emancipation and freedom it sought to achieve. Dominated by the authoritarian figure of its leader, Crowley's utopia emerges less as an achieved reality than as an unfulfilled fantasy. Yet it is a fiction that can still reveal something about the unresolved contradictions of the society we live in.

* * *

Where Koester finds utopia in those interstices of modernity that have been spared for some time the pressure of rationalisation, New York-based filmmaker Matthew Buckingham searches for those moments in history when cinema offered the conditions for an alternative, democratic public sphere.[32] Between 1999 and 2007 he produced a group of works – *Situation Leading to a Story* (1999), *One Side of Broadway* (2005) and *False Future* (2007) – that investigates the early history of the moving image. *Situation Leading to a Story* relates the artist's attempt to track the owner of four short home movies that he accidentally found on a New York street. Dating back to early twentieth century, they depict a family in their cottage enjoying moments of leisure time, the construction of a tramway in the Andes by the American mining company Cerro de Pasco, and a bullfight at dusk in Guadalajara, Mexico. The artist finds the owner of the movies, Harrison Dennis, in an outdated Manhattan phone book, but Dennis professes not to remember throwing out the films and hangs up before Buckingham can ask what they contained. The mysteries of the movies remain unsolved, their stories adrift. This lack of narrative closure is presented by Buckingham not as failure but rather as an opportunity for the viewer to construct her own interpretation of the documents and to reflect on their own desires and projections. With its inherent incompleteness, home-movie production epitomises the utopian idea of an active, 'emancipated' spectator who is capable of appropriating previously inaccessible documents and producing her own history against the authority of the narrator as well as official and professional historians.[33] Thus, Buckingham's film hints at the ideal of an open, incomplete archive accessible by anyone, including subaltern and disenfranchised groups. 'Archiving', the artist has declared, 'is in some sense, a utopic project ... which may act as a mobilizing agent, as a catalyst for real change.'[34] With its fragmentary and open-ended narration, *Situation Leading to a Story* attempts to preserve the altruistic quality and social dimension of home-movie making. The slogan 'Make your movie camera the family historian', used by Eastman Kodak to market early home-movie cameras and quoted by Buckingham in one crucial passage of the film, sums up this utopian idea of amateur cinema as a kind of history writing from below.

Also exploring early cinema as a utopian model are Buckingham's *One Side of Broadway* (2005) and *False Future* (2007). Here the artist has re-enacted some forgotten cinematic and photographic experiments from the late nineteenth and early twentieth century. *One Side of Broadway* is a continuous slide installation that recreates Rudolph DeLeeuw's ambitious photographic book *Both Sides of Broadway*. Published in 1910, the book contained photographs of every building on both west and east sides of Broadway, in Manhattan. Buckingham's project depicts every block on the east side of Broadway, as it appears today through a series of black-and-white slides that begins in Bowling Green, in Lower Manhattan, and ends in Central Park (the work is also reminiscent of Ed Ruscha's seminal photo-book *Every Building on the Sunset Strip*, a foldout panorama of each house on both sides of Sunset Boulevard in Los Angeles). The projection is accompanied by a voiceover narration consisting of Buckingham's scattered reflections on DeLeeuw's fascination for Broadway, the invention of cinema and the widespread presence of nickelodeon and movie theatres in early twentieth-century New York. While the narrator describes DeLeeuw's Broadway as an energetic space teeming with working-class people, the slides portray the contemporary street as an empty and almost forlorn avenue: in Buckingham's pictures bystanders aggressively refuse to be photographed, and it has now become illegal to take photographs of many buildings. In *False Future* the artist has imitated one of August Le Prince's cinematic experiments: a still shot of a bridge in central Leeds captured by Le Prince in 1886, nine years before the Lumière brothers announced the invention of cinema. However, twenty-first-century Leeds, as shot by Buckingham, is not the lively and chaotic space of Le Prince's movie. Its traffic is orderly and few pedestrians walk on the bridge. Both *One Side of Broadway* and *False Future* suggest that modern urban space has been radically transformed throughout the twentieth and twenty-first centuries. From the stage where potentially transforming chance encounters could have happened and where different social and ethnic groups used to mingle, the city has turned into a space of frictionless monotony and surveillance.

Buckingham, of course, is not the first artist to appropriate early cinema. In the late 1960s and 1970s numerous avant-garde filmmakers turned to cinematic archives as a creative resource. In Ken Jacobs' film *Tom Tom the Piper's Son* (1969) and Ernie Gehr's *Eureka* (1979), early cinema was appropriated and manipulated through a variety of techniques. In *Tom Tom the Piper's Son*, Jacobs dissected a 1905 film through slow-motion, stop-motion, frame enlargement, cropping and repetition. And in *Eureka* Gehr re-photographed and slowed down by seven times a 1903 documentary film shot from the front of a trolley in San Francisco. For many of these filmmakers early films embodied a time when a low-budget, experimental cinema offered an alternative practice to the later conventional Hollywood one. Importantly, early films epitomised a model of filmmaking seemingly unburdened by the pressures of narrative, a taboo for structural filmmakers largely influenced by sculptural and phenomenological models. As film historian Tom Gunning has pointed out, the avant-garde has always been attracted to early cinema for 'its freedom from the creation of a diegesis [and] its accent on direct stimulation'.[35] Likewise, as we have seen, Buckingham's nostalgic fascination for home movies is a product of their spontaneity, their diversity and their capacity to capture the contingent moments of everyday life. In addition, early cinema represented a more inclusive and democratic public sphere. A social event attended by peripheral and disenfranchised groups and ethnic minorities, early film exhibitions were a mix of live performance and recorded spectacle that allowed for a margin of improvisation, interpretation and unpredictability in stark contrast to the structured form of subsequent Hollywood cinema.[36]

Through the reference to early cinema, Buckingham advocates the return to a visual culture capable of offering a proletarian public sphere. Nevertheless, a trademark of the artist's work is that his films always shun straightforward depictions of the past and always avoid providing representations of what a 'perfect society' could look like: while introduced as utopic sites, Le Prince's Leeds or DeLeeuw's Broadway are conjured up by the evocative voiceover narration but are not shown by the artist. Buckingham conceives utopia as an impossible, unrealisable and, therefore, always fictive model. Just as for Foucault, utopias are, for the artist, only imaginary constructions. 'I think it is important to look at Utopia not as something that is intended to succeed,' he has declared, 'but as a fiction that is meant as a critique of the present moment.'[37] Also emerging as a 'fiction' is the free town of Christiania in Buckingham's *Sandra of the Tulip House or How to Live in a Free State* (2001).

Made in collaboration with Joachim Koester, *Sandra of the Tulip House...* is an 86-minute, five-channel video projection and sound installation that explores the space and history of Christiania, a community of squatters founded in Copenhagen in 1971 by a group of social-housing activists. Inspired by anti-capitalist and anarchic principles, the group broke through the fences of an abandoned seventeenth-century military base that occupies 32 hectares of land owned by the Danish Ministry of Defence. Buckingham 'fictionalises' Christiania through various strategies. One of them is to describe the place as if seen through the eyes of an imaginary traveller. The images and voiceover of Buckingham's film convey a first-person narrative about an invented character named Sandra, a young student from Goteborg who takes a trip to Copenhagen and incidentally finds hospitality in Christiania. Travel to a foreign place and to another time is indeed a central trope of the literary genre of utopian fiction from Thomas More to H. G. Wells. Indeed, Christiania becomes also the point of departure through which to explore different times and histories. While wandering around the free town, Sandra weaves together a constellation of stories tangentially related to the site: the construction of Christiania as a military base in the seventeenth century; the function of harbour fortifications in European urban history; the invention and commercialisation of heroin by a German pharmaceutical industry; the obsolescence and symbolic use of armour in the eighteenth century; the adventurous life of Dutch captain Jan Janszoon, who became the governor of the Corsair Republic of Salé, in Morocco, and whose flag resembles the flag of Christiania. Disparate footage accompanies this intricate narration: old photographs of Christiania military headquarters and Danish soldiers; black-and-white portraits of the squatters who founded the hippie community in the 1970s; Peter Isaascz's portrait of Prince Frederik of Denmark holding a rifle from 1615; maps and architectural renderings of late seventeenth-century European city fortifications. Christiania then emerges as a sort of unpredictable and somehow even chaotic time machine. The sense of dispersion and fragmentation provided by the voiceover narration is further amplified by the raw editing of the footage and by the spatial form of the installation: different segments of the films are projected onto five screens and replayed within each projection according to a random order. In addition, dome-shaped speakers create slightly overlapping but distinct pools of sound in front of each screen.

Fig. 8. Matthew Buckingham and Joachim Koester, Installation view, *Sandra of the Tulip House or How to Live in a Free State*, Statens Museum for Kunst, Copenhagen, 2001 (Courtesy Matthew Buckingham and Joachim Koester; Gallery Murray Guy, New York)

Buckingham's representational strategies turn Christiania into an opaque and labyrinthic place in order to suspend and confound clear-cut interpretations. The camera never offers the viewer a clear sense of Christiania's location in relation to the city of Copenhagen. It creates a sense of mystery and suspense through the darkness of the cinematography: Buckingham films the path traversing the town's green areas at dawn or sunset (we do not know exactly when); glimpses of the interiors of the squatters' houses alternate with slow panoramic shots of the colourful barracks; however, we are never shown the members of the community, and as a result the city ultimately emerges as a mysterious ghost town. Buckingham's camera focuses on the backyards – cluttered with trash, disintegrating objects and debris, offering only fragmentary clues about the lives of the city's inhabitants; Christiania's flag, three yellow dots over a red ground, is everywhere, but its meaning is no more clear. In a crucial sequence of the film, Sandra, the protagonist and a temporary visitor to the community, discusses the meaning of the flag. This strange sign, she surmises, is an 'ellipsis, or points of suspension', that indicates 'an omission, faltering speech, or an incomplete thought in a printed text. [...] Wherever one of these ellipses appears, it

Figs. 9, 10, 11, 12. Matthew Buckingham and Joachim Koester, *Sandra of the Tulip House or How to Live in a Free State*, 2001, continuous five colour channel video projection with sound, 86 minutes, screen dimensions variable (Courtesy Matthew Buckingham and Joachim Koester; Gallery Murray Guy, New York)

seems to interrupt its surroundings – punctuating it with doubt.'[38] Like its flag, Christiania appears less as a determined and univocal site than as an enigmatic, coded message waiting to be deciphered.

Likewise, Buckingham does not offer a clear-cut response to the issue of whether or not Christiania is a failed utopia. Despite providing a wealth of information about parallel and sometimes farfetched histories, Buckingham's film does not dwell on the specific ideology of the community's founders, and neither does it address the conflicts between Christiania and the Danish government.[39] Since its inception Christiania has been the object of scathing criticism from mainstream media and conservative parties, which consider the place as a shelter for drug pushers and very profitable drug trafficking, and call for the restitution of the land to the state. Over the past fifteen years, in a climate of increased conservativism, the government has tried to implement a 'normalisation plan' which will introduce individual property ownership and a gradual shift towards market values for the formerly collectively-owned property. Christiania's inhabitants have reacted by building walls and other physical separations to prevent intrusions from outsiders and the police. The community is under attack even from the Left: according to some critics, the governance of Christiania is far from democratic, as older members have more decisional power than younger ones; in addition, the group of drug pushers living in the community represents an egoistic, aggressive and materialistic culture that is indifferent to the sense of solidarity and responsibility that pervaded the declarations of its founders. The values originally embodied by Christiania seem to have been betrayed in its short but contentious history. Therefore, the squatter town has often been discussed in Scandinavia as a 'failed utopia'.

If Buckingham's film does not dwell on much of this criticism, neither does it romanticise Christiania. In fact, the voiceover narration and montage draw a parallel between the squatter town and its military past. 'Historians of ideas', Sandra informs us, 'usually attribute the dream of a perfect society to philosophers, but there is also a military dream of society, a dream that depends on artificial kinship relations that can be created in military bases. [...] Spaces like this are not meant to be perfect social environments, but, instead, places in which society itself can be perfected.'[40] Buckingham thus suggests that Christiania resonates historically and politically with its site, an ex-military base. As in all utopian social experiments, there is an authoritarian and exclusionary dimension within all free cities. Like Foucault's heterotopia, the free town is not the epitome of absolute radical difference: rather, it is a site that mirrors the contradictions and limitations of the society to which it belongs and cannot escape from. Buckingham's Christiania also parallels Foucault's notion of heterotopia for another reason. 'Heterotopias', wrote Foucault, 'desiccate speech, stop words in their tracks, contest the very possibility of grammar at its source.'[41] Heterotopias are exceptions that differ so greatly from all categories that they cannot be fitted and fixed into any rigid taxonomy. Likewise, in *Sandra of the Tulip House…* Christiania appears as a detonator of order, logic and language, an almost unrepresentable arrangement. Against the notion of utopia as a closed and orthodox system of knowledge, Christiania is, for Buckingham, a figure of the momentary suspension and inconclusiveness of meaning.

* * *

Are all utopian projects animated by an authoritarian 'will to order'? So argued French novelist George Perec. 'All utopias', he wrote, 'are depressing because they leave no room to chance, to difference, to those who are "different".'[42] The problem with utopia is that its believers, while attempting to transcend the limits of the present, end up imposing their blueprints for a better and alternative world on the rest of society. Utopian thinking is just a parlour game for intellectuals who set themselves the task of designing a future society without leaving their ivory towers. However, as Perec would remind us, what is utopian for a particular segment of society is dystopian for another and, therefore, utopian dreams are tragically doomed to fail, crashing against the complexity of the real world. Through their films and photographic essays, contemporary artists challenge this negative notion of utopia. Revisiting the abandoned sites of unrealised dreams of the past, they turn them into spaces of contingency that anticipate the becoming of new forms and orderings. Artists' ruins symbolise utopia not as perfect stasis but as difference and becoming. That's why Foucault's concept of heterotopia is a productive lens through which to discuss these artists' practices: with its etymological root in the word 'hetero' (another), the term implicitly suggests the idea of radical difference. As heterotopic space, contemporary artists' ruins, we might conclude, evoke the notion of radical otherness and the complete erasure of the normative and disciplinary power of modern reason. They are utopias of difference and immanence.

Yet by coining the term 'heterotopia', Foucault was not suggesting that radical difference is possible. This reductive interpretation of the concept owes to the appropriation of Foucault's lecture by postmodernism – an academic discourse celebrating above all heterogeneity and otherness. Although circulating in the architectural field more as a rumour than as a codified concept since the late 1960s, Foucault's essay remained fairly unnoticed until 1984, when it was finally published and suddenly became popular in urban and spatial theory at the climax of postmodernism.[43] Heterotopia was the antidote to the erasure of differences by global capitalism – capitalism whose logic, according to Jameson, is the homogenisation of all cultures.[44] While deploying the term as a periodising concept, Gianni Vattimo nevertheless invested it with straightforwardly positive connotations. He claimed that the movement from modernity to postmodernity entails the passage from utopia to heterotopia, that is, the transition from a linear conception of time and history to one characterised by the coexistence of multiple transient events and different temporal narratives.[45] The ruined landscape of the post-apocalyptic city of Ridley Scott's *Blade Runner*, Vattimo remarked, represents heterotopia as a condition of generative chaos and possibility.

In architectural discourse and geography, Foucault's term was appropriated for its alleged potential to be the foundation for a new conception of urban planning, based on the principles of other spaces that contest the spaces we inhabit. Influenced by postmodernism, urban theorists and geographers imbued the notion of heterotopia with excessively positive connotations, applying the term to those neglected spaces inhabited by minority and marginal subgroups. They endowed all extravagant formations with almost mythical, ideal capacities, and the subtle nuances of Foucault's term have been somehow lost. Indeed, part of the difficulty – but also the intricacy and fascination – of this concept is that it involves thinking difference as a relation. Heterotopias are not completely separated from the regimented spaces of the society they belong to: despite their apparent distinctness, they are these spaces' inverted mirrors and share with them some characteristics and limitations. That is why heterotopias should not be overtly romanticised: their value stems not from any intrinsic property they might possess but from the critical insights they can offer about the context in which they are located.

Transforming abandoned modern sites into heterotopic spaces, the aesthetic of ruins of contemporary artists can be problematic if it neglects the relational dimension of heterotopias in favour of an uncritical and purely formalist celebration of contingency and marginality. The virtues of decay and entropy can be excessively extolled, ignoring the contextual economic and social devastation that ruins evidence and the role of finance and government in their creation. This risk has become more pronounced as, in the post-recession time, images of urban hopelessness and industrial decay have become extremely popular in art and visual culture – enough so that the term 'ruin porn' has been coined to designate this pervasive genre. To borrow the words of a critic, much ruin photography and ruin film 'aestheticizes poverty without inquiring of its origins, dramatizes spaces but never seeks out the people who inhabit and transform them, and romanticizes isolated acts of resistance without acknowledging the massive political and social forces aligned against the real transformation, and not just stubborn survival, of the city'.[46]

The danger of aestheticising ruins and decay is perhaps more pronounced in the works of Tacita Dean than in the films of Joachim Koester and Matthew Buckingham. Lacking voiceover commentary, Dean's seductive cinematography and richly layered soundtrack construct the Bubble House as a heterotopic space of chance and flux which resonates well with the celebration of alterity typical of postmodernism. However, the relation between the ruin and late capitalism is missing as the artist's minimalist film style withdraws crucial information about the historical and economic context of the ruin. The house is located in an island that is one the major financial centres and tax havens in the world, and its developer was himself a wealthy banker who was sentenced to 35 years in prison for embezzling money from the United States government. Emphasising this background information would have allowed the viewer to better understand the function of ruins within late capitalism. The dilapidated construction can be considered both as a space of difference and also as a byproduct of a fraudulent economic and political system in which the Bubble House's owner was an accomplice. And yet this line of enquiry is not pursued by Dean; while she mentions the story of the developer of the futuristic building, this is not central to her film (in the artist's writings and interviews, this man almost emerges as a romantic and tragic figure: 'This Frenchman got arrested for fraud and he is doing 35 years in Tampa Prison, which is an horrific amount').[47]

Other significant historical and political resonances are somehow buried within Dean's film. One of them is the Bubble House's resemblance to one of the most popular objects of countercultural architecture: the geodesic dome. Created in the late 1940s by visionary designer Buckminster Fuller, who envisioned it as a hyper-efficient, repeatable and universal dwelling, the dome became an icon of several hippie and artistic communes across the USA in the 1960s (today, this spherical structure is still widely employed by architects as an argument against eroding the public functions of the city street).[48] Within the American counterculture, the geodesic dome epitomised the utopian project of creating sustainable modes of living through the use of technology. To build these makeshift dwellings, the members of communes such as Drop City, Colorado, deployed and recycled a variety of discarded industrial materials: studs, tarpaper, scavenged railroad ties, factory reject plywood, bottle-tops, junk cars – in other words, the waste products of advanced consumer culture. This history is overlooked by Dean, who prefers, instead, to concentrate on the alluring play of light and sound offered by the Bubble House's interiors.

A more direct precedent for Dean's *Bubble House* can be found in the work of 1960s land artist Robert Smithson. Smithson's artistic, literary and theoretical work is inseparable from the concept of entropy and ruination, and, in an eccentric travelogue of his journey to his hometown Passaic, New Jersey, he coined the crucial term 'ruins in reverse', referring to the dull panorama of unfinished constructions of the suburban American town. 'This is the opposite of the "romantic ruin",' he wrote, 'because the buildings don't fall into ruin after they are built but rather rise into ruin before they are built.'[49] Dean's *Bubble House* recalls Smithson's 'ruins in reverse' insofar as it looks simultaneously old-fashioned and futuristic. The contemplative way in which Dean films the house also recalls the manner in which Smithson deployed the concept of entropy to articulate a theory of time where direction, motion and change are irrelevant. In the famous tour of the monuments of Passaic, he pointed at the futility of attempting to overcome the forces of entropy. Fixing time only momentarily, even film, for Smithson, cannot escape history's relentless destruction.[50]

Commenting on Smithson's philosophy of entropy, historian Jennifer Roberts has observed that Smithson's fascination for ruins ended up proposing an image of eternal stasis and indifference where 'notions of political causality, historical change, or progressive activism are rendered both futile and irrelevant'.[51] 'Smithson's treatment of the horizon theme', Roberts remarked, 'is telling in this regard; the horizon functions as a symbol not of hope or anticipation but rather of apathy.'[52] Buckingham and Koester also define utopia as a horizon.[53] According to them, the three dots of Christiania's flag should be seen as 'a horizon line – a limit that is not a limit – because it is always receding into the distance'.[54] While they would insist that utopian desire acts as a mobilising agent, the ill-defined nature of their visions of utopia, embodied by the figure of the modern ruin and possessing some affinities with Smithson's aesthetics of entropy, betrays a sense of self-doubt regarding the possibility of achieving progressive historical change. In viewing the notion of a better world as a distant and never achievable limit, contemporary artists may inadvertently support the idea of utopia as pie-in-the-sky thinking often used by the proponents of capitalism to discredit every claim that there is an alternative to the ruling politico-economic order. A related question is whether their visions of difference, transience and change come to double, by virtue of an intended consequence, capitalism's own utopian imaginary.

The fragmentary image of utopia provided by the films of contemporary artists may indeed recall Zygmunt Bauman's diagnosis of the condition of utopia in late capitalism. For Bauman we now live in a liquid modernity where any ambitious project aiming at changing the status quo is always seen as impractical and naive and where small improvements in the here and now are treated as more desirable than the radical and structural changes advocated by modern utopian thought. Bauman's slogan to depict the current condition is 'utopia with no topos': within global capitalism place becomes not the fixed site of future transformation, but the temporary location of fleeting moments of happiness. 'The globe is full', Bauman declared. 'There are no as yet undiscovered places left and no places where one could hide from the order (or for that matter disorder) ruling (or for that matter misruling) in places already known and mapped, crisscrossed by beaten tracks, administered and managed. In this world, there is no more "outside".'[55] What lurks beneath this historical transformation of the conditions of utopia is the spectre of a dominant consumer culture which hedonistically emphasises instant and individual gratification over long-term commitment. According to Bauman, under global capitalism utopia has been reduced to a private affair while the happiness of others is no more a condition of one's own felicity.

Contemporary artists can be said to respond to Bauman's ominous diagnosis by trying to find the 'topos' of utopia in the ruins of ambitious social, technological and architectural experiments. Their film installations emerge out of a sense of a failure of the current social and cultural system: for why else revisit failed utopia so feverishly if things did not appear so frightfully dystopian in the first place? However, these artistic practices seem unable to propose a stark and thrilling image of an alternative world. The crumbling frescoes of Thelema, the emptiness of the Bubble House interior and the deserted barracks of Christiania are ultimately faint, if not obscure, anticipations of happiness. Neither purely utopian nor purely dystopian, they do not show a clear alternative to the present or the collective agents of its creation, leaving us the task of imagining or finding some 'other' place. Utopia is, for contemporary artists, a fiction or 'an empty space urging us onward'.[56] Yet can an 'empty space' be effective as a catalyst for social change? Buckingham's, Dean's and Koester's visions of utopia lack the persuasive force of a fully developed picture of the happy world that is expected to result from the application of particular principles.

'At best,' Fredric Jameson once declared, 'Utopia can serve the negative purpose of making us more aware of our mental and ideological imprisonment.'[57] Also serving this critical purpose, the films and photographic projects of contemporary artists invite the viewer to reflect on the present repression of utopian thinking but leave us ultimately unhinged and unknowing. Artists' reluctance to indicate future directions owes something to a certain Foucauldian scepticism towards utopias as transcendental visions and prophetic statements about the future. As we have seen, this scepticism is at the heart of the ambivalence of Foucault's concept of heterotopias which I have used to discuss contemporary artists' aesthetics of ruins. For Foucault all utopias are unavoidably prescriptive and normative. Fifty years ago, when totalitarian ideologies were still confronting each other through the Cold War, this was still a critical insight, and challenges to the triumphalist claims of progress and reason were urgent. But more and more in our contemporary individualistic culture, self-defeating pragmatism and cynicism triumph over the imagination of alternatives; perhaps what we need today is less a critique of utopia than a daring and clear-cut anticipation of a different world.

NOTES

1. Relying entirely on the still take – in a way reminiscent of Michael Snow's *Wavelength* (1967) or Ernie Gehr's *Serene Velocity* (1970) – the film strains the attention of the viewer, making him/her more conscious of the present time of the projection.
2. Tacita Dean as quoted in Roland Groenenboom, 'A Conversation with Tacita Dean', in Roland Groenenboom, ed., *Tacita Dean* (Barcelona: Museum of Contemporary Art, 2001), p. 106.
3. Tacita Dean, 'Bubble House', in Roland Groenenboom, ed., *Tacita Dean* (Barcelona: Museum of Contemporary Art, 2001), p. 52.
4. Thomas More, *Utopia* (1516), trans. Dominic Baker-Smith (London: Penguin Books, 2012). For the iconography of utopia see Laurent Gerverau, 'Symbolic Collapse: Utopia Challenged by Its Representations', in Roland Schaer, Gregory Claeys and Lyman Tower Sargent, eds, *Utopia: The Search for the Ideal Society in the Western World* (New York: New York Public Library, 2000). On the utopian symbolic meaning of spheres, see Peter Sloterdijk, *Bubbles: Microspherology*, trans. Wieland Hoban (Cambridge, MA: MIT Press, 2011).
5. Tacita Dean cited in Marina Warner, 'Interview', in Jean-Christophe Royoux, Marina Warner and Germaine Greer, *Tacita Dean* (London: Phaidon, 2006), p. 36.
6. Tacita Dean, 'Once Upon a Different Sort of Time: The Story of Donald Crownhurst', in Roland Groenenboom, ed., *Tacita Dean* (Barcelona: Museum of Contemporary Art, 2001), p. 40.
7. On the motif of the ruin in the history of Western art and culture, see Brian Dillon, ed., *Ruins* (London: Whitechapel Gallery, 2011); Julia Hell and Andreas Schönle, eds, *Ruins of Modernity* (Durham, NC: Duke University Press, 2010); Michel Makarius, *Ruins* (Paris: Flammarion, 2004); Michael Roth, Claire Lyons and Charles Merewether,

Irresistible Decay: Ruins Reclaimed (Los Angeles: Getty Research Institute for the History of Art and the Humanities, 1997); on Giovan Battista Piranesi's ruins see Andreas Huyssen, 'Nostalgia for Ruins', *Grey Room*, no. 23 (2006), pp. 6–21.

8   Julia Hell and Andreas Schönle, 'Introduction', in Julia Hell and Andreas Schönle, eds, *Ruins of Modernity* (Durham, NC: Duke University Press, 2010), p. 7.

9   See Martin Jay, 'The Trouble with Nowhere', *London Review of Books*, 1 June 2000, pp. 23–4; Judith Shklar, 'The Political Theory of Utopia: From Melancholy to Nostalgia', in Stanley Hoffman, ed., *Political Thought and Political Thinkers* (Chicago: Chicago University Press, 1998), pp. 161–74; on Balibar and utopianism see Molly Nesbit, Hans-Ulrich Obrist and Rirkrit Tiravanija, 'What is a Station?', in Francesco Bonami, ed., *Dreams and Conflicts: The Dictatorship of the Viewer* (Venice: La Biennale di Venezia, 2003), p. 355.

10   Gianni Vattimo, 'Utopia, Counter-Utopia, Irony', in *The Transparent Society* (Baltimore, MD: Johns Hopkins University Press, 1992), p. 82.

11   Tim Edensor, *Industrial Ruins: Spaces, Aesthetics, and Materiality* (New York: Berg, 2005), p. 15.

12   On Foucault's anti-utopianism see Mark Kelly, *The Political Philosophy of Michel Foucault* (London: Routledge, 2009).

13   Michel Foucault, 'Truth, Power, Self: An Interview with Michel Foucault', in Luther H. Martin, Huck Gutman and Patrick H. Hutton, eds, *Technologies of the Self* (Amherst, MA: University of Massachusetts Press, 1988), p. 10.

14   Michel Foucault, 'Of Other Spaces', in Michiel Dehaene and Lieven De Cauter, eds, *Heterotopia and the City: Public Space in a Postcivil Society* (New York: Routledge, 2008), p. 17.

15   *Ibid.*, p. 22.

16   For a critique of Foucault's theory of heterotopic spaces, see Benjamin Genocchio, 'Discourse, Discontinuity, Difference: The Question of Other Spaces', in S. Watson and K. Gibson, eds, *Postmodern Cities and Spaces* (Cambridge: Blackwell, 1995), pp. 35–46.

17   Michel Foucault, 'Of Other Spaces', p. 21.

18   James D. Faubion, 'Heterotopia: An Ecology', in Michiel Dehaene and Lieven De Cauter, eds, *Heterotopia and the City: Public Space in a Postcivil Society* (London: Routledge, 2008), p. 32.

19   Joachim Koester quoted in Hal Foster, 'Blind Spots: The Art of Joachim Koester', *Artforum*, vol. 44, no. 8 (2006), p. 213.

20   Other cinematic references that have appeared in Koester's work are Alfred Hitchcock and George Romero. See for example Koester's *Gentofte Bibliotek/The Birds* (1994) and *Rocent/Dawn of the Dead* (1994).

21   See Lawrence Sutin, *Do What You Wilt: A Life of Alisteir Crowley* (New York: Godalming, 2002).

22   *Ibid.*, p. 280.

23   Anger's documentary was called *Thelema Abbey* (1955) and was produced for the television branch of the English illustrated magazine *Picture Post*. Unfortunately, according to Anger, the film was lost when the magazine had to close. See Kenneth Anger interviewed by Scott MacDonald in *A Critical Cinema: Interviews with Independent Filmmakers* (Berkley, CA: University of California Press, 1989), pp. 16–54.

24 Hugh B. Urban, *Magia Sexualis: Sex, Magic, and Liberation in Modern Western Esotericism* (Berkeley, CA: University of California, 2006), p. 17.
25 *Ibid.*, p. 120.
26 Joachim Koester, 'Morning of the Magicians', in Anders Kreuger, ed., *Messages from the Unseen: Joachim Koester* (Lund: Veenman, 2006), p. 185.
27 *Ibid.*, p. 184.
28 Robert Smithson, 'Hotel Palenque', *Parkett*, no. 43 (1995). The *Parkett* insert is a transcription of Smithson's commentary and a reproduction of the slides from the lecture he gave at the University of Utah in 1972.
29 Joachim Koester, 'Morning of the Magicians', p. 187.
30 *Ibid.*
31 Michel Foucault, 'Of Other Spaces', p. 21.
32 A significant strand of Buckingham's films investigates the relation of monuments to power. On this aspect of Buckingham's work, see Mark Godfrey, 'The Artist as Historian', *October*, no. 120 (2007), pp. 140–72.
33 Buckingham's idea of spectatorship as a creative and subversive activity resonates with the aesthetic theory of Jacques Rancière. See Rancière, *The Emancipated Spectator* (London: Verso, 2009).
34 Matthew Buckingham, 'Archives Are Where You Find Them (2000)'; http://www.matthewbuckingham.net/PT%20ArchivesACCText.html.
35 Tom Gunning, 'Cinema of Attractions: Early Cinema, Its Spectator and the Avant-Garde', in Thomas Elsaesser, ed., *Early Cinema: Space, Frame, Narrative* (London: BFI, 1990), p. 59. On the avant-garde fascination for early cinema see also Tom Gunning, 'An Unseen Energy Swallows Space: The Space in Early Film and Its Relation to American Avant-Garde Film', in John L. Fell, ed., *Film Before Griffith* (Berkeley, CA: University of California Press, 1983), pp. 355–66.
36 On early cinema as an alternative public sphere, see Miriam Hansen, *Babel and Babylon: Spectatorship in American Silent Film* (Cambridge, MA: Harvard University Press, 1991); Miriam Hansen, 'Early Cinema, Late Cinema: Permutations of the Public Sphere', *Screen*, vol. 34, no. 3 (1993), pp. 197–210.
37 Matthew Buckingham, 'Round Table: The Projected Image in Contemporary Art', *October*, no. 104 (2003), pp. 71–96.
38 Matthew Buckingham and Joachim Koester, 'Points of Suspension', *October*, no. 100 (2002), p. 60.
39 See Håkan Thörn, Cathrin Wasshede and Tomas Nilson, eds, *Space for Urban Alternatives? Christiania 1971–2011* (Goteborg: Gidlunds Förlag, 2011).
40 Matthew Buckingham and Joachim Koester, 'Points of Suspension', *October*, no. 100 (2002), p. 58.
41 Michel Foucault, *The Order of Things: An Archaeology of the Human Sciences* (New York: Vintage Books, 1994), p. xviii.
42 George Perec cited in Christian Boltaski and Charles Esche, *Pentimenti* (Milano: Charta, 1997), p. 141.
43 For a discussion of the belated reception of Foucault's lecture, see Daniel Defert, 'Foucault, Space and the Architects', in *Politics/Poetics: Documenta X – The Book* (Ostfilder-Ruit: Cantx Verlag, 1997), pp. 274–83.
44 Fredric Jameson, 'Notes on Globalization as a Philosophical Issue', in Federic

Jameson and Masao Miyoshi, eds (Durham, NC: Duke University Press, 1999).

45 Gianni Vattimo, 'Utopia, Counter-Utopia, Irony', in *The Transparent Society* (Baltimore, MD: Johns Hopkins University Press, 1992), pp. 76–89.

46 John P. Leary, 'Detroitism', in *Guernica: A Magazine of Arts and Politics*, 15 January 2011, np. On post-industrial ruins see also B. Finoki, 'The Anatomy of Ruins', *Triple Canopy*, no. 7 (2009). An example of recent photographic publications aestheticising urban ruins is Yves Marchand and Romain Meffre, *The Ruins of Detroit* (Göttingen: Steidl, 2013). Excerpts of this project were published in *The Observer* on 2 January 2011.

47 Tacita Dean as quoted in Groenenboom, 'A Conversation with Tacita Dean', p. 106.

48 For a history of the geodesic dome within the 1960s counterculture, see Felicity Scott, *Architecture or Techno-utopia: Politics after Modernism* (Cambridge, MA: MIT Press, 2007). For a discussion of recent political uses of this architecture, see Eva Díaz, 'Under the Dome: Architectures of Networked Engagement from Drop City to Rockaway Beach', *Rhizome*, 25 July 2013.

49 Robert Smithson, 'A Tour of the Monuments of Passaic, New Jersey', in Jack Flam, ed., *Robert Smithson: The Collected Writings* (Berkeley, CA: University of California Press, 1996), p. 72.

50 *Ibid.*, p. 74. Perhaps, despite its deadpan irony, there was a Romantic streak in Smithson's celebration of dilapidated architecture, which resonates well with Georg Simmel's philosophy of ruins. In 1911 Simmel discussed the figure of the ruins as a superior redemptive force. 'An equalizing justice', Simmel concluded, 'connects the uninhibited unity of all things that grow apart and against one another with the decay of those men and works of men which now can only yield, but can no longer create and maintain their own forms out of their own strength.' Georg Simmel, 'The Ruin', in Kurt H. Wolff, ed., *Essays on Sociology, Philosophy and Aesthetics*, trans. David Kettler (New York: Harper & Row, 1965), p. 266.

51 Jennifer L. Roberts, 'Landscapes of Indifference: Robert Smithson and John Lloyd Stephens in Yucatán', *Art Bulletin*, vol. 82, no. 3 (2000), p. 562. For a compelling discussion of Smithson's philosophy of history, see Jennifer L. Roberts, *Mirror-Travels: Robert Smithson and History* (New Haven, CT: Yale University Press, 2004).

52 *Ibid.*

53 French philosopher Louis Marin also defines utopia through the figure of the horizon. Marin's theory, based on the semiotic concept of the 'neutral', bears more than a superficial resemblance to Foucault's heterotopia. See Louis Marin, 'Frontiers of Utopia: Past and Present', *Critical Inquiry*, vol. 19, no. 3 (1993), pp. 397–420; Louis Marin, *Utopics: The Semiological Play of Textual Spaces*, trans. Robert A. Vollrath (Atlantic Highlands, NJ: Humanities Press International, 1984).

54 Matthew Buckingham and Joachim Koester, 'Points of Suspension', p. 62.

55 Zygmunt Bauman, 'Utopia with no Topos', *History of the Human Sciences*, vol. 16, no. 1 (2003), p. 22.

56 Matthew Buckingham and Joachim Koester, 'Points of Suspension', p. 62.

57 Fredric Jameson, *Archaeologies of the Future: The Desire called Utopia and Other Science Fictions* (London: Verso, 2007), p. xii.

CHAPTER TWO
Reinventing Propaganda Films

'Nostalgia tells it like it wasn't.'[1] So declared David Lowenthal in the late 1980s. This sentiment, he remarked, is a lopsided view of history whereby the past is imagined as a comfortable refuge and all its negative features are removed. A similar criticism is levelled against utopia: those who imagine perfect worlds ignore the lessons of history, which indicate that utopias are impossible dreams. As Lewis Mumford sombrely remarked: 'History is the sternest critic of utopia.'[2] History provides us with countless examples of ideal political programmes that have never been realised, and, if they have been accomplished, these have become nightmarish dystopias: the attempt to radically change the system and to make utopian visions real is inevitably accompanied by violence and repression. The corollary to this argument is that utopia is, at best, naive and romantic wishful thinking, at worst, dangerous totalitarianism.

Within this one-sided view, the impulse to imagine other worlds is pitted against history as 'fantasy against fact, as the pleasure principle versus the reality principle, as myth against reason'.[3] This criticism operates on the premise that historical facts are not constituted by interpretation and subjective bias: truth is not perspectival and the historian's role is that of 'a neutral, or disinterested, judge; it must never degenerate into that of advocate or, even worse, propagandist'.[4] In this sense, history is the ultimate tribunal, where the feasibility of ambitious alternative visions of the world must be assessed; it provides what can count as the criterion for deciding what is realistic, and what is unrealistic, in any given proposal for an alternative to the here and now. But what happens when we question the assumption that a sharp separation can be drawn between facts and values, reality and imagination, history and fiction? What if we embraced a model of truth that would include utopian hopes and desires, treating history as an amalgam of determinations and possibilities?

Such a model is proposed by Anri Sala (*Intervista* [1999]), Hito Steyerl (*Journal No.1. An Artist's Impression* [2007]) and Ilya and Emilia Kabakov (*The Happiest Man in the World* [2013]). Their films delve into the history of Albania, Yugoslavia and Soviet Russia. They address the twentieth-century event that has most discredited utopianism, as both a concept and an impulse: the failure of communism. The transformation of communism – an economic and political system founded on the utopian ideal of a classless society – into a repressive, authoritarian and violent regime has indeed been considered, especially on the Right, as the indisputable proof of the impossibility of the dream of a fully emancipated and equal society. Against this widespread historical interpretation, the artists at issue here refuse to express a clear-cut and conclusive verdict on communism. In their works there lingers an undercurrent of nostalgia, connecting them with a significant strand of post-1989 European cinema and literature that has attempted to rescue the radical values and dreams of communism from the dustbin of history.[5] This chapter investigates the model of

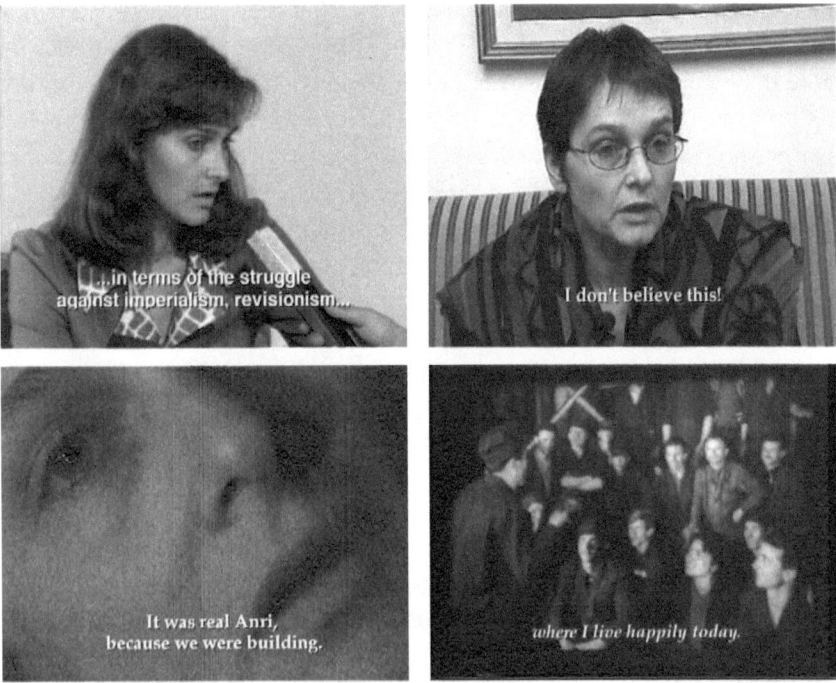

Figs. 13, 14, 15, 16. Anri Sala, *Intervista*, 1998, video projection, colour, sound, 26 minutes (Courtesy Anri Sala and Ideal audiance international, Paris; Galerie Chantal Crousel, Paris; Johnen Galerie, Berlin; Galerie Rüdiger Schöttle, Munich)

truth proposed by the films and will discuss its implications for a theory of utopia and nostalgia.

Truth is also a central category in the discourse of documentary. An inherently plural and elusive genre, contingent on the specific epoch and society in which it was created (the term was coined by filmmaker John Grierson in the 1920s, but examples of documentary cinema date back to the early days of the medium), documentary is inseparable from the idea of revelation.[6] As Olivier Lugon has pointed out, 'the one element that the countless definitions [of documentary] have in common is the very general requirement to respect the subject matter, the desire to reveal "things as they are," to provide reliable, authentic information about them, avoiding any embellishment that might alter the integrity of reality'.[7] In film studies, the expression has come to stand for all those films that are *not* fiction. The distinction between documentary and fiction is blurred by the works at issue here, which deploy a range of representational strategies conventionally associated with theatre, literature and drama: re-enactments, artificial staging of the profilmic, non-indexical media (e.g. animation and drawing), essayistic and autobiographical narratives, repetition and the manipulation of archival documents. More importantly, these films address their historical subject matter through the appropriation of propaganda films: Sala discovers and scrutinises an interview given by his mother for the Albanian state television in the 1970s, where she celebrates the achievements of the communist party; Steyerl examines the past of Yugoslavia through a newsreel reporting on the success of a literacy campaign initiated by the newly formed communist state in 1948, and showing Muslim women confidently removing their headscarves; the Kabakovs deploy propaganda films from the 1930s and 1940s produced under Stalin and depicting enthusiastic young men and women working in the fields and singing patriotic songs. Importantly, these artists' experimental works do not appropriate propaganda materials with parodic intent: their point is not to demonstrate the gap between the misery of actual life under communism and the visions of happiness and freedom formulated by those films; rather, it is to show how propaganda tapped into authentic desires and dreams.

Through the appropriation of propaganda films, the films at issue here tend to 'fictionalise' the genre of documentary, blurring the conventional separation between fiction and non-fiction cinema. This tendency is hardly new: it was active in the post-war period when technological advancements allowed new personal and poetic forms of documentary (e.g. in the *cinéma vérité* of Jean Rouch and the film essays of Chris Marker and Harun Farocki), and it was even more variously active in the 1980s and 1990s, especially as appropriated images and imitation became common idioms.[8] This period also witnessed the emergence of a loose film genre – branded with the term 'mockumentary' or 'mock-documentary'

– that comprises 'fiction films that make use of (copy, mock, mimic, gimmick) documentary style and therefore acquire its associated content (the moral and the social) and associated feelings (belief, trust, authenticity) to create a documentary experience defined by their antithesis, self-conscious distance'.[9] While this genre may offer a salutary critique of those documentary modes which tend to situate the viewer in the role of passive recipient of ostensibly factual information, ultimately, its deconstruction of documentary's claims to truth, if taken to its logical conclusion, ends up suggesting absolute scepticism. Consider Craig Hight and Janet Roscoe's analysis of this genre, which, in my view, exemplifies the dangers of relativism that lurk within the deconstructive parody of documentary.[10] For these authors, mock-documentaries suggest that all documentary images are manufactured and deceptive. The rise of the mock-documentary in visual culture is a phenomenon to be welcomed; this new form has an important critical function in that 'it offers the audience an opportunity to reflect on the wider cultural acceptance of factual and sober discourses and potentially to move towards a position of critical awareness, distrust or even incredulity of such discourses'.[11] Certainly, the positive critical effect of the mock-documentary among the audience remains an assumption to be verified. Yet the authors' trust in the power of the mock-documentary to raise critical awareness is undisputed throughout their work. In a passage of their book, Hight and Roscoe pitch the mock-documentary against the reflexive documentary, which to them is unable to fully critique the authoritative status of factual discourse. They explain: 'Perhaps the reflexive and performative modes are, in fact, not that radical after all, and [don't] have mock-documentary's potential to go to the core of the documentary genre. [...] [t]hey do not question the assumption that there is a truth to be gained.'[12] Ultimately, these authors embrace that kind of postmodern scepticism – so popular in 1990s theoretical discourse as well as in visual culture – which posits that all media images are but empty simulations. Also, their critique falls into a logical contradiction: the parodic quality of the mock-documentary ends by producing the universal and incontrovertible truth that all documentaries are deceptive.

To return to Sala's, Steyerl's and the Kabakovs' films, I would argue that, unlike many 1990s fake documentaries, these artists' films do not propose a sterile postmodern scepticism; rather, truths are preserved in their 'fictional' modes: affective truths and subjective truths which contribute to giving a more complex account of life under Albania's, Yugoslavia's and Russia's communist regimes. These films intimate that only through fiction can an adequate image of the experience of life under communism be created. But, if it becomes clear that these films do not aim to deconstruct the authority and legitimacy of documentary, then to what ends do they blur the boundaries between fact and fiction? Without anticipating my conclusions, the representational strategies adopted by these contemporary artists problematise the dualism of fantasy and reality, fact and fiction, that resides at the heart of the denigration of utopia and nostalgia. I want to read these films through the lenses of the philosophy of Ernst Bloch. Bloch's 'open' ontology considers utopia as an essential element of the real and, consequently, proposes a re-evaluation of this impulse: rather than compensatory and irrelevant fantasy, Bloch conceptualises utopianism as a powerful catalyst for social change. Likewise, Sala, Steyerl and the Kabakovs seek to restore political relevance to the act of dreaming a better future (as well as that of remembering those dreams) against the reduction of utopia to wishful thinking – a reduction which too often results in the affirmation of the status quo. In so doing, they suggest that utopianism can be history's driving force and not just its irrational Other.

* * *

Anri Sala's oeuvre resists being pigeonholed into straightforward categories.[13] Although he has worked mainly with video and photography, Sala has often engaged with very different subject matter. In his videos, he has portrayed a sleepy homeless man in Milan (*Uomoduomo* [2000]), empty billboards (*Blindfold* [2002]), a particular species of crab on a beach in Brazil (*Ghostgames* [2002]), the colourful façades of Tirana's buildings (*Dammi I Colori* [2003]), Senegalese boys learning the Wolof language (*Lak-Kat* [2004]) and various music performances (*Mixed Behaviour* [2003]; *Now I See* [2004]; *Long Sorrow* [2005]). Sala's practice can be described, in the words of artist and critic Liam Gillick, as 'a simultaneous stretching and compression of what we might call the terminology and language of the applied documentary'.[14] Sala's enigmatic realism originates from his awareness that media, even reproductive media, are not transparent windows onto the real. 'Documenting reality', Sala explains, 'involves a process of abstraction, transformation and distance. I cannot accept documentaries that make spectators believe they are witnessing reality as it unfolds, as if there was no mediation on the part of the filmmaker and the medium.'[15] His first work, *Intervista* (1999), released while he was attending the École Nationale Supérieure des Arts Décoratifs, in Paris, is a half-hour-long video that demonstrates how formal questions are also crucial historical questions. In this documentary, truth appears to be inseparable from the mediation of opaque archival images and from an equally obscure language. Nevertheless, *Intervista* does not lead to a postmodernist plunge into cynical relativism. Sala himself declared: 'I did not want to show the final truth about Albania, but certainly I wanted to expose a truth.'[16] As we will see, this truth relates more to the ideals and emotions of those who lived in Albania during the communist regime than to a precise sequence of events. Importantly, Sala prompts us to consider these emotions and ideals, however subjective, to be as significant and truthful as factual events per se.

Intervista deals with the past of Albania, a small country in the Balkan region, which was governed by a dictatorial communist regime from World War II until 1991. After the fall of the regime, the nation witnessed a period of violent unrest and instability due to political fragmentation and the adoption of anarchic free-market capitalism.[17] Like other Eastern European countries, in the 1990s Albania experienced a deep historical amnesia. As Czech critic Vit Havránek has observed, the desire of Albanians to conform to the new capitalist order prompted them to force out historical memory 'as a negative stigma which was useless in the new conditions'.[18] Released in 1998 and awarded numerous documentary awards, Sala's *Intervista* represents one of the first attempts by an Albanian artist to overcome this widespread amnesia.

The video begins with the artist finding a 16mm film roll stored in a box in his Tirana apartment. The roll shows his mother, Valdet, attending a conference of the communist party as the head of the Communist Youth Alliance of Albania some twenty years earlier. It also contains an interview she gave on the occasion of this conference. Unfortunately, Sala also discovers that the soundtrack is missing from the film roll. After showing the film to his mother, she looks amused and claims to have no memory of that particular episode. Later on, Sala tracks down the sound engineer of Albanian national television who recorded the interview. He explains that in 1977 it was impossible with contemporary film technologies to record sound and image on the same reel and that the separate soundtrack had probably been lost. In order to find Valdet's missing words, Sala goes to the institute of deaf people in Tirana, where he has his mother's words lip-read by a deaf person. The recovered speech is a shocking surprise for both Sala and Valdet, as her answers are rife with clichés and party slogans. For example, the 32-year-old Valdet says: 'This meeting was held to clearly express the current political situation of the country in terms of the struggle against imperialism and revisionism and the two superpowers, which is only possible under the guardianship of the Marxist-Leninist Party.' She initially refuses to believe in the authenticity of the reconstructed soundtrack. Later on, Valdet accepts the truthfulness of the interview to the point of proudly claiming that she had truly believed in the ideals of equality underpinning the ideology of communism.

In Sala's work, the binary of fact versus fiction is undermined in numerous ways and so is the opposition between relativism and naive realism. First of all, Sala refuses to present Valdet's original film interview as transparent evidence. *Intervista* is an investigation of Albanian life under the communist regime as well as a video about the reconstruction of an incomplete and forgotten document. Its narrative bears more than a superficial resemblance to Agnès Varda's

Ulysse (1982), a 22-minute film essay that recounts the filmmaker's attempt to reconstruct the meaning of a single still that Varda herself took 28 years prior to the production of the film.[19] The famous essay ruminates upon the capability of photographic images to recall authentic memory. But while Varda's film, despite the hopeful tone, concludes with a dose of scepticism regarding the truth status of her speculations, Sala's work seems more sanguine about the possibility of retrieving truthful knowledge about the past through filmic documents.

This reconstruction is made possible by Sala's conversation with other witnesses, such as the journalist and the sound technician who recorded the interview. Most of all, the reconstruction of the document is made possible by Sala's reliance on deaf people. One of the most significant sequences in the video is shot at the institute for deaf people in Tirana. In one of the institute's rooms the images of the old reel are screened on a television monitor in front of Sala and a deaf person. Surprisingly the archival images of Valdet's 1977 interview are significantly distorted, as, in order to facilitate the lip reading, Sala enlarges Valdet's mouth by reshooting the film reel with his video camera. As a result, the document is transformed into a gigantic and wordless mouth that occupies almost the entire screen. The manipulation of the document, however, facilitates the recovery of Valdet's 'lost' words – it is in fact crucial for the effectiveness of the lip reading. At the end of the scene, the camera cuts to a shot of Valdet's enlarged mouth as it appears on the television monitor. In this suggestive shot we see her mouth moving in slow-motion while the image of the deaf person is also reflected on the television screen. As the deaf person gesticulates, translating Valdet's speech into sign language, viewers are confronted with an unexpected relay: Valdet's words seem dictated by somebody else's body, as if her mouth was like that of a ventriloquist's dummy.

This scene does not simply suggest the perhaps tautological recognition that language and representation are crucial means for the production of truth. It shows that fiction and a certain degree of artificiality constituted an essential part of the reality of Albanians under communism. The restoration of Valdet's lost soundtrack leads not to the return to a truthful speaking but to the discovery of the fictive quality of her language. Her tortuous syntax demonstrates how constricted the public sphere was, with the media closely controlled by the communist party through the exercise of vigorous censorship.[20] Likewise, while the images of the film reel show Valdet standing next to the dictator Enver Hoxha, applauded by an audience of loyal party members, she recalls that the delirious enthusiasm of congresses and ceremonies of state was a forced enthusiasm, that it was a crowd's hysteria for its leader, who was like an icon. Later on in *Intervista*, the television reporter Pushkin Lubonja explains how predictable the television interviews were for the audience and how each question implied a predetermined answer.[21] All of this demonstrates that public life in Albania under the communist regime was a performance staged according to an invented script that did not correspond to the real situation of the country. In order to grasp the truth of Albania's past, Sala demonstrates, it is fundamental to consider the artificial rhetoric of the regime as something that was embedded in everyday life and subjectivity. In short, a language that effectively structured the experience of reality in Albania during the regime cannot be dismissed as simply false.

Moreover, Valdet's interview is not dismissed as an inauthentic document because it is considered to be a trace of her political dreams and convictions. In *Intervista*, Sala presents the dreams of social equality of his mother's generation – that is, the ideal of justice and emancipation underpinning communist rhetoric – as deep personal truths that need to be acknowledged. Although Valdet refuses to believe in the opaque and absurd language she used in the archival interview, she does not deny its political content. 'That was real', she declares at some point. 'If I could go back, I wouldn't act differently. I believed in what I was doing, that much I can say.' Thus, the goal of Sala's enquiry into his mother's past is not simply to recover the memory of what she actually said on a certain public occasion, but to retrieve the memory of her ethical drive. In light of her testimony, the images of television footage showing idyllic images of Albanian workers, women and children listening to the revolutionary songs of freedom do not appear only as propaganda footage. Rather, they allude to the desires and hopes of those Albanians who, like Valdet, spontaneously embraced the ideals of communism. Although these ideals never became reality, Sala shows that they have to be considered as part of the truth about Albania's past. *Intervista* overcomes a dogmatic reduction of documentary to ideology. Sala's video proposes an expanded notion of truth that comprises not only factual events but also virtual, imaginary ones such as political ideals: 'I am interested in the truths that originate from our needs and the hopes and wishes or the things we don't need or we don't wish', the artist once declared.[22]

Sala also foregrounds the process of representation or fiction by showing his presence onscreen. In a recent interview, critic Gerald Matt asked Sala whether he considers himself as a storyteller. Sala replied: 'Maybe I could define myself as a catalyst, a starting point.'[23] In *Intervista*, Sala does indeed appear as a catalyst and an intercessor. He makes his presence visible from the beginning of the video, when we see him examining the forgotten film roll, but we also see him in other scenes when he interviews Valdet and other witnesses. Far from being a new documentary strategy, incorporating the presence of the filmmaker onscreen can be traced back to the works of *cinéma vérité* pioneer Jean Rouch. In films like *Chronique d'un Eté* (1960), co-directed with sociologist Edgar Morin, Rouch portrayed himself in conversation with his subjects, performing a very similar role to that of Sala in *Intervista*. In *Chronique d'un Eté* we see Rouch constantly provoking a group of Parisians through questions about their personal happiness as well as political opinions about the war in Algeria. The film represents an example of reverse ethnography through which Rouch turned the camera onto French subjects instead of using it to document the ethnographic other.

Yet, according to art historian Tom McDonough, *Chronique d'un Eté* hides 'a metaphysics of reality' because, despite Rouch's presence on screen, the intervention of the camera is actually concealed.[24] McDonough's argument is based on the fact that Rouch's innovative documentary was the first film of its kind to record synchronous sound on location, due to the miniaturised and portable film technologies invented in the late 1950s. For McDonough, Rouch exploited the new technologies as a 'means of hiding the work of the camera and the microphone, of seeming to restitute the lived in a raw manner and eliminating any intervention of the filmmaker and his technique'.[25] Also, McDonough contrasts Rouch's work with Guy Debord's anti-documentary *Critique de la Séparation* (1961). Produced only one year later than *Chronique d'un Eté*, Debord's film is characterised by an extreme fragmentation that renders impossible any attempt at creating a coherent diegetic world. For this fragmentation, McDonough argues, Debord's film proposed a 'cinematic topology of the everyday' that 'insisted on its own imbrication within the social and psychic structures it set out to represent, as against [Rouch's] *cinéma vérité*'s metaphysical claim of a disinterested observation'.[26] For Debord, as for McDonough, documentary cinema deceives its spectators by providing them with the illusion of a coherent rational world in which a dialogue between subjects is possible. 'The function of the cinema, whether dramatic or documentary', Debord declares at the beginning of *Critique de la Séparation*, 'is to present a false and isolated coherence as a substitute for a communication and activity that are absent'. However, I believe McDonough too hastily dismisses Rouch's documentary. In fact, the French ethnographer does not frame the representation within a discourse of scientific objectivity but casts doubts on the truth of the representation in the final sequences of *Chronique d'un Eté*. In one of these sequences, Rouch shows the footage of the interviews to his subjects in a Paris cinema. A beam of light from a projector is visible before turning off. Lights come on to reveal an auditorium where many of the film's interviewees have just seen themselves in a rough cut of previous footage. A discussion of the rough cut follows, with differences of opinion concerning the truth of the interviews. In other words, Rouch problematises the outcome of his ethnographic experiment and the difficulties of communicating experience in an authentic way.

Like Rouch, Sala insistently avoids framing *Intervista* within a discourse of impassive, scientific observation. His peculiar editing and camerawork contribute to the reflexive quality of the representation. Numerous scenes of his video are characterised by a theatrical quality, and look as if they were already staged. Take, for example, the opening sequence depicting the artist's discovery of the 16mm reel in his Tirana apartment. The scene is filmed through a close-up of Sala, who is bending over a box. The camera being set up inside the box, Sala's face is framed from a very low angle. Directing his gaze towards us, Sala makes us aware of our condition as spectators. Apparently, this constructed scene was scripted and planned in advance. Yet the camera makes itself present in other sequences as well. For example, Sala's encounter with Valdet is filmed with a fixed camera placed inside Valdet's apartment in a manner more akin to a fictional film than a documentary. Given the staged quality of this scene, the spectator realises that their encounter was actually arranged in advance.

Also, *Intervista* displays the same dialogic and inquisitive quality of Rouch's *Chronique d'un Eté*. The meaning of the discovered archival footage is not presented as a certain and indisputable fact but is constructed through the dialogue between Sala, Valdet and the other interviewees. Unlike Valdet's television statement, which is never challenged by the journalist, Sala's interviews raise questions. Valdet's initial rejection of the authenticity of the archival interview is indeed firmly questioned by Sala, who invites her to reconsider her relationship with the document. Across the video this found film reel sets off a mnemonic process of reconstruction of the past in which truth will emerge in all its complexity. Thus, in *Intervista* truth appears less as a transcendental entity than as a laborious process of interrogation.

* * *

Like Sala, Hito Steyerl began making videos in the mid-1990s. Unlike Sala's works, however, her videos can be said to belong more firmly to the tradition of the video essay, which has as its progenitors artists such as Chris Marker, Harun Farocki and Jean-Luc Godard.[27] A very loose category, the video essay can be defined as a multi-layered product where an amalgam of fictional and documentary images and sounds are linked through a voiceover or through intertitle text. Steyerl's works are characterised by an eclectic montage that combines fictional and non-fictional materials such as animations, drawings, movie snippets, newsreel footage, interviews and other documentary images. As film historian Nora Alter has observed, this hybrid documentary form is often characterised by an open-ended, evaluative search, as '"to essay" means "to assay", "to weigh", as well as "to attempt".'[28] Two of Steyerl's most exhibited works, *November* (2004) and *Lovely Andrea* (2007), take the form of a quest related to the artist's own experience. In both videos the artist engages in a search for images that have been lost or have travelled through different media and geographical contexts, often shifting their meanings. Steyerl's 23-minute-long video *Journal No. 1. An Artist's*

Impression similarly narrates the search for a missing film: the first newsreel produced in Bosnia after World War II.

Entitled 'Journal No. 1', the lost newsreel was part of a series produced by the socialist government of Yugoslavia in order to provide selected news about the state's production efforts and social reforms.[29] 'Journal No. 1' was destroyed during the 1992–95 war that split Bosnia into two autonomous states, the Federation of Bosnia and Herzegovina, inhabited mostly by Muslims and Croats, and Republika Srpska, of Serbian majority. According to Steyerl, the film was stored on the premises of the film studio Sutjeska on the outskirts of Sarajevo, but was later moved to the house of a local family, which was then hit by a grenade during the war. In an attempt to reconstruct the lost document, Steyerl asks the director of Sarajevo's Film Museum, Devleta Filipovi, and its projectionist, Halid Buni, to recount one of the scenes from 'Journal No. 1'. The scene depicts a literacy class: a young teacher stands next to a blackboard in front of a classroom crowded with old veiled women. A picture of Tito, at that time the head of the communist party, hangs on the wall. Steyerl attempts a visual reconstruction of the newsreel scene by asking a graphic artist to sketch out the recollections of the two witnesses on separate white paperboards. Surprisingly, as the artist films the process of drawing, the reconstructions turn out to be quite different, even though they are based on the same scene. The museum director and the projectionist do not agree on numerous details and confuse the classroom scene with images from popular Yugoslav feature films. Finally, Steyerl interviews the graphic artist Arman Kulaši. Kulaši, a young member of the Bosnian Muslim community, was forced to leave school and escape from his home town during the 1992 war for fear of internment in a prison camp. As a result, the contrast between the optimistic image of the past represented by the newsreel and the dismal present of Bosnia, a country still struggling to overcome the effects of civil war, becomes more and more evident.

Steyerl has often declared the importance of avoiding too much emphasis on the constructed and mediated quality of documentary images. 'Although we basically cannot trust documents, we still need them', she has stated in an interview.[30] Produced with the support of Boris Buden, an expert on Yugoslavia's cultural and political history, *Journal No. 1. An Artist's Impression* represents Steyerl's attempt to probe the contemporary reality of Bosnia and to show the effects of the war on the population. Unsurprisingly, then, almost one-third of the documentary is devoted to the graphic artist's testimony, in which he movingly relates his traumatic experience of the war. Steyerl writes that in *Journal No. 1. An Artist's Impression* she aimed for a 'creative fictionalisation' of the missing newsreel.[31] Importantly, this fictionalisation is not meant as a statement of relativism in that the video does not question the reality of the Bosnian War. On

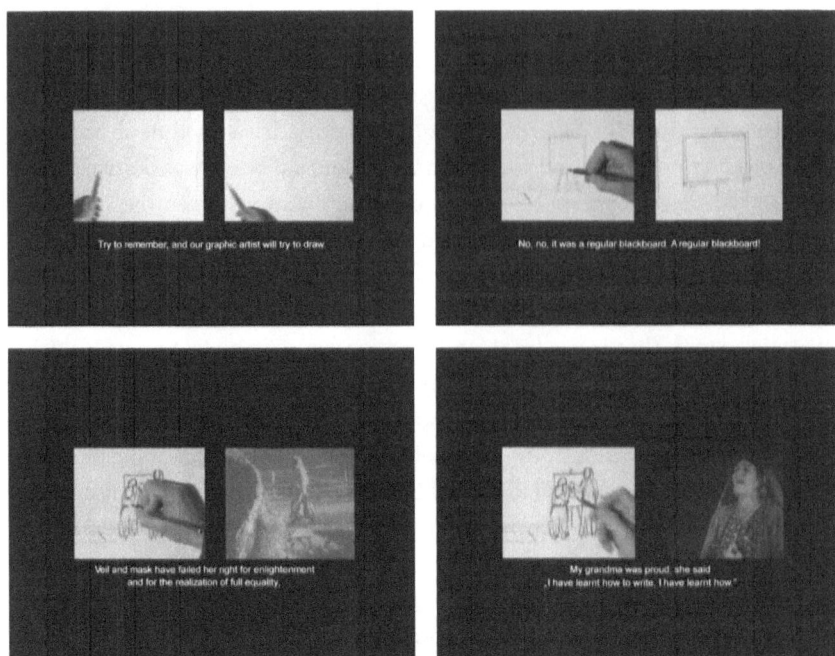

Figs. 17, 18, 19, 20. Hito Steyerl, *Journal No.1. An Artist's Impression*, 2007, video projection, colour, sound, 22 min (Courtesy Hito Steyerl)

the contrary, the fictionalisation of the lost newsreel is an attempt on behalf of the artist to represent documentary images as afterimages that are imbricated with collective fantasies and private memories. Steyerl's camera is less concerned with verifying the factual content of the lost film than in detecting its traces in the collective memory of contemporary Bosnians. Importantly, the truth-value of 'Journal No. 1' resides in its affective and political connotations. The film expresses the fulfilment of desires of equality and justice that, for Steyerl, are particularly relevant today in the current context of Bosnia, with its division along ethnic and cultural lines.

Steyerl achieves the fictionalisation of the missing film through the use of three representational strategies: the use of the split-screen, the appropriation of feature films and the deployment of drawing as a technique for the reconstruction of the lost document. A single channel video, Steyerl's work is divided into two frames separated by a vertical black border. The split-screen is hardly new in avant-garde cinema, and the technique was often used in experimental films to lay bare the material properties of the medium and to break the cinematographic image's illusion of reality.[32] A reflexive device, the split-screen draws attention to the act of framing itself. In Steyerl's video the split-screen also allows viewing of both white-boards on which the reconstructions are drawn, so that the contradictions between the testimonies of the archive director and film projectionist are underscored. As the graphic artist completes the drawings, their reconstructions of the newsreel present more and more contrasting details. For instance, the number and position of the pupils in the classroom differs, as does the shape of a pendant lamp.

One might view the split-screen as a suggestion of relativism since the technique emphasises the incongruence of the two witnesses' reconstructions. Yet I would argue that in *Journal No. 1. An Artist's Impression* the split-screen functions less as a reflexive strategy than as a mimetic device and that its effect is not that of undermining the reliability of the reconstructions. As we keep watching the film, the screen remains constantly divided and it becomes clear that this division is a metaphor for Bosnia's current cultural and political fragmentation. Despite being the main cause of the civil war, division along ethnic lines is a defining aspect of contemporary political and cultural life in Bosnia. Today, tensions among Bosnian Serbs, Croats and Muslims remain and the conflict has shifted to the field of cultural heritage and education as each minority seeks to protect its cultural identity by founding its own cultural institutions and archives, a policy condemned by Steyerl as a form of 'ethnic marketing' or 'segregationist multiculturalism'.[33] To return to the split-screen, rather than a device introduced to emphasise the opacity of documentary images, the technique should be interpreted as a device that effectively represents the lack of a unified collective memory in Bosnia.

In the field of the essay video, the use of the split-screen is a trademark of Harun Farocki. A key influence for Steyerl, Farocki's video essays are often structured as dual channel projections. According to him, the technique produces a kind of 'soft-montage', whereby images are more loosely linked, allowing viewers to enjoy a greater freedom in the construction of meaning.[34] Farocki writes, 'in split-screen, what is at issue is a general relatedness rather than a strict opposition or equation', and 'one image does not take the place of the previous one [as in traditional montage], but supplements it, re-evaluates it, balances it'.[35] Likewise, in *Journal No. 1. An Artist's Impression*, the split-screen does not establish contradictions or precise chronological links between the different visual materials that Steyerl combines. Rather, clips drawn from different films and moments in Yugoslavian history are juxtaposed so that their similarities, their common representational contents, are moved to the foreground. For example, while on the left-hand section of the screen we see the reconstruction of the classroom scene depicted in the newsreel, on the right-hand section we see a brief clip from the movie *The Battle of Neretva* (1969). In this clip a teacher writes on a blackboard the word *AVNOJ* (*Antifašisti ko V(ij)e e Narodnog Oslobo enja Jugoslavije*), meaning 'the antifascist people's liberation council founded in the Yugoslavia of the early 1940s'. Children slowly repeat the word aloud. Although not identical, these two clips are strikingly similar. By their juxtaposition through split-screen, the video suggests that this classroom scene is a sort of archetypical image of Bosnian collective memory. The split-screen 'fictionalises' the archival newsreel in that it shows its connection with a wider repertoire of documentary and fictional images that circulate in the country's culture.

Another important strategy adopted by the artist to fictionalise the document is the use of drawing for the reconstruction of the lost film reel. Although in specific legal contexts drawing may be invested with evidential status (e.g. forensic art), it remains quite an unconventional representational choice for a documentary, as in visual culture this medium is often associated with the construction of fictional or fantastic worlds. Moreover, apart from a few exceptions, the index of the hand-drawn mark is usually connected to the artist's expressive subjectivity rather than the purported objective world of documentary lenses. Likewise, in classic film theory, animation has often been considered as a cinematic form unable to achieve the truth status of photo-based cinema.[36] However, by deploying the medium of drawing, Steyerl's aim is to portray the mnemonic life of the lost newsreel. Although 'Journal No. 1' is lost, it survives in the memories of those people who saw it or heard about it. Its essence lies not in its materiality, which is unfortunately irretrievable, but in its mnemonic afterlife. Thus, drawing is deployed as a means of showing the missing documentary's continuous presence in memory; a memory that, for Steyerl, is real. The third 'fictionalising' strategy adopted by Steyerl in *Journal No. 1. An Artist's Impression* is the appropriation of fiction cinema. Steyerl appropriates clips from popular Yugoslavian feature films such as *The Battle of Neretva*, *Walter Defends Sarajevo* (1972) and *Do You Remember Dolly Bell?* (1981). *The Battle of Neretva* and *Walter Defends Sarajevo* belong to a very popular genre in Yugoslavian cinema history that narrates, in a melodramatic and spectacular manner, the heroic acts of the local partisan resistance over the Nazi occupation in World War II. *Do You Remember Dolly Bell?* describes Sarajevo in the 1960s, a time in which a dissatisfaction with Tito's regime started to grow among the young generation.[37] Importantly, clips from these movies intersect with the reconstructions of the lost newsreel. For example, when the archive director describes the lamp in the classroom scene of the newsreel to the graphic artist, she compares it with the lamp she saw in a sequence from *Do You Remember Dolly Bell?*. This shows the protagonist of Emir Kusturica's film, an old communist, and his sons singing a Yugoslavian patriotic song in the family's dining room at night. The allusions the witnesses make when reconstructing the newsreel clearly demonstrate the importance of cultural representations such as those provided by movies in shaping the historical memory of a country. Steyerl's appropriation of these popular movies does not undermine the truth of the archival document, as once again the truth that the artist is interested in showing is the collective memory of the people in Sarajevo. The point is not whether the reconstructions of the newsreel are identical or whether they are similar to the scenes of fiction films, because the artist is not primarily concerned with factual and physical details. Steyerl is more crucially interested in the emotional and political value of the classroom scene.

For Steyerl, film history is a reservoir of memories, dreams and premonitions to be taken as true. She owes this conception of cinema to her teacher – and former editor of *Filmkritic* magazine – Helmut Farber. Drawing on film theorist Siegfried Kracauer and philosopher Ernst Bloch, Farber argued that films constitute 'a rich memory, a productive, pre-inventing unconscious' and they articulate 'codified messages about the daydreams of society, their otherwise suppressed desires, dark forces, deep-rooted premonitions'.[38] Likewise, the lost newsreel, with its classroom scene, should be viewed as the expression of the desire for women's political empowerment. In fact, 'Journal No. 1' showed women liberated through education and knowledge. This becomes more evident when Steyerl inserts a brief sequence from a surviving (and supposedly similar) Bosnian newsreel, in which women throw their veils away in a gesture of empowerment and liberation. 'Veil and mask have failed her right for enlightenment and for the realisation of full equality', a voiceover proclaims. The sheer exhilaration radiating from the Muslim women's faces in these scenes testifies to an age of optimism and change. Likewise, enthusiasm and joy are expressed by the testimony of the film projectionist, who describes the happiness of her grandmother, herself a participant in the 1940s literacy classes, after she had learnt to write her name. He recounts: '[After going to the literacy classes] my old grandma was so proud: "I can now write and don't have to sign my name with little crosses anymore!" she said.'[39] Thus, the missing newsreel becomes the symbol of a more equal and just society.

Given the political and emotional value of 'Journal No. 1', we can now better understand the purpose of the hand-drawn reconstructions and, more generally, the function of representation or fiction in Steyerl's work. Fiction here is deployed as a decoy to access collective memories and hopes and to stress their contingent, processual quality. By asking to recreate the lost film, Steyerl invited Bosnians to reanimate and express their desire for a free and equal society. In this sense, the reconstructions are to be taken as projections of a better future more than evidence of a past event. 'The reconstruction process', Steyerl writes, 'becomes interesting because it is no longer about uncovering a lost truth from the past, but about inventing a new truth from the future.'[40]

The drawings represent 'the literacy class they wanted to have in the future, which would be opposed to the reactionary process of indigenisation of the present'.[41] Once again, the 'fictionalisation' of the document performed by the artist's appropriation strategies does not function to deconstruct the idea of truth, because truth is considered less as a fact than as a memory and social ideal. Unsurprisingly, then, Steyerl defines documentary as a 'language of practice' that is 'not only a possible arena of public debate' but also a form capable of 'anticipat[ing] alternative forms of social composition'.[42] Documentary is thus charged not only with the task of conveying knowledge about the past but also with the potential of providing anticipatory knowledge about possible and better futures.

* * *

Ilya and Emilia Kabakov's installation *The Happiest Man in the World* develops and takes to an extreme elements that were already contained in Sala's and Steyerl's documentaries: the tendency to elicit empathy with unreliable witnesses (see the long close-ups on Valdet's face in *Intervista*) and the tendency to indulge in the spectacle of propaganda and popular cinema (see the repetition of popular cinema clips in *Journal No. 1. An Artist's Impression*). But where Sala and Steyerl present 'truth' as a retrospective event and thus distance viewers from the fantasy world of communism, the Kabakovs want to make the communist utopia present and palpable, eliciting immediate identification and awe. Appropriating 1940s Soviet musical films without providing much contextual explanation, *The Happiest Man in the World* entices viewers to take delight in the sumptuous beauty and splendour of Stalinist spectacle. In so doing, it shuns the sobriety and didacticism that are typical of conventional documentary.[43] This strategy, however, may be risky, as it assumes a competent and informed spectator, capable of perceiving the subtly ironic quality of the artists' careful staging of Soviet propaganda.

Set in the vast cavernous space of the London gallery Ambika P3, the installation plunges the spectator into a pitch black environment dominated by a monumental screen and tight rows of old cinema seats, stretched out like a ghostly audience.[44] Excerpts from Stalin's favourite movies – Ivan Pyriev's popular musicals *The Kuban Cossacks* (1949) and *A Tale of the Siberian Land* (1948) – are projected in an enchanting loop. The ravishing colours of the cinematography, the catchy tunes and the carefully choreographed camera movements are deeply enthralling, and so are the actors' performances: in *The Kuban Cossacks* handsome young Russians from a 'kolkhoz' – a Soviet collective farm – enthusiastically sing while labouring amid golden fields of grain; peasant women are surrounded by tall pyramids built of gorgeous watermelons; an army of tractors and machinery rapidly gather, chop and discharge crops under a vivid blue sky; in *A Tale of the Siberian Land* a man on a barge sailing away down a river sings a lilting, bittersweet lament to a group of ordinary folks. On one side of the gallery, next to the cinema seats, is a little room with its door ajar. Its unassuming environment recalls the decor of late Stalinist domestic interiors: the furniture includes a single narrow bed, an armchair, a chest of drawers, a solid wood cabinet, a round table covered with a traditional hand-knit cloth, some silverware, a couple of simply decorated ceramic plates and a cup of tea, and a flower-embroidered floor lamp. Mid-size amateurish paintings – depicting idyllic rural landscapes, romantic marine views at sunset and a white horse carriage – adorn the walls. The bed is neatly made, and some old books (among them Herman Hesse's *Siddartha* and Theodor Dreiser's *Sister Carrie*) are stacked on a night table. The small apartment has a window facing the screen: it is as if its dweller has built a home right there to get the perfect view, to live as close as possible to the silver screen.

The installation evokes the idea of utopia as the flight from reality into a perfect world – a theme which has run through Ilya Kabakov's oeuvre since the early 1970s. Some of Kabakov's well-known albums of this period are based on fictional narratives about anonymous individuals dreaming imaginary perfect worlds. For example, *The Flying Komarov* (1972–75) – the sixth in his well-known series of albums *Ten Characters* – depicts the story of a fictional hero who wakes up one morning and sees from his balcony a multitude of people hovering around him in the greying sky (the story, Matthew Jesse Jackson has pointed out, bears more than superficial affinities with passages from Nikolai Chernyshevsky's novel *What Is To Be Done?* [1905], a staple of Russian political radicalism which contains dreams of a presumably post-revolutionary future inhabited by a new kind of humanity).[45] Also exploring the theme of utopia is Kabakov's installation *The Man Who Flew in Space from His Apartment* (1988). The work consisted of a small apartment plastered with Soviet posters designed to communicate a sense of historical optimism, where there lies a bed and the remains of a technical apparatus. According to Kabakov's narrative, the apparatus catapulted the mysterious dweller straight from his bed into outer space. Utopian consciousness is also the subject of *The Palace of Project* (1998): a construction composed of a warren of small rooms where absurd and impossible projects devised by bogus characters are displayed (one of them is ironically entitled 'To Escape from Oneself'). Similar to Kabakov's previous works, *The Happiest Man in the World* relates the story of a person living in a condition of constant retreat from reality: from his apartment window the 'happiest man' sees only the idyllic images of Stakhanovite and supremely conscientious workers who sing 'We grew our wheat / for labour's honour' and are surrounded by material abundance.

It is tempting to consider the hero of the installation as an avatar of the artist Ilya Kabakov.[46] Born in 1933 in Ukraine, Kabakov must have been very familiar with Pyriev's movies, watching them as a teenager studying at the Leningrad Academy of Art. After becoming one of the leading figure of Soviet conceptualism in the 1970s, Kabakov escaped from the USSR on the wave of *perestroika* in 1987, settling first in Austria and then in the USA, and did not return to Moscow for almost twenty years.[47] Svetlana Boym has defined Kabakov's total installations as his 'refuge from exile'.[48] While the artist's diasporic experience is certainly a relevant element of his biography, this emphasis on the impact of Kabakov's exile from the Soviet Union on his practice is not, however, a useful way of thinking about the artist's work. In my view, this approach deflects our attention from the documentary nature of Kabakov's installations. Far from epitomising the artist's longing for home, *The Happiest Man in the World* addresses the central role played by cinema in shaping Soviet people's perception of reality. Kabakov's 'total installations', Boym has also remarked, 'reveal a nostalgia for utopia, but they return utopia to its origins – not in life, but in art'.[49] *Pace* Boym, I would argue that Kabakov's work blurs the distinction between life and art, imagination and truth, and shows how intertwined they were in the everyday experience of the Soviet Union.

Fig. 21. Ilya and Emilia Kabakov, *The Happiest Man in the World*, 2000–2013, mixed media video installation, dimension variable (Courtesy Ilya and Emilia Kabakov and Sprovieri Gallery, London, photograph by David Freeman / University of Westminster)

Fig. 22. Ilya and Emilia Kabakov, *The Happiest Man in the World*, 2000–2013, mixed media video installation, dimension variable (Courtesy Ilya and Emilia Kabakov and Sprovieri Gallery, London, photograph by David Freeman / University of Westminster)

Watched by millions of people, Pyriev's movies were produced under tight control of the Communist Party and were made during a time of incredible hardship for the Soviet Union: because Stalin forced collectivisation of the land, between the 1930s and the 1940s millions of people died in the country. Villages refusing to join a collective were occupied by the army, and the villagers were usually executed as enemies of the revolution. The land, now freed from ownership, was handed to the nearest collective farm. Dissidents of the communist regime died in the gulag; World War II compounded this already extreme hardship: the war's casualties – some historians have argued – were over twenty million. Devoid of any explicit reference to this grim historical context, Stalinist musicals have been dismissed, by critics and historians, as kitsch propaganda. 'From the opening of the chorus amid fields of grain to the fairbooth bulging with melons, bikes, books, and shoes,' Richard Stites has argued, '[*The Kuban*] *Cossacks* mystified the economic life of rural Russia.'[50] Ilya Kabakov experienced first-hand the gap between official propaganda and the reality of life under the Soviet regime. As he has succinctly put it, 'everything Soviet that was produced is always a lie, an abomination'.[51] 'From childhood, everyone knew what was necessary to survive in this country', he has remarked; 'How you had to lie, how to adapt, what to draw, what to sing, how to dance: by the 1950s, the entire repertoire, the whole menu, was sketched out.'[52] And yet, although not oblivious to the misery of those living under the Soviet regime, Kabakov does not dismiss Stalinist musicals as mere propaganda. Similarly to Steyerl's approach to Yugoslavian post-war cinema, the artist contemplates Stalinist musicals as a mechanism for introspection and analysis, as a probe into the political unconscious of the Soviet people. Importantly, this was defined and shaped by images of happiness and abundance: indeed, one of the principal functions of Socialist Realism, whose aesthetic philosophy was formalised and theorised as early as the First Congress of Soviet Writers of August 1934, was the production of anticipatory utopian fantasies. According to the influential Anatolii Lunacharskii – playwright, film critic, party member and minister responsible for Soviet culture and education until the early 1930s – the task of the artist was to provide the people with an anticipation of the future communist society:

> The Socialist Realist is in complete harmony with his surroundings and with the tendencies in their development as a warrior for the morrow that is in the process of realisation. But he does not accept reality as it really is. He accepts it as it will be. [...] The Socialist Realist is not obliged to stick to the limits of realism in the sense of verisimilitude [but may] resort to all sorts of

Fig. 23. Ilya and Emilia Kabakov, *The Happiest Man in the World*, 2000–2013, mixed media video installation, dimension variable (Courtesy Ilya and Emilia Kabakov and Sprovieri Gallery, London, photograph by David Freeman / University of Westminster)

hyperbole, caricature and utterly improbable comparisons – not to conceal reality but, through stylisation, to reveal it. A Communist who cannot dream is a bad Communist. The Communist dream is not a flight from the earthly but a flight into the future.[53]

The films appropriated by the Kabakovs exemplify Lunacharskii's theory of Socialist Realism. One innovation of Pyriev's films was 'the construction of the entire dialogue in rhyming couplets, stylizing even the spoken word, so that the film moves from spoken to sung words and back without difficulty'.[54] This allowed the film to further smudge the boundaries between the narrative and the number, and between reality and fantasy. More importantly, Pyriev's highly stylised and overtly staged *mise-en-scène*, the carefully choreographed camera movements and the overt bonhomie of the characters were not supposed to conceal the reality of communism but, instead, to reveal its essential outlines: the perhaps too idealistic image of a society where everybody was capable of working generously for the collective interest.

According to Richard Dyer, the dualism between fact and fiction lies at the heart of the potentially critical and subversive dimension of the Hollywood musical film. Drawing attention to the gap between what is and what could be, the musical, he suggests, may constitute a powerful threat to the dominant ideology, revealing inequalities and power structures and society's real needs. However, this genre is produced from within the boundaries and control of capitalism's elites; therefore, while it may give rein to the imagination of alternative systems, it must also defuse somehow the potentially subversive effects and implications of the utopian fantasies it contains. 'While entertainment is responding to needs that are real,' Dyer concludes, 'at the same time it is also defining and delimiting what constitutes the legitimate needs of people in this society.'[55] Thus, the Hollywood musical offers alternative solutions to real social problems and shortcomings within the terms of the socio-economic order that generates them, that is to say, capitalism. In this genre, 'abundance becomes consumerism, energy and intensity personal freedom and individualism, and transparency freedom of speech'.[56] Also weakening the potentially anti-ideological message of the musical is, according to Dyer, the tendency of the genre to separate the world of the narrative from the world of the musical numbers, that is, utopia from present reality. This was achieved in various ways: for instance, by representing the numbers as mere escapist dreams of the characters, or by removing the whole film in time and space and setting the story in a remote period of history, or in an exotic faraway community.

Unlike its American counterpart, the Soviet musical strived to collapse the separation between reality and utopia. Pyriev's films enacted the ideal of

Fig. 24. Ilya and Emilia Kabakov, *The Happiest Man in the World*, 2000–2013, mixed media video installation, dimension variable (Courtesy Ilya and Emilia Kabakov and Sprovieri Gallery, London, photograph by David Freeman / University of Westminster)

a communist society in the here and now. In the Stalinist musical, wrote one historian, 'the 'personal' is entirely submerged by the 'collective': virtue (the socialist attitude to work-cum-perseverance, represented by the central characters) is bound to triumph over vice (selfishness, philistinism or conservativism, represented by their antagonists)'.[57] Another way to look at the difference between the Hollywood and the Soviet musical is to consider the distinct role played by 'self-reflexivity' in both genres. In the Hollywood film, direct address to the audience, usually at the end of the movie, shows the 'constructed' or fictional quality of the cinematic fantasy. In the Stalinist musical, instead, this and other self-reflexive devices – such as the unveiling of façades, the insertion of documentary footage, or the pulling back of the camera in a 'reveal' – summon the audience to join the spectacle and aim to integrate the film into the viewers' world. As Trudy Anderson has pointed out, in Stalinist musicals, 'the aperture [to the audience] is also not self-reflexive in the traditional sense of demystifying representation but rather is a part of the Socialist Realist project of mystifying reality'.[58] Thus, where in the Hollywood musical self-reflexivity suggests the 'unreality' of the fiction, in the Soviet musical it is the spectator's world that is conveyed as unreal while the 'reality' of the fiction is posited as the only true reality. Far more than American entertainment, the Soviet musical coerced viewers into believing that the spectator's reality could be created or constructed just like a filmic reality. In a sense, the blurring of fact and fiction was a representational and ideological effect that was unique to Soviet film.

It is this effect that the Kabakovs' installation addresses: here the dream world of the screen is brought into close proximity with the space of the spectator. The withdrawal of the 'happiest man' into the imaginary landscape of Stalinist cinema is not as absurd a conceit as it might seem at first sight; rather, it is a metaphorical representation of the sort of virtual, artificial reality in which the Soviets used to live. In a world like the Soviet Union – the installation implies – there was no other depiction of reality than that offered by the highly manipulated world of communist propaganda. Socialist Realism penetrated every realm of culture so that the positive and ideal image of communism expressed in it began to achieve a sort of independent and autonomous life. This is the argument proposed by Russian historian Evgeny Dobrenko. For Dobrenko, one of the consequences of the ideology of state socialism in the Soviet Union was the 'de-realization of the every-day'. Socialist Realism produced a system of signs, an alternative discursive space in which to live – in effect, the 'real' space of socialism. Insofar as it proclaimed to be utopia realised, and substituted the ideal for the real, Socialist Realism obliterated the distinction between image and its referent, language and the real. 'The goal of Socialist Realism', Dobrenko concludes, 'is the de-realization of everydayness: available reality must cease to exist in order to appear in the form of socialism.'[59]

Indeed, Dobrenko's discussion of Socialist Realism bears more than superficial affinities with the effects elicited by *The Happiest Man in the World*. Consider, for instance, how the installation encourages the identification with the fantasy world of its hero and tends to invade the space reserved for the audience. As we enter the 'happiest man' apartment the room is striking for its intimacy: indeed, no museum official guards the objects, and no physical barriers discourage us from touching the furniture; instead, we are let free to wander through the space and maybe even to sit on the bed and the chairs. Adorned with long red curtains, reminiscent of film theatres, the cinemascope-proportioned window offers a perfect, unhindered vision of the movies projected onto the screen a few metres away. The viewers are surreptitiously coerced to join the *mise-en-scène*. But the neat order of the apartment inevitably sounds contrived: its theatrical appearance reflects back on the space outside, that is, on the area of the movie seats, which is also the space of the spectator. This is absorbed into the fictive world of the installation.

To put it differently, the Kabakovs lure the audience into the utopia of communism not through the raw realism of its images and props but, instead, through the overt staging of the installation space. Their work's expansive theatricality recalls the mechanics of Socialist Realism *qua* Dobrenko: blurring the distinction between the screen and the spectator, utopia and reality, *The Happiest Man in the World* re-enacts on a small scale the de-realisation of everydayness sought by the ideologues of Soviet culture. Yet Dobrenko's thesis is more radical than it would seem at first look: not only does he argue that the ideology of the Communist Party aimed to substitute idealised depictions for reality, he maintains that socialism as an entity could not have existed without its cultural production, its language and set of images, that is, without Socialist Realism. For Dobrenko the traditional view that Soviet official culture was an industry for manufacturing lies or a propaganda machine is mistaken. This view implies that a pre-existing truth was still within the grasp of the Soviet people, and yet this was not the case. 'We should keep in mind', Dobrenko insists, 'that this enormous production of images, which occupied the entire Soviet media, began to shape not only the political unconscious but the entire sphere of the imaginary as well' and that 'years later, for subsequent generations, all these images would become "the truth," for that is how people had come to see the world.'[60] He explains:

> Socialist Realism was a machine for transforming Soviet reality into socialism. That's why its basic function was not propagandistic but aesthetic and transformative *par excellence*. The mystical political economy of socialism, which lacks any foundation in human nature, can be understood only in terms of aesthetics. From the start, it was a project of the imagination and of political aesthetics. Aesthetics did not beautify reality, it *was* reality.[61]

Dobrenko's provocative thesis seems corroborated by the Kabakovs. Withdrawing any contextual explanation and plunging the viewer into the darkness of a movie theatre, their work imagines Soviet reality as a fleeting and bi-dimensional world, devoid of real substance.

We might object to the Kabakovs' analysis by arguing that it does not consider the extent to which specific social practices and places might have resisted Socialist Realism. Indeed, like Dobrenko, the Kabakovs might seem to overestimate the power of culture and aesthetics to shape and create reality. Moreover, the artists seem ambivalent about the possibility of escaping the demystifying power of ideology. In their reluctance to provide background information in the form of wall texts or captions, the Kabakovs suggest that it is impossible to fully distinguish between images and their referents. In their view, irony becomes the only possible form of truth. In *The Happiest Man in the World* a streak of irony can be detected in the somehow excessively conventional nature of the films' narratives. As Richard Taylor has observed, the opening sequence of Pyriev's *The Kuban Cossacks* 'in some ways ... also approaches self-parody. The characters move in a slower and more deliberate way than in pre-war films; they are, of course, older, and they are more stately, perhaps even grandiose ... the aging process of the lead players also became the aging process of the genre itself.'[62] On closer examination, the films selected by the artists may appear as imitations of previous films, simulacra of other simulacra. This self-irony involuntarily and subtly falsifies the representation, detaching images from any concrete material grounding. Nevertheless, there seems to be no directly accessible reality for the Kabakovs. For the artists, truth is entangled with language and conventions but also with dreams, hopes, ideas, projects and possibilities; and the ideal of a bare and absolute truth, devoid of fantastic and imaginary elements, is itself a naive illusion. As Ilya Kabakov has remarked:

> the elimination of 'utopianism' – alas, is also yet another form of utopianism. The creation of projects, project thinking, the formulation of all kinds of utopias is immanently inherent in us, our consciousness, and furthermore, it rests as a stimulus and as a basis for any of our actions as long as we remain human beings. In other words, we can exist only in the mode of the creation and realizations of utopias no matter what they might turn out to be 'in actual fact.'[63]

Kabakov's recognition of the impossibility of drawing a clear line between facts and fictions, fantasies and reality, is not necessarily an assertion of nihilism and despair. As *The Happiest Man in the World* demonstrates, dominant ideologies tap into utopian human aspirations and ideals which are not by default regressive. In a sense, the after-life of Stalinist musicals is a proof of the inherent validity of the ideals portrayed by these movies. Pyriev's films continue to strike a chord today, exerting a particular fascination among audiences in a post-Soviet Russia threatened by growing corruption and extreme individualism. While dismissed as kitsch propaganda by critics, the genre was resurrected in the late 1990s and early 2000s by countless popular movies that appropriate its popular motifs with critical intents. As Rimgaila Salys has pointed out, 'Contemporary quotations from Stalinist musicals contrapose the positive (in the absolute sense) idealism, optimism and semiotic wholeness of the Stalinist era to the demoralized, corrupt and fragmented post-Soviet present.'[64]

* * *

In Steyerl's, Sala's and the Kabakovs' film installations the fictionalisation of documentary is – rather than a formalist avant-garde gambit – the outcome of a new conceptualisation of truth which does not prioritise factual information as the main focus of knowledge. These artists' film installations invite the viewer to consider utopian dreams, memories, desires and political ideals: elements that are traditionally eschewed by empiricist notions of documentary. For the artists, these elements articulate significant layers of the truth that should not be neglected. The recognition of these affective and imaginary dimensions adds complexity to our knowledge of the past and the present rather than simply suspending them in relativism – fiction and representation are precisely the loci where these layers can be made visible. The model of truth that emerges from the experimental documentaries possesses significant affinities with Jacques Rancière's reading of Chris Marker's essay films in his book *Film Fables* (2006). Rancière argues that we need to view fiction not as 'a pretty story or evil lie, the flipside of reality that people try to pass off for it'.[65] Rather, we should look at it as a productive construction as in the Latin root of the word. 'Fiction' comes from the Latin *fingere*, which means not 'to feign' but 'to forge'. Rancière suggests that truth should not be understood according to the Platonic distinction so central to Western thought between *eidolon* – that which provides a mere likeness or semblance (*eilon* or *phantasma*) – and *eidos*, or 'idea', as that in which the true essence of the (only apparently) material universe is crystallised. In contrast, historical truth is inseparable from appearance or representation; it is not a pattern that waits to be found and discovered by the professional historian, independent from mediation, but is an entity that is entangled with subjective elements such as imagination, affect and desires, including utopian impulses. Rancière's reading of Marker's film essays appears valid for the artists at issue in this chapter. In these artists' works, fiction appears not only as a device to access the 'affective' content of truth but also as the metaphor for the dialogic process of historical enquiry. In this process, images are interrogated as fragments that can lead to the reconstruction of the past. Although this process of reconstruction is presented as open-ended, it is generative of new meanings. New insights into history as well as into the present result from it: far from demonstrating the futility of historical research, the foregrounding of representation here conveys the processual quality of truth. In other words, unlike 'mock-documentaries', these artists' films do not deploy fiction to deny the possibility of authentic knowledge and do not advocate for a pernicious relativism.

Importantly, Sala's, Steyerl's and the Kabakovs' experimental documentaries posit utopia firmly within the real. In them this impulse emerges as the expression of humanity's innate tendency to reach forward to a possible future. Judgements on the failure of utopias are theorised as always retrospective: those doing the hoping and the dreaming – these artists suggest – could not possibly have clairvoyant knowledge of the outcome of their projects and, therefore, to recover an authentic sense of history one has to be capable of reintroducing the openness of the future into the past, to grasp what was in its process of becoming. In this sense, history, rather than being the tribunal where the validity of utopian visions is assessed, appears as a repertoire of unfulfilled possibilities that could still be valid today. More specifically, contemporary artists suggest that to take the failure of communism as incontrovertible proof of the futility of utopian thinking is equivalent to throwing the baby out with the bathwater.

Steyerl's, Sala's and the Kabakovs' works demand critical attention for the way in which they foreground the transformative power of utopia and nostalgia. Their approach to these impulses approximates Ernst Bloch's philosophy.[66] For Bloch, one has to be able to rescue those elements that are forward-looking within the past and the failure of previous utopias does not invalidate the credentials of a particular vision. He argues that some of the greatest utopias have been constantly defeated, representing as they do a fundamental challenge to existing power relations, and that, rather than reject the failures of the past, we need to build on them. Bloch called for a re-evaluation of the role of the imagination, emotion and desire within an emancipatory politics; he was opposed to the rationalism of Marxism, for which utopia was a neglected political category. Indeed, the attitude of Marxists to utopian culture has generally been to consider it as at best an irrelevance and an irrational behaviour, at worst a dangerous distraction from the class struggle. In contrast, Bloch maintained that utopian desires and hope should not always be reduced to wishful thinking but may function as catalysts for social change. Hope, he remarked, is to be understood not only as emotion 'but more essentially as a directing act of a cognitive kind'.[67]

Bloch also proposed a capacious notion of utopia that included a range of materials that orthodox Marxists would have quickly dismissed as false consciousness or bourgeois ideology. According to him, traces of utopia can be found in a wide range of cultural forms – from day-dreams to fairy tales, from myths to travellers' tales, to various forms of art, literature and even religion – that Marxists tended to dismiss as unscientific and deceptive knowledge. Bloch posited, amidst the ideological, a 'utopian surplus' – the gold bearing strata of hope and promise. For him ideologies, even the most horrific ones, contain emancipatory-utopian elements, together with illusory ones. As Douglas Kellner has pointed out, according to Bloch, 'critique of ideology should not only be merely unmasking or demystification but also discovery of hidden potentials and values'.[68] Or, as Jürgen Habermas put it, 'within the ideological shell Bloch discovers the Utopian core, within the yet false consciousness the true consciousness'.[69] Criticising German socialist parties for having underestimated Nazism's capacity to address and mobilise the hopes and desires of the people, Bloch called for a Marxist politics that not only unveiled the mystifications and manipulations of bourgeois ideology but also could recognise and marshal the positive emotional and ideal energies embedded within a mass culture usually narrowly defined as the expression of the dominant class.

Bloch's nuanced concept of ideology bears more than a superficial resemblance to Steyerl's, Sala's and the Kabakovs' approach to communist propaganda. Appropriating propaganda films without resorting to parody, these artists point at the authentic dreams contained within it. Their works intimate that, to oppose false liberation, one should learn to recognise in ideology the authentic utopian core and to view propaganda materials and popular commercial cinema less as a distorted or manipulative form of knowledge which departs from a criterion of objectivity than as the expression of positive desires for communal living and human warmth.

At stake in these artistic experimental practices is the distinction between ideology and utopia, truth and fiction, and the very same possibility of a politics of utopia. Since every political project is based on some sort of truth claim, it cannot do without a criterion distinguishing between antiquated modes of belief contributing to the preservation of the status quo and those visions aimed at the progressive transformation of society.[70] For Bloch, this criterion is Marxism:

> Socialism as the ideology of the revolutionary proletariat is generally true consciousness in respect to the movement that is comprehended and in respect to the tendency of reality that is apprehended. Marx made an interesting comment to Ruge in 1843 about the relation of true ideology to the anticipation within the false consciousness of the former ideology that is not entirely false: 'Our slogan has to be: the reform of consciousness not by dogmas but by analyzing the mystical consciousness that is still vague about itself. Then it will become clear that since long ago the world has the dream of a thing and the world only has to have consciousness to really possess the thing. It will become clear that it is not a matter of a great connecting line between the past and the future but a matter of the fulfilment of the thoughts of the past.[71]

Nevertheless, Bloch's distinction between false and true consciousness is based on nothing other than an evaluative analysis of the content of utopia/ideology and its consistency with Marxist politics. As Ruth Levitas has noted, the grounds of the distinction between true and mystificatory knowledge are not sufficiently spelt out and ultimately rest upon a questionable teleological belief that humanity is 'naturally' reaching forward to a socialist society. 'To have pursued [this distinction] further', Levitas concludes, 'would have revealed the intrinsically political nature of the dichotomy and undermined the pretensions of Marxism to absolute verity and scientificity.'[72] Levitas has a point here: Bloch's theory is based on an excessive faith in the epistemological grounds of Marxism and does not consider the risks of it sliding into dangerous orthodoxy and blind acceptance of its dogmas.

This is also one of the challenges and possible weaknesses facing documentary practices that seek to reanimate past social utopias which underpinned authoritarian regimes such as the Soviet Union or Albania. Do these documentaries inadvertently risk glossing over the use (or misuse) of utopian fantasies by party elites to justify and conceal reactionary politics? The artists' overall response to this challenge is to defamiliarise propaganda films and to treat them as enigmatic objects open to multiple and different readings. But there are also significant differences between Sala's, Steyerl's and the Kabakovs' appropriation strategies. While they do not ridicule or dismiss the hopes and ideals informing communist rhetoric, Sala and the Kabakovs are more reluctant than Steyerl to celebrate their countries' pasts. Their more cautious attitude *vis-à-vis* communist propaganda can be easily explained by considering the artists' biographies: émigrés who left their countries in the midst of the disintegration of communism or in its immediate aftermath, Sala and the Kabakovs directly experienced their nations' blatant economic and political failure and the gap between state propaganda and the dismal reality of their countries. Hence, their work betrays a more pronounced ambivalence: Sala and the Kabakovs appear to identify with the communist utopia even as they distance themselves from it. In contrast, German-born Steyerl seems to sidestep the question of whether the Yugoslavian communist regime misused utopianism to preserve the status quo and prefers to shift the focus onto Bosnia's difficult present. For Steyerl this question is irrelevant because, according to her, the 'truth' of the lost newsreel resides in its being the model for a peaceful and secular Bosnia, freed from the sectarianism of identity politics. Steyerl's seemingly arbitrary approach certainly has some advantages: it offers concrete political solutions to current problems instead of vague answers. More importantly, Steyerl suggests that the validity of the Marxist ideology owes to an intrinsically normative and evaluative choice: this choice would still remain true even if every evidence of the positive achievements of communist regimes were completely obliterated, as it actually happened in the case of the destruction of the Sarajevo film archive. In other words, while truth should determine politics rather than politics determining truth, Steyerl points out that truth is also the outcome of a value-based choice that is 'fictional' in the sense of epistemologically unassailable.

NOTES

1. David Lowenthal, 'Nostalgia Tells It Like It Wasn't', in Christopher Shaw and Malcolm Chase, eds, *The Imagined Past: History and Nostalgia* (Manchester: Manchester University Press, 1989), pp. 18–32.
2. Lewis Mumford, 'Utopia, the City and the Machine', in Frank E. Manuel, ed., *Utopias and Utopian Thought* (Boston, MA: Beacon, 1967), p. 12.
3. Hayden White, 'The Future of Utopia in History', *Historein: A Review of the Past and Other Stories*, vol. 7 (2007), p. 12.
4. Peter Novick, *That Noble Dream: The 'Objectivity Question' and the American Historical Profession* (Cambridge: Cambridge University Press, 1988), pp. 1–2.
5. On the politics of nostalgia for communism in European culture, see Charity Scribner, *Requiem for Communism* (Cambridge, MA: MIT Press, 2003); on memory in post-re-unification German cinema, see Anthony Enns, 'The Politics of Ostalgie: Post-Socialist Nostalgia in Recent German Film', *Screen*, vol. 48, no. 4 (2007), pp. 475–91.
6. For a discussion of the epistemological claims made by documentary cinema and a history of the term and its usage, see Brian Winston, *Claiming the Real: The Griersonian Documentary and Its Legitimations* (London: British Film Institute, 1995).
7. Olivier Lugon, 'Documentary: Authority and Ambiguities', in Maria Lind and Hito Steyerl, eds, *The Green Room* (Berlin: Sternberg Press, 2008), p. 29.
8. This impulse is also at work internationally in contemporary art. See Maria Lind and Hito Steyerl, eds, *The Green Room* (Berlin: Sternberg Press, 2008). On the philosophical and epistemological implications of contemporary artists' use of fiction, see Vered Maimon, 'The Third Citizen: On Models of Criticality in Contemporary Artistic Practices', *October*, no. 129 (2009), pp. 85–112; Carry Lambert-Beatty, 'Parafiction Make Believe: Parafiction and Plausibility', *October*, no. 129 (2009), pp. 51–84.
9. Alexandra Juhasz and Jesse Lerner, 'Introduction: Phony Definitions and Troubling Taxonomies of the Fake Documentary', in Alexandra Juhasz and Jesse Lerner, eds, *F is for Phony: Fake Documentary and Truth's Undoing* (Minneapolis, MN: University of Minnesota Press, 2006), p. 7.
10. Craig Hight and Janet Roscoe, *Faking It: Mock-Documentary and the Subversion of Factuality* (Manchester: Manchester University Press, 2001), p. 188.
11. Ibid.
12. Ibid., p. 182.
13. For an extensive survey of Sala's work, see Mark Godfrey, 'Articulate Enigma: The Works of Anri Sala', in Mark Godfrey, Liam Gillick and Hans Ulrich Obrist, eds, *Anri Sala* (London: Phaidon, 2006), pp. 33–102.
14. Liam Gillick, 'Now I See, One Work by Anri Sala', in Mark Godfrey, Liam Gillick and Hans Ulrich Obrist, eds, *Anri Sala* (London: Phaidon, 2006), pp. 103–10.
15. Personal conversation with the artist, May 2009.
16. Ibid.
17. For an account of the history of Albania, see Miranda Vickers, *The Albanians: A Modern History* (London: I.B. Tauris, 1999); and James Pettifer, *The Albanian Question: Reshaping the Balkans* (London: I.B. Tauris, 2006).
18. Vit Havránek, 'The Documentary Ontology of Forms in Transforming Countries', in Maria Lind and Hito Steyerl, eds, *The Green Room* (Berlin: Sternberg Press, 2008), p.

136.
19 For an analysis of this film in the context of Varda's cinema, see Ari J. Blatt, 'Thinking Photography in Film, or the Suspended Cinema of Agnès Varda and Jean Eustache', *French Forum*, vol. 36, nos. 2–3 (2011), pp. 181–200
20 Before 1990, all individuals who worked in the mass media, whether editors, film directors or television and radio producers, were subject to strict party discipline and rigid guidelines. See Raymond E. Zickel and Walter R. Iwaskiw, eds, *Albania: A Country Study* (Washington: U.S. Government, 1994).
21 As Sala remembers, because of the controlled nature of television programmes, 'everything was so unreal [on Albanian television] that I remember the only realistic thing was the weather forecast'; Sala as quoted in Massimiliano Gioni and Michele Robecchi, 'Anri Sala, Unfinished Histories', *Flash Art*, 214, (2001), p. 107.
22 Sala as cited in Gerald Matt, *Interviews: Vol. 2* (Köln: Walther König, 2008), p. 298.
23 *Ibid.*, p. 292.
24 Tom McDonough, 'Calling from the Inside: Filmic Topologies of the Everyday', *Grey Room*, no. 26 (2007), p. 12.
25 *Ibid.*
26 *Ibid.*, p. 14.
27 On the history of the film essay, see Nora Alter, 'Translating the Essay into Film and Installation', *Journal of Visual Culture*, vol. 6, no. 1 (2007), pp. 44–57.
28 *Ibid.*, p. 45.
29 See Hito Steyerl, 'From Ethnicity to Ethics', in Maria Lind and Tirdad Zolghadr, eds, *A Fiesta of Tough Choices: Contemporary Art in the Wake of Cultural Policies* (Oslo: Torpedo, 2007), pp. 58–70.
30 Hito Steyerl as cited in Catrin Lundqvist, 'Journal No. 1. An Artist's Impression'; http://www.modernamuseet.org/v4/templates/template1.asp?lang=Eng&id=3661 (accessed June 2009). For a more articulated explanation of Steyerl's position regarding postmodernist theories of documentary, see also Steyerl, 'Documentary Uncertainty', *A Prior*, no. 15 (2007), pp. 304–6.
31 Hito Steyerl, 'From Ethnicity to Ethics', p. 69.
32 The 1960s and 1970s witnessed a proliferation of experiments with split-screen and multiple projections. See, for example, the film works of Andy Warhol and Stan Van der Beeck. For a history of the projected image in America, see Chrissie Iles, *Into the Light: The Projected Image in American Art 1964–1977* (New York: Whitney Museum, 2001); see also Malcolm Turvey et al., 'Roundtable: The Projected Image in Contemporary Art', *October*, no. 104 (2003), pp. 71–96; Tamara Trodd, ed., *Screen/Space: The Projected Image in Contemporary Art* (Manchester: Manchester University Press, 2011).
33 Hito Steyerl, 'From Ethnicity to Ethics', p. 60. Indeed, according to historians such as Alexander Pavkovic and Ann Lane, one of the causes of the disintegration of Yugoslavia in the early 1990s was the inability of the communist leadership of Tito and his followers to build a unified school system with common textbooks and school curricula, and thereby create a sense of commonality between Yugoslavia's ethnic groups. See Alexander Pavkovic, *The Fragmentation of Yugoslavia: Nationalism in a Multinational State* (Basingstoke: Palgrave, 1997); Ann Lane, *Yugoslavia: When Ideals Collide* (Basingstoke: Palgrave, 2004).

34 Harun Farocki in Farocki and Kaja Silverman, eds, *Speaking about Godard* (New York and London: New York University Press, 1998), p. 142.
35 Farocki as cited in Rembert Huser, 'Nine Minutes in the Yard: A Conversation with Harun Farocki', *Senses of Cinema*, no. 21 (1999), np; see also Harun Farocki and Kaja Silverman, eds., *Speaking about Godard*, p. 142.
36 See André Bazin, 'The Ontology of the Photographic Image' and 'Theater and Cinema', in *What Is Cinema?* (Berkeley, CA: University of California Press, 1967), pp. 9–16 and pp. 76–124. Siegfried Kracauer, *Theory of Film: The Redemption of Physical Reality* (Princeton, NJ; Chichester: Princeton University Press, 1960). See also Tom Gunning, 'Moving away from the Index: Cinema and the Impression of Reality', in *Differences*, vol. 8, no. 1 (2007), pp. 29–52.
37 For an account of the history of Yugoslav cinema, see Daniel Goulding, *Liberated Cinema: The Yugoslav Experience, 1945–2001* (Bloomington, IN: Indiana University Press, 2002).
38 Helmut Farber, 'Das Unentdeckte Kino', in Alexander Kluge, ed., *Bestandsaufnahme: Utopie Film* (Frankfurt am Main: Zweitausendeins, 1983), p. 26 (my translation).
39 Steyerl herself has openly declared her fondness for the ideals expressed in the lost newsreel. 'The grenade which destroyed "Journal No. 1"', Steyerl writes, 'also symbolically destroyed the socialist-modernist ideal of education and empowerment of women in secular institutions, as imperfect as they may have been' (Steyerl, 'From Ethnicity to Ethics', p. 63).
40 *Ibid.*, p. 69.
41 *Ibid.*
42 Hito Steyerl, 'A Language of Practice', in Maria Lind and Steyerl, eds, *The Green Room*, p. 231.
43 Documentary film, in the words of Bill Nichols, is one of the discourses of sobriety that include science, economics, politics and history: discourses that claim to tell the truth, to describe the real. See Bill Nichols, *Introduction to Documentary* (Bloomington, IN: Indiana University Press, 2001).
44 My description of the installation is based on the Kabakovs' 2012 exhibition of the same title at Ambika P3 in London. A previous version of the work was displayed in Paris in the collective exhibition 'L'autre moitié de l'Europe' presented at the Galerie Nationale du Jeu de Paume in Paris from 8 February to 21 June 2000.
45 Matthew Jesse Jackson, *The Experimental Group: Ilya Kabakov, Moscow Conceptualism, Soviet Avant-Gardes* (Chicago: University of Chicago Press, 2010), pp. 151-6.
46 Likewise, Boris Groys reads the character of Kabakov's installation *The Man Who Flew into Space from His Apartment* as a stand-in for the artist. 'Not so very long after the making of this installation,' writes Groys, 'Ilya Kabakov was himself propelled over the borders of the Soviet realm towards the West, in much the same way that his hero hurtled into outer space'; Boris Groys, *Ilya Kabakov: The Man Who Flew into Space from His Apartment* (London: Afterall, 2006), p. 3.
47 On the philosophical origins and principles of Russian conceptualism, see Mikhail Epstein, 'The Philosophical Implications of Russian Conceptualism', *Journal of Eurasian Studies*, no. 1 (2010), pp. 64–71.
48 Svetlana Boym, *The Future of Nostalgia* (New York: Basic Books, 2001), p. 312. See also

Svetlana Boym, 'On Diasporic Intimacy: Ilya Kabakov's Installations and Immigrant Homes', *Critical Inquiry*, vol. 24, no. 2 (2008), pp. 498–524. For a similar approach to Kabakov's work, see Boris Groys, 'Ilya Kabakov: The Theatre of Authorship', in *History Becomes Form: Moscow Conceptualism* (Cambridge, MA: MIT Press, 2010), pp. 105–23. For a survey of Kabakov's art in the Soviet era, see Matthew Jesse Jackson, *The Experimental Group: Ilya Kabakov, Moscow Conceptualism, Soviet Avant-Gardes* (Chicago: University of Chicago Press, 2010).

49 Svetlana Boym, *The Future of Nostalgia*, p. 324.
50 Richard Stites, *Russian Popular Culture* (Cambridge: Cambridge University Press, 1992), p. 221. For an alternative interpretation of Pyriev's cinema, see M. Turovskaya, 'I. A. Pyr'ev i ego muzykal'nye komedii. K probleme zhanra' [I. A. Pyriev and His Musical Comedies. On the Problem of Genre], *Kino-vedcheskie zapiski* [Scholarly Film Notes], no. 1 (1988), pp. 111–46.
51 Ilya Kabakov as cited by Anton Vidolke, 'Interview with Ilya and Emilia Kabakov', in Charles Esche and Boris Groys, *Utopia and Reality: El Lissitzky, Ilya and Emilia Kabakov* (Eindhoven: Van Abbemuseum, 2012), p. 29.
52 *Ibid.*, p. 30.
53 Anatolii Lunacharskii as cited by Richard Taylor, 'Singing on the Steppes for Stalin: Ivan Pyr'ev and the Kolkhoz Musical in Soviet Cinema', *Slavic Review*, vol. 58, no. 1 (1999), p. 145.
54 *Ibid.*, p. 155.
55 Richard Dyer, *Only Entertainment* (New York: Routledge, 1992), p. 26.
56 *Ibid.*, p. 27.
57 Maria Enzenzberger, '"We were born to turn a fairy tale into reality": Grigori Alexandrov's *The Radiant Path*', in Richard Taylor and Derek Spring, eds, *Stalinism and Soviet Cinema* (New York: Routledge, 1993), p. 99.
58 Trudy Anderson, 'Why Stalinist Musicals?', *Discourse*, vol. 17, no. 3 (1995), p. 44.
59 Evgeny Dobrenko, *Political Economy of Socialist Realism*, trans. Jesse M. Savage (New Haven, CT: Yale University Press, 2007), p. 14.
60 *Ibid.*, p. 6.
61 *Ibid.*, p. 4.
62 Richard Taylor, 'Singing on the Steppes for Stalin: Ivan Pyryev and the Kolkhoz Musical in Soviet Cinema', *Slavic Review*, vol. 58, no. 1 (1999), p. 158. See also Taylor, '"But Eastward, Look, the Land Is Brighter": Toward a Topography of the Utopia in the Stalinist Musical', in Evgeny Dobrenko, *The Landscape of Stalinism: The Art and Ideology of Soviet Space* (Seattle: University of Washington Press, 2003), pp. 201–15.
63 Ilya Kabakov as cited in Ilya and Emilia Kabakov, *Dvorets Proektov/Der Palast der Projekte/The Palace of Projects* (Essen: Kokerei Zollverein, 2001), p. 191.
64 Rimgaila Salys, *The Strange Afterlife of Stalinist Musical Films* (Washington D.C.: National Council for Eurasian and East European Studies, 2006), p. 9.
65 Jacques Rancière, 'Documentary Fictions: Marker and the Fiction of Memory', *Film Fables* (Oxford: Berg, 2006), p. 158.
66 Ernst Bloch, *The Principle of Hope*, trans. Neville Plaice, Stephen Plaice and Paul Knight, three volumes (Oxford: Basil Blackwell, 1986).
67 *Ibid.*, p. 12.

68 Douglas Kellner, 'Ernst Bloch, Utopia and Ideology Critique,' in Jamie Owen Daniel and Tom Moylan, eds., *Not Yet: Reconsidering Ernst Bloch* (London: Verso 1997), p. 84.
69 Jürgen Habermas as quoted in James Bentley, *Between Marx and Christ: The Dialogue in German Speaking Europe: 1870–1970* (London: Verso, 1982).
70 I am borrowing this definition of the difference between ideology and utopia from Karl Mannheim, *Ideology and Utopia* (London: Routledge and Kegan Paul, 1979).
71 Ernst Bloch, *The Principle of Hope*, pp. 155–6.
72 Ruth Levitas, 'Educated Hope: Ernst Bloch on Abstract and Concrete Utopia', *Utopian Studies*, vol. 1, no. 2 (1990), pp. 13–26.

CHAPTER THREE
Archives of Commodities

Consider a gigantic installation of 412 photographs depicting used television sets, worn-out shoes, shop signs, storefronts, second-hand clothes and market stalls in Poland, Uganda, Cuba, Mexico, Palestine and Manhattan. Or, a sequence of 57 digital photographs of kitsch and colourful souvenirs, window mannequins, statuettes and pictures of celebrities taken in various shops across the world. Or, in a more pristine register, consider a series of well-crafted images of various mass-produced objects made by French workers on strike. However different in presentation, these photographic works – *Analogue* (1998–2009) by Zoe Leonard, *Voyage of the Beagle* (2007) by Rachel Harrison and *Vingt-quatre Objets de Grève* (1999–2000) by Jean-Luc Moulène respectively – share an interest in the affective and symbolic values of commodities.

Given the subject matter of these projects, we could be tempted to situate them within a post-war artistic and critical tradition that treated advertisement and commercial photography as irrefutable evidence of the amnesiac effects of capitalism.[1] One of the most significant and well-known examples of this tendency is Gerard Richter's *Atlas* (1964–present). *Atlas* is a large album containing a heterogeneous array of photographic sources: amateur snapshots together with reproductions from newspapers and popular magazines, portraits, advertisements, pornographic imagery, and pictures of famous historical figures and events such as concentration camp survivors and Adolf Hitler. Richter does not make any attempt to offer an overriding interpretation, thus denying any promise of comprehensibility, objectivity and definitiveness of the kind evoked by scientific or archaeological archives. Hence, according to Benjamin Buchloh, Richter's *Atlas* is an 'anomic' archive which acknowledged that, in the world of late capitalism, photography cannot return as an unproblematic tool of knowledge.

'Richter's *Atlas*', Buchloh concluded, 'seems to consider photography and its various practices as a system of ideological domination, more precisely, as one of the instruments with which collective anomie, amnesia, and repression are socially inscribed.'[2] Moreover, the *Atlas* points at the obsolescence of Weimar and Soviet theorisations of photography and avant-garde practices, which had a clear agitational and emancipatory dimension, originating from the utopian desire for the radical transformation of society's power structures. The disordered juxtaposition of diverse imagery in the photomontages of Rodchenko and Hannah Höch suggested such a transformation, while the chaotic and inconclusive nature of Richter's archive – rife with banal imagery culled from the mass media – functioned as a socially enforced legitimation of the historical repressions of German society. The significance of *Atlas* lies, according to Buchloh, in its capacity to reflect the complicity of photography in the construction of an escapist, reified culture that furthered acquiescence to the status quo.

Buchloh's reading of Richter's seminal work extends a critical framework originating from the 1968 political movement that regarded the photographic archive as an instrument of capitalistic power and governmental institutions.[3] Consider Allan Sekula's influential essay 'Reading an Archive: Photography between Labour and Capital' (1983), which, in my view, epitomises this conceptualisation. Writing at a time of increasing incorporation of photography within an art world perceived as elitist and the expression of capitalistic hegemony, Sekula argued that photographic archives ended up reinforcing the formalist discourse of mainstream art criticism; their mystifying authority dovetailed with a superficial attention to the aesthetic qualities of documentary images that undermined authentic and potentially subversive contextual knowledge. The working class's uses of the medium and the exploitative and hierarchical social relations that constitute capitalistic production are dissolved under the illusion of objectivity and completeness provided by the photographic archive. The '*semantic availability* of pictures in archives', Sekula wrote, 'exhibits the same abstract logic as that which characterizes goods in the marketplace'.[4] It is easy to see the influence of Marx's notion of commodity fetishism on this theory: for Marx, the commodity is a cipher for amnesia as it veils the use value of objects and the memory of their production, that is to say, the memory of the workers' labour.[5] Defining the archive as a 'clearing house of meaning' that is akin to the reifying logic of the capitalistic market, Sekula evoked a rather monolithic vision of documentary photography – one which reduces it to an ideological machine at the service of the bourgeois elite and ultimately confined the historian to the study of anything but hegemonic practices and discourses.

Harrison's, Leonard's and Moulène's series seem to be informed by a more ambivalent attitude toward consumer and advertisement culture than that suggested by Buchloh and Sekula. Like Richter's *Atlas*, their photographic archives seem to acknowledge the intensified flood of images and amnesiac tendencies of late capitalism; however, their works also tend to animate commodities with affect and singularity. An element of mimicry is present in all these projects: their repetitive format (*Analogue*), pristine look (*Objets de Grève*) and parodic excess (*Voyage of the Beagle*) mirror the formal strategies of cheap consumer culture and advertisement. Leonard's, Moulène's and Harrison's projects suggest that in contemporary society, 'the stuff of consumer culture is an integral component of the structures of feeling and affect of our times'.[6] Their projects imply a move from an emphasis on the figure of the commodity as a cipher of amnesia to a reappraisal of the commodity as a site where popular and utopian desires can be found. Leonard's, Moulène's and Harrison's 'mimetic archives' intimate that there is some life and creativity within capitalism and that it is, therefore, possible to detect a utopian impulse within its products and culture.

The artists at issue here also propose the kind of hermeneutic approach described by Fredric Jameson at the very beginning of his *Archaeologies of the Future*. Here Jameson distinguishes between utopian planners and utopian interpreters.[7] Where the former propose a systematic blueprint for radical political transformation, the latter attempt to decipher the unconscious utopian desires at work in contemporary popular culture. Utopia may be found in those aspects of society that might look to be the most affected by the reifying logic of capitalism:

> The utopian impulse, therefore, calls for a hermeneutic, for the detective work of a decipherment and a reading of utopian clues and traces in the landscape of the real; a theorization and interpretation of unconscious utopian investments in realities large or small, which may be far from utopian. The premise here is that the most noxious phenomena can serve as the repository and hiding place for all kinds of unsuspected wish fulfilments and utopian gratifications.[8]

Following Jameson, we may consider Moulène, Leonard and Harrison as 'utopian interpreters' who rummage through the utterly commodified landscape of postmodern society in search of fragments that may be read as allegories of alternative social formations. Like Jameson's 'utopian interpreters', they invest utopian desire 'in a variety of unexpected, disguised, concealed and distorted ways'.[9] Looking for utopia in the 'most noxious phenomena', the artists at issue here deliver an image of capitalism that does not conform with the monolithic approaches to the photographic archive discussed earlier. In Harrison's, Leonard's and Moulène's works, capitalism emerges as a dynamic and differentiated reality that may offer openings and some hope for social change. But if it becomes clear that Harrison's, Leonard's and Moulène's archives attempt to decipher a revolutionary desire within the destructive nature of capitalism, then what is the content of this impulse? These artistic projects raise a second crucial question: when everyday consumer culture is presented as an allegory of utopia, what are the implications for the idea of utopia as radical difference?

* * *

Leonard decided to begin *Analogue* in the late 1990s when, returning to New York after a period spent in Alaska, she found the Lower East Side of Manhattan (LES) –the neighbourhood where the artist lived for over three decades – to be increasingly gentrified. In fact, in less than twenty years, the LES was gradually transformed into an area of luxury developments destined for the middle and upper class employed in the growing service and financial industry of the city. This process of gentrification caused the displacement of the local population from a neighbourhood traditionally occupied by blue-collar workers of ethnic background.[10] Importantly, this phenomenon was not determined by upward social mobility: unlike the Jewish, Italian and Irish immigrants who lived in the neighbourhood at the beginning of the twentieth century, the black, Puerto Rican and Dominican communities who inhabited the LES at the beginning of the gentrifying developments moved out of the area not because of their improved financial conditions but because of the increased cost of living, and at times forced eviction. One of the most visible signs of this process of gentrification was the disappearance of the unassuming local markets, beauty shops, discount stores and second-hand shops that catered to the immigrant community. Like the inhabitants of the neighbourhood, these small businesses were forced to close down because of the rising rents and the competition of big store chains, sleek bars and trendy boutiques, which have increasingly occupied the area. 'It was only when these old shops began disappearing', Leonard remarked, 'that I realized how much I counted on them – that this layered, frayed and quirky beauty underlined my own life. I felt at home in it.'[11] For the project Leonard chose to only use analogue photography; her old Rolleiflex camera seemed appropriate for the task: like the shops, in the late 1990s analogue photography was on the verge of disappearing and was being replaced by more functional digital cameras. One of Leonard's most significant projects to date, *Analogue* has appeared in three different versions: as a portfolio of dye transfer prints that can be shown individually or in groups; as a book of ninety photographs; and as an installation of more than four hundred photographs, as displayed in *Documenta 12* at Kassel in 2007, at the Hispanic Society of America

Fig. 25. Zoe Leonard, installation view, *Analogue*, Museo Nacional Centro de Arte Reina Sofia, Madrid, 2008 (Courtesy Zoe Leonard and Galerie Gisela Capitain, Cologne)

in New York, and at Reina Sofía in 2008. It is this latter version that I will focus on here.

Produced over a decade, the project has a monumental quality: it comprises more than four hundred photographs, which are arranged into grids divided into twenty-five separate panels; in its installation form it occupies multiple walls of a large gallery room, overwhelming the viewer with images. Contextual information is absent, contrary to the book version, wherein each of the eighty images is captioned by the city, date and street where the photograph was taken. Given the size of Leonard's archive, it is difficult to provide an exhaustive description of its content. Suffice it to say that the first half of the installation represents the vanishing economy of small discount stores of the LES. In one picture of a shop window, colourful bottles of detergent – labelled 'Joy' – are serially arranged in front of the viewer. In another photograph, air-fresheners, washing-up liquids and other household items stand over a fake golden background made up with drab decorating paper. Other pictures depict the shop fronts of butchers, 99-cent stores, TV repair shops, and hairdressers for the local black and Latino community. The arrangement of the materials seems ordered according to similarities in content: thus one panel contains photographs of shop signs, another of closed stores, another one of household and furniture stores, and so on. As we move on towards the next panels, the focus shifts from New York to markets in foreign cities in Mexico, Cuba, Uganda and Poland. In this section, which occupies half of

Fig. 26. Zoe Leonard, *Analogue*, 1998–2009 (detail), 412 C-prints + gelatin silver prints, 28 x 28 cm. (Courtesy Zoe Leonard and Galerie Gisela Capitain, Cologne)

the installation, the subject matter becomes the global market of used products. One large panel depicts only bundles of used clothes. These were donated by charities across the USA and sent to Africa and East Europe, where they are sold in local markets. These appear in panels that portray small storefronts and stalls in cities such as Kampala, Trinidad, Mexico City and Warsaw. Leonard's camera documents them with the same straight frontality of her LES photographs. Tidily arranged second-hand clothes, detergents, shoes, meat and poultry, used TV monitors and radios parade in front of the viewer. One small panel shows similar bright red ramshackle outdoor cafés, with the brazen declarations of Coca-Cola. Some of the photographs are in black-and-white; others are high-contrast and saturated colour prints. One of the specifics of the installation version is that it invites both an intimate relation with the images *and* a more distanced vision of the totality. While the small format of the singular pictures suggests proximity, the grid-like arrangement of the installation, sprawling across multiple walls, encourages viewers to indulge in the global spectacle of the flow of commodities from one country to another.

Three similar interpretations informed the reception of Leonard's work. The series was discussed as a lament about the vanishing of the LES working-class community, as a poignant critique of globalisation as a homogenising force erasing local identities, and as a self-reflexive project interrogating the losses produced by the rapid obsolescence of analogue photography.[12] All three readings framed

Fig. 27. Zoe Leonard, *Analogue*, 1998–2009 (detail), 412 C-prints + gelatin silver prints, 28 x 28 cm. (Courtesy Zoe Leonard and Galerie Gisela Capitain, Cologne)

Analogue as a critique of capitalism, viewed, in turn, as an inherently destructive force. My purpose here is not to dismiss the interpretations proposed by the reception of *Analogue*: indeed, I believe that they are valid. However, one wonders whether critics, in the hope of finding elements of 'criticality' in the artist's work, have 'imagined everything and projected it' into Leonard's images, reducing the work to a rather straightforward critique of capitalism.[13] These critics' emphasis on loss and mourning downplays the pleasurable affective and aesthetic investments that can be extrapolated from Leonard's representational strategies and downplays the work's ambiguous mimicry of consumer culture. Mimesis occurs in the archive: *Analogue* not only portrays a highly commodified culture in the process of been displaced, it also mirrors it by adopting some of the conventions of advertisement.

Take for example the artist's use of colour photography: some of her pictures depart from the tradition of black-and-white photography – strongly associated with social documentary – to embrace brash colours in order to grab the viewer's attention and to mirror advertisement techniques. Since we have emotional and psychological connections with colours, the archive aims not only to inform and preserve memory but also to enchant. In addition, Leonard's framing departs from the more 'objective' wide shot in favour of close-ups that magnify the commodities, inviting the viewer to move closer. Likewise, the small size of the pictures (11 x 11 inches) suggests a kind of emotional, almost tactile engagement with the objects depicted. Leonard skilfully deploys natural lighting techniques to evoke a magical and uncanny atmosphere. Shot under the dim morning light, the objects often appear to pop-up from the darkness. Or, in other cases, Leonard produces a chiaroscuro effect by shooting at night, under the atmospheric neon lights of the stores. Several other pictures show a variety of exhortative signs (e.g. 'Meats, Meats, Meats Fresh Everyday'). One sign reads 'Mr. Shoe' and then hints at a fantastic anthropomorphisation of the products.[14] Finally, the uncanny animation of an inert material world of cheap goods is achieved by the exclusion of human beings from the representation – a strategy that recalls the street photography of Eugène Atget.[15] As in Atget's pictures of early twentieth-century Paris shops, people are consistently absent in Leonard's photographs: it is as if they have suddenly and mysteriously disappeared into the phantasmagorical world of kitsch and second-hand commodities. Finally, mimesis occurs in the seriality of the archive: while, as many critics have pointed out, this may be a reference to photoconceptualism, the serial form of the installation can also be read as Leonard's strategy to mirror the ordered and symmetric arrangement of products as seen in the numerous market stalls and shop windows of *Analogue*. The sheer number of Leonard's same-size pictures mirrors the sense of profusion conveyed by the number of commodities on display in some of the pictures.

This ambivalent mimetic approach is symptomatic of an affective investment in the commodity world at the centre of the archive. Tom McDonough, one of the few writers to have subjected Leonard's work to a trenchant ideological critique, questioned *Analogue*'s affective investment in the LES small-shop economy by arguing that it generates a distorted image of the socio-political reality that caused the neighbourhood's gentrification. McDonough compared *Analogue* with Hans Haacke's well-known *Shapolsky et al. Manhattan Real Estate Holdings, a Real Time Social System, as of May 1, 1971* (1971). Haacke's photographic project deployed photographic documents together with explanatory wall panels, maps and charts to describe the obscure connections between various dummy companies that together controlled an exploitative market for lower-income housing in Lower Manhattan. According to McDonough, *Shapolsky et al....* adequately exposed corporate business's greed and ruthless profiteering and should be taken, then, as a significantly more successful artistic intervention than Leonard's. In contrast, *Analogue*'s sentimental elegy ends up suggesting that large companies are uniquely responsible for the gentrification of the area. 'Leonard's stark dichotomy of small business/large corporation', McDonough claimed, 'implies what we might call an ecological view of the urban economy, with local stores that created a responsive equilibrated ecosystem being eradicated by the invasive species of multinational brands, the "honest" commerce of the former undone by the wastefulness of the latter.'[16] As a matter of fact, the destruction of the

Fig. 28. Zoe Leonard, *Analogue*, 1998–2009 (detail), 412 C-prints + gelatin silver prints, 28 x 28 cm. (Courtesy Zoe Leonard and Galerie Gisela Capitain, Cologne)

LES working-class community was caused not only by big chains taking over the area, but also by the pressure of other small entrepreneurial shops now serving an entirely different social class. In sum, *Analogue* is an 'amnesiac' archive, which forgets that small business is not an external reality to capitalism but one of its components. In McDonough's words, the project fails to show that 'waste, ruin, destruction are constitutive of present order, not mere surplus negativity'.[17]

McDonough certainly has a point in arguing that Leonard's photographs focus too much on detail, excluding much of the wider economic and political background that determined the gentrification of Lower Manhattan; but I take his critique less as a shortcoming of the project than as a symptom of the provocative ambivalence of *Analogue*. What is really scandalous, for uncompromising Marxists like McDonough, is that *Analogue* intimates at the identification between the working class – the 'revolutionary' class according to Marx – with the body of the commodity, conventionally considered as a symbol of the mystifying nature of the capitalist ideology. Yet Leonard's project seems animated by what sociologist Arjun Appadurai has called 'methodological fetishism', or the need to approach consumption closely as an overdetermined process whereby commodities are not inert objects but 'things-in-motion', capable of engendering, across their life, multiple and contradictory meanings.[18] In other words, as *Analogue* seems to propose, an examination of the desires invested in consumption can reveal hidden utopian impulses *within* capitalism.

McDonough's critique is based on the notion that documentary is at its best when it dispassionately unmasks ideology and disenchants capitalism. Yet this reductive concept of documentary betrays a bias against affect and emotion as effective critical strategies.[19] Indeed, the personal and the informational, reason and emotion, and the private and the political are not opposed in the 1980s and 1990s queer and feminist activism – one significant matrix of Leonard's work. At the start of her career, Leonard produced several propaganda posters for numerous feminist and lesbian civil rights organisations of which she was a member. One of her early projects included billboards where she used photographs of her second-grade class to which she added the captions 'Are you a boy or a girl?' (*Are you a boy or a girl?* [1992–95]). In other posters, she combined her friends' children's photo-booth portraits with captions like 'Find the dyke in this picture'. These works acknowledged the conservative notion that homosexuality is toxic to children: but the appropriation of private albums was also a means by which to gain control of their past. As she has remarked, 'for us it was a chance to rewrite our own experiences, and to claim them'.[20] Also exploring autobiographical modes of address were works such as *Strange Fruit* (1992–97) and *The Fae Richards Photo Archive* (1993–96). The latter is a fictional photographic archive that relates the story of an imaginary black Hollywood actress, Fae Richards, through the images of her personal album. The aged, ripped and sepia-toned pictures showing the actress's close friends, lovers and siblings fostered the viewer's affective identification with the protagonist and, through the captions, evidenced the discriminations experienced by Richards (because of the colour of her skin, the film studios tended to cast her in minor or stereotyped roles, fitting with the conventional image of the 'Watermelon Woman'). As in her posters and billboards, in *The Fae Richards Photo Archive* the use of private memories was a strategy to reveal the mutual imbrication of the affective and the political – a tactic that was also typical of many feminist videos of the time.[21]

If Leonard's early work reclaimed a queer and black subjectivity forgotten and repressed in mainstream culture, *Analogue* aimed to give an outlet to the desires and aspirations of a class of low-income consumers. Traces of them could be found in the shop window signs featuring slogans such as 'True Desires for Beauty' and 'Money is Life'; or they could be discovered in the wall murals of Kampala's stores, depicting large bales of used clothes coming from the USA or the UK that look about to explode. It is a fantasy of material abundance that is evoked by these murals and is reflected in the overwhelming quantity of clothes, brooms, textiles and household goods that crowd many local stores. Indeed, Leonard's archive reveals a world that is unified by the consumption of similar products; but this also appears as a world that has overcome scarcity and extreme poverty. *Analogue* recalls anthropologist Karen Tranberg Hansen's research on the global trade in second-hand clothes. The commerce grew exponentially in the 1990s in wake of the liberalisation of third world economy, and it is often taken as an example of globalisation's destructive effects. For the critics of globalisation the trade has obliterated local textile industries, causing unemployment and misery. In fact, as Hansen's ethnographic study showed, in many instances the opposite is true: the flow of used clothing into third world countries such as Zambia, India and the Philippines has created employment and stimulated the local textile industry, which depends on the recycling of used clothes. More importantly, it brought affordable goods to low-income rural and urban consumers and enabled them to buy not only more, but better quality clothes, 'for not only does [the international trade in used garments] give people what they need, namely clothing they can afford; it also gives them what they want, namely the ability to dress rather than wear rags.'[22] Hansen's research gives us a more nuanced account of globalisation's impact on local cultures and economies, one which reminds us of its complexities and warns us against an uncritical and hasty embrace of the paradigm of globalisation as a homogenising, imperialistic process.

Analogue seems to follow Hansen's warning as it delivers an image of the global flow of commodities that eschews easy catastrophism. But is there a critical function in the utopian desires that Leonard locates in thrift stores, flea markets and 99-cent shops? Is this utopian impulse just a compensatory escape from reality and a celebration of individualistic pleasure? There can be no questioning of the distance that separates Leonard's project from the works of 1980s pop artists, such as Jeff Koons, Haim Steinbach, Takeshi Murakami and Ashley Bickerton, who, in their installations and pictures, also appropriated consumer objects and the language of advertisement.[23] Koons, for example, used kitsch consumer objects as a strategy to evoke an imaginary world of hedonistic self-regeneration and eternal being, and one of his most famous projects, *The New* (1981), showed brand new vacuum cleaners under glass vitrines and included a photograph of the artist as a young, self-assured boy. In contrast, novelty and youth is not conjured up by Leonard's archive, as its objects are rarely brand new. Rather, most of the products that appear in *Analogue* are second-hand, refurbished and recycled. In countries such as Uganda and Poland, discarded old things that would have been thrown out in the West are resurrected into something new and useful. Indeed, the economy celebrated by Leonard is not one of luxurious and unrestrained consumption but one of thrift and recycling, and her project might be read as an exhortation to parsimonious consumption and solidarity.

In *Analogue* Leonard deploys the figure of the cheap commodity as the allegory for a transnational, global populism. Traversing and bridging different national contexts, the commodity – like photography itself – emerges as the stand-in for a proletarian multitude. The installation elicits a mode of spectatorship wherein the viewer is asked to identify, if only momentarily, with the mobile and the transitory commodity object, and, in turn, with the subjectivity of this mass of anonymous consumers. 'There is something more here than quaintness, or nostalgia', Leonard declared; 'It is a feeling of connectedness to the rest of the world: to language and economy, to history and struggle – to the endless supply of human solutions to the problem of survival.'[24] If the feeling of connectedness animates the artist's documentary project, then its title may evoke, rather than an obsolescent media, the idea of reciprocity: analogy as an affective relation and a correspondence between distant but equal subjects. Yet the work also suggests that equality comes with a price: the series' repetitive format projects the ambivalent image of a world that seems to become increasingly homogenous and therefore gloomily dystopian; at the same time, however, this homogeneity can be interpreted as a declaration of equality, a levelling of social differences and hierarchies: a 'feeling of connectedness'. Whether or not this ambivalence can be read as a dialectical analysis of capitalism that sheds light on its internal contradictions, *Analogue* has a scandalous message which lies in its ironical conclusion that a certain degree of 'capitalistic' destruction might lead to universal equality.

* * *

Also revealing a deep fascination for the aesthetic of low consumer culture is the art of Rachel Harrison. Speaking of Harrison's installations, John Kelsey observed that they 'assault the viewer's attention with the same gimmicks any 99-cent store uses to promote discounted merchandise'.[25] Her brash abstract sculptures are combined with a variety of cheap commodities and ready-made objects: supermarket shelves, magazine racks, mannequins, Styrofoam apples, Slim-Fast cans, garish wigs, air fresheners, bananas, mosquito nets, VCRs, worn-out carpets, carnival masks and plastic bags – just to name a few. Found photography and video also populate her dazzling installations. Culled from tabloids, lifestyle press and celebrity magazines or retrieved through random Google searches, they refuse the pristine aesthetic quality of fine art photography, and its obsession with obsolescence.[26] Where in Leonard's photography the material culture of junk stores appears as dignified and neat, in Harrison's sculptural practice it is debased and chaotic. Mixed with references to minimalism, pop art and abstract expressionism, this kitsch consumer culture is neither elevated or redeemed nor fused into a superior or coherent synthesis.[27] Harrison's aesthetic of chaos, nevertheless, is not nihilistic and melancholic in tone, recalling the excess and carnivalesque pleasure of Bakhtinian inversion.

Harrison's sculptural work possesses significant affinities with the practice of artists such as Haim Steinbach. Combining the geometric seriality of minimalism with the fascination for the figure of the commodity of pop art, Steinbach's 1980s installations consisted of prefabricated wooden shelves reminiscent of supermarket racks. On these Steinbach arranged a variety of products that he purchased in large shops or flea stores.[28] Like Harrison, Steinbach has a penchant for the unusual combination of ancient and contemporary objects. In Steinbach's *Related and Different* (1985), for example, a pair of trendy Nike shoes was arranged next to medieval goblets. However, the minimalist regularity of Steinbach's displays differed significantly from the chaotic quality of Harrison's installations. Unlike her predecessor, Harrison does not explore consumer culture as a synchronic symbolic system structured around binary differences; rather, she seems interested in playing with notions of authenticity and fakery and in exploiting the deceptive and flashy quality of cheap products. Harrison's sculptures have been regarded as 'stand-ins' and 'imposters': 'standing in for men, they perform their statuesque act in drag, and verticality as a sort of camp routine'.[29] Many of her works are dedicated to famous performers such as Marilyn Monroe, Fats Domino, Johnny Depp or Richard Pryor, and – besides supermarket shelves – they resemble movie or theatrical sets. Some of her installations parody contemporary culture's obsession with historical re-enactments. Consider for instance *Snake in the Grass* (1997/2009), which epitomises the tongue-in-cheek humour of Harrison's practice: here John Fitzgerald Kennedy's 1963 tragic death is represented through a labyrinthic structure of movable walls, a tray filled with discarded olive pits – an oblique reference to the Mafia's alleged involvement in the president's assassination – and a picture of a blurred poster depicting a policeman running on Dallas Grassy Knoll taken in the aftermath of Kennedy's killing. The poster is clearly fading away, and the only thing that stands out is the garish yellow price tag. In a gesture of mockery, a dramatic episode in American official history – which has generated endless speculations and conspiracy theories and a plethora of best-selling books and Hollywood movies – is degraded to the status of banal and corny commodity.

The central role played by parody and humour in Harrison's practice signals a crucial difference between her and Leonard's appropriation of consumer culture. As we have seen, there is an element of mimicry in *Analogue* as its repetitive and ordered accumulation mirrors the neat display strategies of 99-cent stores. Nevertheless, Leonard's imitation does not result in parody and excess. In contrast, Harrison deploys trivial consumer culture and subjects it to further degradation and defilement. She exaggerates the theatrical and vulgar materialism of the cheap and kitsch commodity – but to what end? If it becomes clear that the artist's practice cannot be understood dialectically as a Marxist critique of commodity fetishism, then what are the targets of Harrison's parodic appropriation? Her photographic archive *Voyage of the Beagle* (2007) represents an answer to this question.³⁰ Here mimicry fulfils two functions: on the negative side, it enacts a strategy of subversion of the binary of high and low; on the positive side, it evokes a populist utopian world, bulging with life and energy.

Voyage of the Beagle is a collection of fifty-seven digital pictures of various figurative and anthropomorphic sculptures and souvenirs, which were taken by the artist during her travels to London, Texas, Washington DC, Brooklyn, New York, Los Angeles, Cologne and Corsica. Lacking captions, the photographs recall the style of vernacular, non-fine art photography and are arranged horizontally: from left to right, the first image in the series is that of a menhir – an ancient monolithic sculpture dating back to around 3000 BCE that can be found on the Mediterranean island of Corsica; next, an immensely diverse series of objects parades in front of the viewer: taxidermied animals, store mannequins, a wooden cigar store, Indian mortuary angels, a bust of Marilyn Monroe, a mounted deer head, a Barbie doll, a discarded picture of Hollywood actor Kevin Bacon, a sculpture of Abraham Lincoln from a New York steakhouse – only some of the weird objects forming Harrison's archive. Shots of 'real' sculptures are also present: a twelfth-century standing Hanuman from Tamil Nadu, a Janus figure from the Victorian and Albert Museum in London, a shot of the bust of the French King David dating back to 1145 CE and photographed by the artist off a reference computer at the Metropolitan Museum, commemorative statues of the eighteenth-century English judge William Blackstone, President Lyndon Johnson's wife Lady Bird Johnston, and modern art collector and writer Gertrude Stein. Harrison's archive also includes sculptures such as August Rodin's *Les Bourgeois de Calais* (1884–95), Brancusi's *Bird in Space* (1923), Aristide Maillol's *La Nuit* (1909) and Jean Dubuffet's *Brio de Flètri* (1960). Except for these few art pieces, most of the objects photographed by Harrison were taken outside the space of the museum in nondescript sites such as parking lots, steakhouses, cigar stores, souvenir shops and supermarkets. Unlike Leonard's carefully composed shots, Harrison's pictures look intentionally dingy and unrefined – a nod to Ed Ruscha's and John Baldessari's 1960s photography. To convey the anti-aesthetic look of the archive, Harrison decided to rely exclusively on one small automatic digital camera: 'I carried a point-and-shoot camera with me for a year, to see what would happen', she recounted. 'I was also interested in the limits of pedestrian digital photography, accepting what I would get with limited technical means and an automatic setting.'³¹ The flat and drab appearance of her images redoubles the cheap quality of some of the found objects she photographed.

As is typical of Harrison's work, the highly idiosyncratic nature of this collection is puzzling and even off-putting. The title of the series is borrowed from Charles Darwin's well-known book *The Voyage of the Beagle* (1839). The scientist's five-year journey to the Pacific on board HMS *Beagle* provided him with the

Fig. 29. Rachel Harrison, installation view, *Voyage of the Beagle*, Greene Naftali Gallery, New York, 2007 (Courtesy Rachel Harrison and Greene Naftali, New York)

empirical evidence for his famous and groundbreaking theory of natural selection and evolution.

Darwin's notion of natural history is evoked by the sequential arrangement of Harrison's photographic series. However, looking closely at the work, it becomes clear that the order in which the objects are arranged is not chronological: throughout *Voyage of the Beagle* we shift from prehistoric to contemporary sculptures and back again to the remote past of ancient monoliths. The absence of verbal explanation does nothing to defuse the banal and ordinary quality of the series. Harrison's found sculptures, critics have claimed, retain their 'idiotic singularity' and the archive is an anti-taxonomy, a parody of nineteenth-century archival reason and a critique of the impact of commodification on culture.[32] For its apparent inconclusive quality, the project was compared to Gerard Richter's *Atlas* and to Michael Schmidt's sombre archive of German reunification *Ein-heit* (*U-ni-ty* [1996]).[33] For David Joselit, Harrison's series thwarts our common-held assumptions about photography's capacity to survey and classify, and questions our belief in the medium's documentary veracity.[34] Yet, as its critical reception suggests, is scepticism the only lesson imparted by Harrison's archive? Does *Voyage of the Beagle* really depict a historical consciousness broken down in the face of the pure facticity of the commodity?

Rather than placing Harrison's project within the tradition of anomic archives such as Richter's *Atlas*, we could read *Voyage of the Beagle* through a different genealogy: that of Dada. As Hal Foster has explained, during and in the aftermath of World War I Dada artists such as Hugo Ball devised the persona of the traumatic mime; a key strategy of this traumatist was 'mimetic adaptation', whereby 'the Dadaist assumes the dire conditions of his time – the armouring of the military body, the fragmenting of the industrial worker, the commodifying of the capitalist subject – and inflates them through hyperbole or "hypertrophy".'[36] Although with Harrison the element of trauma, violence and shock is less prominent than in the nihilistic Dada performance – arguably, because of the very different historical contexts of the two artistic practices – buffoonery and mimesis are key components of Harrison's work. Like the Dada mime, Harrison's humorous photographic series assumes the commodification of contemporary culture and turns it into an affirmation of equality. Indeed, mimicry is the conceptual category that unifies the disparate sources in the archive. Harrison's particular mode of framing, lighting and sequencing suggest a preposterous chain of resemblances between the objects in the series: thus, for example, the stern look of the statue of judge Blackstone mirrors the hard stare of the ape following in the series; the degraded quality of Bacon's fading picture and the actor's angular face parallels the rough texture and irregular head of the bronze bust by Dubuffet; with his hand on his forehead, a wooden American Indian found outside a cigar store in Manhattan strikes the same pose of one of the Calais burghers by Rodin; a detail of Maillol's nude woman possesses striking formal affinities with the shape of an indigenous mask. Each object seems to mimic the previous or following one. But who is doing the mimicking, the highbrow object or the campy commodity? Is the tacky souvenir imitating the modernist sculpture or the other way round? *Voyage of the Beagle* stages what is effectively a competition in miming between artefacts belonging to different cultural hierarchies and registers: 'art' and 'commodity' and 'primitive' and 'modern', but also 'animal' and 'human' and 'female' and 'male'. Indeed, many of the sculptures in *Voyage of the Beagle* are hybrid figures: anthropomorphic animals (e.g. a polar bear wearing a bow-tie), half-human and half-monkey deities (e.g. the Tamil Hanuman), androgynous figures (e.g. the bearded woman), Janus-faced statues (e.g. the Janus from the Victoria and Albert Museum) and rock formations whose function and figurative purpose is vague and uncertain (e.g. the Corsican menhirs).

Playing the game of visual analogy, *Voyage of the Beagle* suggests bewildering reciprocities between animal and man, man and savage, animate and inanimate objects. When seen in this light, the title of Harrison's project emerges less as a pun than as a reference to Darwin's discussion of mimicry. In a well-known

Fig. 30. Rachel Harrison, Voyage of the Beagle, 2007 (detail), 57 pigmented inkjet prints 46.8 x 34 x 3 cm. (Courtesy Rachel Harrison and Greene Naftali, New York)

passage of his eponymous travelogue Darwin described the encounter with the inhabitants of the remote land of Tierra del Fuego thus:

> [The Fuegians] are excellent mimics: as often as we coughed or yawned, or made any odd motion, they immediately imitated us. Some of our party began to squint and look awry; but one of the young Fuegians (whose whole face was painted black, excepting a white band across his eyes) succeeded in making far more hideous grimaces. They could repeat with perfect correctness each word in any sentence we addressed them, and they remembered such words for some time. Yet we Europeans all know how difficult it is to distinguish apart the sounds in a foreign language. Which of us, for instance, could follow an American Indian through a sentence of more than three words? All savages appear to possess, to an uncommon degree, this power of mimicry. [...] How can this faculty be explained? Is it a consequence of the more practised habits of perception and keener senses, common to all men in a savage state, as compared with those long civilized?[36]

This passage expresses a commonly held view in nineteenth-century Europe according to which mimicry was considered as 'aping': mimicry was, for Darwin, the skill of the savage man, an unsophisticated and impulsive tendency that was connected with the vulgarities of the grimace tradition and the lack of civilisation;

as an ability mimicry was among the lowest in the scale of human activity, since it crossed the threshold between human and animal species. By staging a competition in miming between artefacts belonging to different symbolic hierarchies, Harrison's archive evokes their inversion and, consequently, a suspension of the privileges implicit in these cultural distinctions. *Voyage of the Beagle* provides an image of a topsy-turvy world where the levelling of hierarchies marks the liberation from the prevailing truths, norms and prohibitions about what is good and bad sculpture, good and bad desire, the civilised and the uncivilised.

In addition, Harrison's photography turns its quest concerning the origins of sculpture into a survey of the 'contemporary grotesque'. The artist photographed most objects head-on and from very close so that their textural and material imperfections are magnified as well as their monstrous, freakish features. These hybrid figures have strange and exorbitant bodies: their hair is too long or too colourful, their trunks are bulky and plump, their ears and eyes are either minuscule or enormous, their make-up is gaudy, their mouths are gaping – reinventing the tradition of the carnivalesque for a postmodern commodified world. This was at the centre of Mikhail Bakhtin's analysis of the language of Renaissance novelist François Rabelais. Bakhtin remarked that one of the key subversive strategies of the carnivalesque as a literary mode was grotesque realism. Grotesque realism imagines the human body as corpulent excess: the grotesque body is bulging, multiple, over- or undersized, protuberant and incomplete.

Figs. 31, 32. Rachel Harrison, *Voyage of the Beagle*, 2007 (detail), 57 pigmented inkjet prints, 46.8 x 34 x 3 cm. (Courtesy Rachel Harrison and Greene Naftali, New York)

Figs. 33, 34. Rachel Harrison, *Voyage of the Beagle*, 2007 (detail), 57 pigmented inkjet prints, 46.8 x 34 x 3 cm. (Courtesy Rachel Harrison and Greene Naftali, New York)

Of all the features of the human face, the nose and mouth play the most important part in the grotesque image of the body; the head, ears, and nose also acquire a grotesque character when they adopt animal form or that of inanimate objects. The grotesque body ... is a body in the act of becoming. It is never finished, never completed; it is continually built, created, and builds and creates another body. [...] Thus the artistic logic of the grotesque image ignores the closed, smooth and impenetrable surface of the body and retains only its excrescences (sprouts, buds) and orifices only that which leads beyond the body's limited space or into the body's depths.[37]

The grotesque body is, for Bakhtin, a 'double body': a never coherent and unitary self, it suggests movement and metamorphosis. More importantly, it is the subversion and inversion of the 'classical body', represented by the idealised beauty of the classical statue. Like the classical statue, the classical body is always mounted on a plinth, elevated and distanced from the crowd; it shows emotional restraint and assumes passive admiration from below. We gaze up at the classical figure and wonder. According to Bakhtin, the classical body denotes the inherent form and the authority of the high official culture and language and expresses the transcendental individualism of the bourgeois subject. In contrast, the grotesque, carnivalesque body is placed at the level of the ground and is open to the world through its many orifices and protuberances. In the grotesque, 'the material bodily principle is contained not in the biological individual, not in the bourgeois ego, but in the people, a people who are continually growing and renewed', Bakhtin observed; 'this is why all that is bodily becomes grandiose, exaggerated, immeasurable'.[38] The grotesque body represents the revolutionary, subversive spirit of the people and contains the anticipation of a better world. The carnivalesque, he optimistically concluded, 'discloses the potentiality of a different world, of another order, of a different way of life'.[39]

An inventory of grotesque buffoonish bodies is offered by Harrison's series. Mounted in a single sequence like stills in a filmstrip, *Voyage of the Beagle* evokes not a linear evolutionary movement but a collectivising movement; the archive reveals not historical progress but a relation of kinship between distinct subjects. We might read the series as the affirmation of a mobile, unrestrained, plural subjectivity which, following Bakhtin, would represent the people. The function of the artist's appropriation of cheap commodities is the evocation of a carnivalesque, populist utopia. Similarly to Leonard, Harrison invests the cheap commodity with positive connotations: rather than symbolising homogeneity, destruction and capitalistic anomie, the commodity is turned into a figure of equality. Commenting on Bakhtin's utopia of the carnival, Terry Eagleton wrote that its radical inversion of established cultural values and norms had, as its most significant political function, the production of a generative uncertainty. The carnival, he wrote, 'is, in effect, a kind of fiction: a temporary retextualizing of the social formation that exposes its "fictive" foundations'.[40] The exhibitionist, debased and inauthentic nature of low consumer culture is re-functioned by Harrison as a carnivalesque, counter-hegemonic tool for the subversion of conventional symbolic binaries of high and low. The artist pushes the masquerade of late capitalist culture to its limits in order to show the dominant system that generated it as itself fragile and unstable.

* * *

The idea of equality informs the utopian impulses of Leonard's and Harrison's projects, leading them to the construction of, respectively, a world of parsimonious consumption and a world of carnivalesque transgression. Their mimesis of commodity culture ultimately suggests equality as the erasure of economic, cultural and geographical differences and hierarchies. Equality is also central to Moulène's practice: at stake in his series *Vingt-quatre Objets de Grève* is the equality between the artist and the factory worker. Moulène shares with Harrison and Leonard the tendency to mimic the strategies and design of consumer culture. His images imitate and disrupt the conventions of advertisement and commercial photography through small but relevant modifications. As he declared, 'I would say that my works lie on the side of serious farce rather than grim ardour.'[41]

The subtly ironic quality of Moulène's art owes to the artist's interest in performance art. Indeed, performance art had a strong influence on Moulène's practice: while taking evening classes at the Académie des Beaux-Arts in Versailles in the early 1970s, the artist worked as an actor and photographer for performance artist Michel Journiac.[42] Journiac treated photography as an integral part of performance works rather than as an instrument of their documentation and used to call his interventions 'photographic actions', because they were specifically made to be recorded on camera. Journiac's 'photo-actions' were devastating parodies that criticised social inequalities and gender stereotypes. His *Vingt-quatre Heures dans La Vie d'un Femme Ordinaire* (*24 Hours in the Life of an Ordinary Woman* [1974]) is a photographic series that portrays the artist posing in drag as his mother and going through the everyday rituals of a lower-middle-class woman. Although Moulène's photographs are less grotesque than Journiac's performances, they nevertheless share a manifest fascination for parodic imitation. In *Les Filles D'Amsterdam* (2004), for instance, Moulène took the display of female genitalia typical of pornography to an extreme. The series portrays naked prostitutes with their legs open in front of violent red backgrounds. The frontality of these photographic portraits, and the direct, almost confrontational gaze of the women, contradict one of pornography's main features, namely that of constructing the (male) viewer as an invisible observer.

Moulène's expert knowledge of commercial photography is owed to his stint in the advertising industry in the 1980s. In this period, before embarking on a career in the arts, Moulène worked as a creative director for the military manufacturer Thomson-Sintra, designing product presentations and advertising materials. An advertising aesthetic persists as a leitmotif of his later practice. As he remarked in an interview, 'the product became my commonplace'.[43] *Documenta X Project, Media Plan, Kassel* (1997) exemplifies his ambivalent approach to photography. Commissioned in 1997 by curator Catherine David for Documenta, the series was printed in German newspapers and displayed on billboards prior to the show's opening. These pictures depict colourful and pristine tomatoes, vine leaves, marrowbones and washing-up liquid containers all arranged frontally on monochromatic backdrops. These nondescript objects remain devoid of any text that could clarify their meaning.

The commodities depicted in *Vingt-quatre Objets de Grève* are similarly presented against such uniform backdrops. The series documents products that were made by French factory workers during strike occupations in the period between 1968 and 1999.[44] They range from scarves, dresses and maps to watches, cigarette packets, newspapers and train tickets.[45] Each of them represents a different dispute. Some were circulated to the general public in order to raise awareness about the workers' grievances (the map of the Paris metro); some were used to demonstrate the workers' technical skills (the Novacore suite); others had a merely symbolic function (the doll symbolising the dispute 'Bella'). Despite their differences, they all stand for the workers' appropriation of the means of production. The strike objects distinguish themselves from standard commercial goods in that they were manufactured in small quantities and were supposed to express craft, know-how and the pleasure of work. They were clearly marked as 'different' from reified commodities through visible details. So, for example, the cigarette packet 'La Pantinoise', made in 1982 by the workers of the Pantin tobacco factory in Jacno, differs from Gauloises packets through the inscription 'Not For Sale. Made by the workers in dispute'; the Manufrance frying pan has the slogans 'Relax' and 'Employment, solidarity, liberty, justice' engraved on its back. Moreover, several of the objects are red, the colour of revolution. While it is true that some of the goods looked like counterfeits of standard commodities, their ambiguous appearance never reached a point of total uncertainty. The form of the products made ostensibly clear that they were made by workers on strike.

Instead of highlighting the difference between strike objects and ordinary commodities, Moulène's photographs depict them as ambiguous things. In *Vingt-quatre Objets de Grève*, the objects have a kind of mute, opaque presence that is quietly unsettling. The artist shot the products in front of grey backgrounds, using a high contrast and highly saturated colour film. He printed the images on large-sized Plexiglas, which gives photographs a glaring, almost reflective

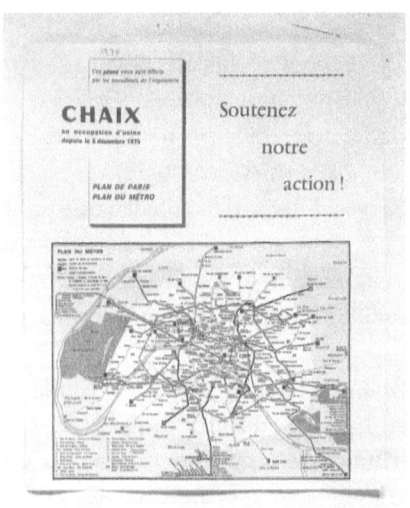 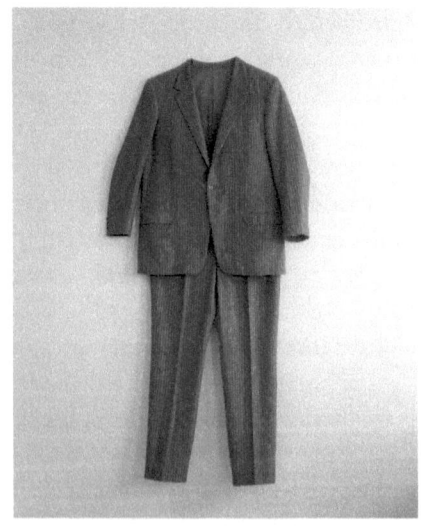

Figs. 35, 36. Jean-Luc Moulène, *24 Objets de Grève présentés par Jean-Luc Moulène*, 1999–2000 (detail), 24 cibachrome prints, Diasec, plexiglas 3mm., 47 x 36 cm. (Courtesy Jean-Luc Moulène and Galerie Chantal Crousel, Paris)

 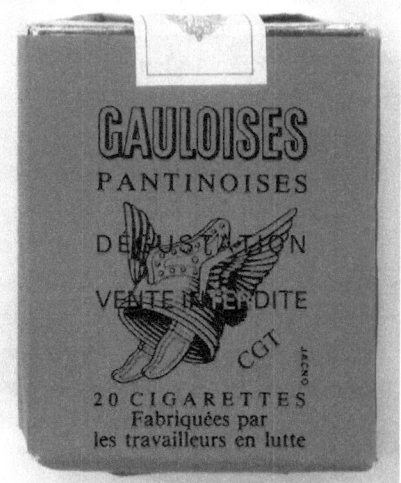

Figs. 37, 38. Jean-Luc Moulène, *24 Objets de Grève présentés par Jean-Luc Moulène*, 1999–2000 (detail), 24 cibachrome prints, Diasec, plexiglas 3mm., 47 x 36 cm. (Courtesy Jean-Luc Moulène and Galerie Chantal Crousel, Paris)

surface, reminiscent of advertisement billboards; it is only through understated captions – printed in the exhibition catalogue – that the viewer can learn about the singular history of the products. As a consequence, the strike objects emerge from Moulène's images as pristine goods, waiting to be collected and consumed. The photographs downplay the strike objects' difference from everyday commodities. They elicit an uncanny feeling that was alien to the objects in the first place. When the project is exhibited in gallery and museums, this feeling is exacerbated by the lack of captions. This is another trademark feature of the artist's photography. In his previous works, Moulène rarely deployed textual supplements to explicate the content of his images, and he is well known for exhibiting them without wall texts and narrative explanations. Several of his photographs are indeed untitled, and others have poetic names (e.g. *Image Blanche, Image Noire*) or dry and deadpan titles (e.g. *Les Vaisseaux Verseurs, 1000 Litres de Jus Allemande*). The uncanny effect of his work is a consequence of these strategies. 'Presented in random order without explanatory text or slogans or a signature,' wrote one critic, '[Moulène's] images become as enigmatic as a whispered conversation.'[46]

However, when published in magazines and exhibition catalogues, *Vingt-quatre Objets de Grève* made extensive use of textual supplements. In these versions, the photographs are accompanied by lengthy captions describing the objects in every minute detail. Importantly, the information provided by the captions often appears unnecessary and irrelevant. For example, the caption of the 'LIBR Doll' reads:

Bril, a factory manufacturing men's ready-made clothes, Loiret. Tall, Slender Barbie-type doll; height dressed 41 cm, diameter of skirt 62cm, gilt chain necklace, dress with a black long-sleeved bodice and a check skirt, with a matching wide-brimmed hat.[47]

Why provide the exact dimensions, weight and materials of the objects? The verbose quality of these textual supplements brings to mind less photojournalism than product catalogues and, therefore, could be viewed as another tactic through which Moulène disrupts expectations by imitating commercial photography. As art historian Yve-Alain Bois has remarked, the captions give the series an 'overtly documentary and slightly parodic tone'.[48] In sum, the project retained, in all its different formats, a laconic quality which, as already noted, seems to echo the ambiguity of Moulène's previous works. Why choose such opacity to represent the history of the strikes?

One possible answer to this question is that the project's enigmatic appearance implies a relation of equivalence between Moulène's artistic practice and the practice of the workers. Critics have argued that one of *Vingt-Quatre Objets de Grève*'s greatest achievements is the effacement of the artist's individuality. Sophie Duplaix, curator of Musée National d'Art Moderne in Paris, claimed that Moulène's photographs 'hide themselves behind the objects' and that he 'denies the idea of the creation of a work by the artist'.[49] For Duplaix the impersonal form of the title ('Twenty-four Strike Objects Presented by Jean-Luc Moulène') demonstrates the artist's will to obliterate any mark of authorship. In my view, the matter cannot be put to rest so quickly. Indeed, Moulène's opaque photographs, rather than effacing themselves, risk taking over the objects. It is fair to say that the artist's individuality emerges precisely *because* of the pictures' enigmatic quality – as we have seen, a trademark of Moulène's entire *oeuvre*. But ambiguity and irony are also part of the subdued, ordinary appearance of the objects themselves: both strike objects and Moulène's photographs resemble everyday commodities, but they also betray them through subtle changes that invert their meaning. To put it differently, both the industry products and the photographs are detourned objects.

Firstly theorised in France by Guy Debord within the context of the Situationist International, the strategy of détournement involved the 'selective and cunning (mis)appropriation of elements from the dominant culture that could then be put to critical or subversive use'.[50] In détournement an advertising poster might be appropriated and written over, or altered in some way, so as to transform its capitalist, consumerist message into a radical statement. A related notion of détournement is found in Michel De Certeau's seminal book *The Practice of Everyday Life*. It is central to the workers' practice called *la perruque*:

> *La perruque* is the worker's own work disguised as work for his employer. It differs from pilfering in that nothing of material value is stolen. It differs from absenteeism in that the worker is officially on the job. *La perruque* may be as simple a matter as a secretary's writing a love letter on 'company time' or as complex as a cabinetmaker's 'borrowing' a lathe to make a piece of furniture for his living room. Under different names in different countries this phenomenon is becoming more and more general, even if managers penalize it or 'turn a blind eye' on it in order not to know about it. Accused of stealing or turning material to his own ends and using the machines for his own profit, the worker who indulges in *la perruque* actually diverts time (not goods, since he uses only scraps) from the factory for work that is free, creative, and precisely not directed toward profit. In the very place where the machine he must serve reigns supreme, he cunningly takes pleasure in finding a way to create gratuitous products whose sole purpose is to signify his own capabilities through his work and to confirm his solidarity with other workers or his family.[51]

For De Certeau *la perruque* is an act of resistance against capitalism whereby workers surreptitiously transgress their routines, appropriating the means of production to their own use. De Certeau's analysis of *la perruque* brings to mind the strike objects. As the ethnographer of the Archives National du Monde du Travail in Roubaix has pointed out, they can be assimilated to this phenomenon in that the production of the objects involved the diversion of manufacturing techniques to a purpose other than that for which they were conventionally used. The objects simultaneously appropriate and divert the language of commodity culture and advertising. The workers imitated a pre-existing 'product' such as, for example, a Galouises cigarette packet, but also betrayed it through a slight, but nevertheless visible addition such as the label 'La Pantinoise' – meaning made by the strikers of the Pantin tobacco factory. Likewise, Moulène's photographs are an example of détournement: in the artist's photographs this tactic is more subdued since it operates less by addition than by subtraction. *Les Vaisseuax Verseurs, 5 février 1992* (1992), from the series *Produits* (1992–96), shows detergent bottles whose labels have been stripped by Moulène. Another well-known work by Moulène, *Blue Galouise Blues – 441* (2000), is based on a similar strategy of détournement. This sculpture comprises a pile of blue cigarette packets, devoid of any inscription.

To return to *Vingt-quatre Objets de Grève*, the conceptual affinities between the artist's photographs and the strike objects – both being the outcome of strategies of détournement – suggest a resemblance between the artist and the worker. A left-wing artist, Moulène has often expressed his solidarity with the struggles

 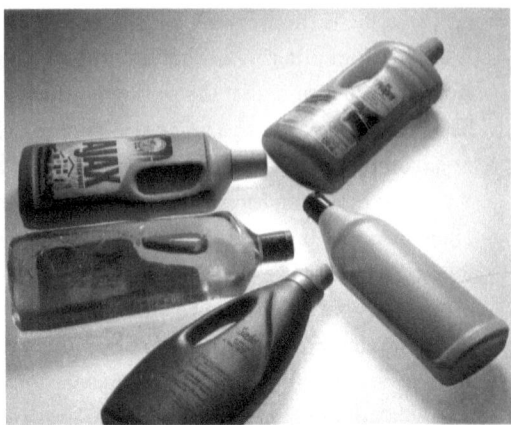

Fig. 39. Jean-Luc Moulène, *Bleu Gauloises Blues – 441*, 2000 (detail), 441 monochromatic packets of Blue Galouises, special manufacture, each packet 7 x 5 x 2 cm. (Courtesy Jean-Luc Moulène and Galerie Chantal Crousel, Paris). Fig. 40 Jean-Luc Moulène, *Les Vaisseaux Verseurs*, 5 février 1992, silkscreen on paper, 300 × 400 cm. (Courtesy Jean-Luc Moulène and Galerie Chantal Crousel, Paris).

of the French workers. 'In making the photographs,' he once remarked, 'I wanted to be a good worker.'[52] Or, elsewhere: 'the photographer is a worker, he works with a machine'.[53] These statements reveal Moulène's utopian desire to identify with the figure of the striker. This identification is also evoked by Moulène's rarely discussed video *+ d'ordre, – d'ordre* (1994). The 26-minute-long video shows Moulène performing a series of rather dull actions in his own kitchen. We see his hands carrying supermarket bags and placing them on a clean white table. He unpacks various items – some salad, coffee, pasta and potatoes, all contained in colourful plastic packaging – places one next to the other on the table in serial arrangements and then shifts their order and position. This cryptic and repetitive performance casts the artist less as a creative genius and more as a worker on a dull assembly line. Likewise, *Vingt-quatre Objets de Grève* implies a relation of resemblance between the figure of the artist and the figure of the worker: like the worker, who produced the strike objects by surreptitiously and unlawfully appropriating the means of production, the artist unduly appropriated the slick language of commercial photography to make an advertisement in service of striking workers.

As a statement of radical equality between artist and worker, Moulène's series resonates with the project of a Rancierian emancipatory aesthetic. In a conversation with Fulvia Carnevale and John Kelsey in 2007, the influential philosopher argued that Moulène's series epitomises an attempt 'to give form to a continuity between artistic creativity and the forms of creativity manifested in objects and behaviours that testify to everyone's capacities and to our inherent powers of resistance'.[54] For Rancière, Moulène's photographs exemplify the model of a truly emancipatory art, whereby the conventional division of competences – such as those between artist and spectator, producer and consumer of images – are overturned.

Research on the history of nineteenth-century utopianism is at the heart of Rancière's aesthetics. His interest in utopian social and pedagogical experiments harks back to the 1970s, when Rancière began his study on the revolutionary educational method of Joseph Jacotot, which resulted in his book *The Ignorant School Master*.[55] If in this book the philosopher posited absolute equality between the teacher and the pupil as the central tenet of a radical, alternative pedagogy, it was in his previous work, *The Nights of Labor*, also known as *Proletarian Nights*, that he sketched out the foundations for his idea of emancipatory art.[56] First published in 1981 and developed from his doctoral thesis, the book narrates the stories of lock makers, tailors, cobblers and typesetters in the 1830s and 1840s, many of whom were converts to the utopian socialism of Saint Simon. Rancière's workers appear as intellectuals, poets and philosophers, capable of devising emancipatory systems for themselves, in the scattered late-night moments that their tight work schedules allowed. For the philosopher, the artistic and intellectual activities of these nineteenth-century workers represented truly political and revolutionary acts in that they transgressed and disturbed the established (but arbitrary) division of labour. 'A worker who had never learned to write', writes Rancière in one of his early articles, 'and yet tried to compose verses to the taste of his times was perhaps more of a danger to the prevailing ideological order than the worker who performed revolutionary songs.'[57] Significantly, *The Nights of Labor* prefigures Rancière's later writings on the relationships between art and politics.[58] For Rancière, the emancipatory value of a work of art resides not in the explicit content of the message it conveys but, rather, in the ways that the common divisions of labour and competences are unsettled. In other words, the problem of an emancipatory, political art has to do with the question: who has the right to produce art? Politics is conceptualised by Rancière as a dissenting event enacted by those 'who have no place' and 'no time', by which he means those who, on the one hand, are defined as deprived of *logos*, and yet, on the other, are taken to share in the universal capacity of aesthetic judgement. 'Politics occurs', he writes, 'when those who have no time take the time necessary to front up as inhabitants of a common space and demonstrate that their mouths really do emit speech capable of making pronouncements on the common which cannot be reduced to voices signalling pain.'[59] In relation to Rancière's aesthetics, *Vingt-quatre Objets de Grève* emerges as an example of an emancipatory and political art. The project describes the strikers as subjects capable of occupying a different place from that usually prescribed to them by the capitalist order and, therefore, it affirms the universal claim of equality that constitutes the radical message at the heart of his aesthetics. In *Vingt-quatre Objets de Grève* the strikers appear as ingenious producers and their creations as conceptually sophisticated works of art. Elaborating on this Rancierian reading, one can argue that Moulène's aestheticisation of the strike objects does not abstract them from their social history but, on the contrary, makes a statement that calls for the equality of all subjects.

One may wonder whether this reading is too optimistic. The photographs in *Vingt-quatre Objets de Grève* may, in fact, convey less the subjectivity of the anonymous strikers than that of the artist. Representing the strike objects according to his trademark style, Moulène, perhaps inadvertently, transforms them into an allegory of his own practice. As critic Stephen Wright acutely observes, Moulène's project may constitute an act of reification, which further obscures the agency of the workers. 'In making images of non-artistic creativity artistically visible by signing his name to his photographs,' Wright argues, 'the artist underscores the fundamental disparity between the striking workers' anonymous creativity and his own authored artwork, as he turns around and sells his images of their objects.'[60] Wright rightly asks whether or not Moulène's appropriation of the strike objects is 'on the symbolic level ... all too similar to the sort of exploitation that the objects' producers set out to denounce in the first place'.[61] Therein lies the ambivalence of the archive. Rather than acting as testimony to the workers' capacity for resistance, as Rancière suggests, *Vingt-quatre Objets de Grève* may be viewed as an undue appropriation of the strikers' work which serves to conceal class hierarchies. The series resonates with the practice of some other contemporary artists who deploy anonymous assistants as labour to produce works of art, while retaining their authorship and ownership. Ultimately, it is impossible to decide which one of these conflicting readings is more appropriate. Perhaps, part of *Vingt-quatre Objets de Grève*'s considerable achievement is that it can operate within and reveal these different, contradictory interpretations, and, perhaps, Moulène's work should be seen as an art of subversive mimesis. Stewart Martin has argued that, instead of condemning commodified culture and occupying a purist position of autonomy and separation, art gains criticality when it reflects on its own contradictory relations with the forces of capital. 'Within a society in which commodification is dominant,' he writes, 'everything that is external to this commodification becomes marginal, liable to be socially irrelevant or merely yet-to-be-commodified. This predicament recommends an alternative, immanent critique: the generation of art's autonomy from *out of* commodification; the refusal of commodification by a subversive mimesis of it.'[62] *Vingt-quatre Objets de Grève* may epitomise such an immanent critique.

* * *

'Consumption as spectacle is – in parody form – the anticipation of a Utopian situation.'[63] So declared writer Hans Magnus Enzenzberger in his essay 'Constituents of a Theory of the Media' from 1970. Enzenzberger took issue with the Frankfurt School's wholesale dismissal of mass culture and Adorno's critique of the culture industry. For him, the fraudulent nature of capitalist spectacle lies in its promise of abundance and fulfilment for everyone; but its sway is not due to manipulation of the consumer and the imposition of false needs: in fact, the power and ubiquity of commercial culture shows the depth of the needs that capitalism exploits and the wishes for another life that permeate capitalist societies. Although ignored and dismissed by critics for being complicit with power and the interests of the elites, spectacle and entertainment, Enzenzberger claimed, address an authentic 'mass need': 'This need – it is a utopian one – is there', he declared; 'it is a desire for a new ecology, for a breaking down of environmental barriers, for an aesthetic which is not limited to the sphere of the artistic'.[64]

Leonard's, Harrison's and Moulène's documentary projects seem to echo Enzenzberger's optimistic statement. Here commodity culture emerges as an opaque visual field that, nevertheless, can disclose critical elements and subversive and transformative desires. Harrison invests campy commodities with the democratic exuberance of the carnival; Moulène and Leonard celebrate the ordinary and anonymous man, turning him into a hero, for his way of escaping his role as 'consumer' by a multiplicity of microscopic ruses. Contemporary artists' mimetic appropriation of consumer culture confounds attempts to understand their practices as straightforward critiques of commodity fetishism. Yet, in their refusal to dismiss the world of consumption, Leonard's, Harrison's and Moulène's works seem to share in the dialectical and materialist approach to utopia that, for Terry Eagleton, distinguishes Marxism from pie-in-the-sky utopianism. As Eagleton has remarked, Marxists do not project the future in some distant and fanciful world or some 'metaphysical outer space'. Rather, for them, the alternative to capitalism has to spring forth from the system's immanent contradictions: 'Authentic utopian thought concerns itself with that which is encoded within the logic of a system which, extrapolated in a certain direction, has the power to undo it.'[65] Eagleton's analysis seems valid for the works of the artists at issue here. By showing the simultaneous coexistence of negative and positive, within capitalism, their photographic archives are faithful to Marx's commitment to immanent critique. By focusing on the here and now of consumer culture, they seem to evade the 'double bind' that, according to Eagleton, utopianism sets for the unwary: 'the fact that its affirmative images of transcendence rest upon a potentially crippling sublimation of the drives necessary to achieve it in practice'.[66] Leonard, Harrison and Moulène eschew the representation of utopia as radical and absolute transcendence and suggest that we could find the way to alternative social formations in the fissures and cracks within capitalism.

Yet the artists' embrace of a commodity aesthetics is not immune from dangers. In their projects the figure of the cheap, dumb and debased commodity tends to emerge as the empty signifier for the figure of the 'underdog' or the 'oppressed people'. As Ernesto Laclau has observed, 'populism means putting into question the institutional order by constructing an underdog as an historical agent – i.e. an agent which is an *other* in relation to the way things stand'.[67] Hence, the spectre of a romantic populism hovers over all the three projects examined in this chapter. Leonard's, Harrison's and Moulène's archives possess significant affinities with a loose artistic trend that has vigorously emerged in contemporary art over the last decade and that seems to take to an extreme the 'aesthetic populism' that Jameson located in postmodern art.[68] Among its most prominent features are the emphasis on participation over critical distance, the enthusiastic engagement with commercial mass culture, the reliance on familiar advertising techniques and the ostentatious lack of pretension (populist art does not pretend not to be a commodity).[69] Some of these elements can be found, as we have seen, in the documentary works at issue here. Their populist spirit is not necessarily negative: as Laclau suggested, a populist dimension is inherent to politics as such. But the problem with populism is precisely that it embraces a range of diverse and often contradictory beliefs; movements as varied as Maoism and Fascism, and leaders as distinct as Hugo Chávez and Margaret Thatcher, have all been described as populist in one way or another. In fact, the immense variety of populisms demonstrates that 'there is no *a priori* guarantee that the "people" as a historical actor will be constituted around a progressive identity (from the point of view of the Left)'.[70]

This brings us to a second, related problem: does consumer aesthetics legitimise utopian desires that are, ultimately, conservative? If we only look at the plethora of TV programmes about home improvement and the property market or the proliferation of talent shows, we evince an image of happiness and optimism that is counted in cold hard cash and commodities. Arguably, the dreams of a better world have become dreams of a better world for oneself or one's family. *Pace* Enzenzberger, commodity culture may well be the vehicle for the expression of selfish impulses: it can celebrate indifference to the consequences of consumption on the environment, rather than a desire for a new ecology; greed, rather than solidarity; narcissistic individualism rather than the need for an anti-elitist aesthetic. All these are aspirations that are, what is more, compatible with the free-market ideology of neoliberal capitalism. It is thus unclear how it is possible to detect and unravel positive desires from consumer culture; perhaps utopia, in order to be a catalyst for social change, needs to provide the imagination of a substantially different world, which is not offered by the works of the artists examined in this chapter.

The affirmative function of consumer utopias was already clear to Ernst Bloch in the 1940s. Writing from the USA, at the peak of the American Dream, Bloch saw a positive utopian impulse in commercial culture but also acknowledged that shop windows and advertisement promises are 'a beautifying mirror which often only reflects how the ruling class wishes the wishes of the weak to be'.[71] For Bloch, the image of happiness emerging from the high street store and the mall was largely compensatory: here the wish of the capitalist subject 'also demonstrates, of course, that it merely wishes to break out of the world somewhat, not that it wants to change it'.[72] The consumerist utopia is an image of private happiness whereby the world remains as it is except for the dreamer's changed place in it – perhaps by a large win in a lottery. Nevertheless, for Bloch, the positive aspirations invoked by consumption could be sifted through conscious reflections and, ultimately, a Marxist education. The intoxicating desires triggered by the fancy world of advertisement could be politically directed through Marxism. Only *docta spes* – meaning 'educated hope' – was capable of being really transformative; only conscious reflection could turn the immature, escapist nature of the consumer dream into a concrete utopia and turn its energies into wilful and effective action.

Now, we may wonder whether hope is 'educated' by Moulène's, Harrison's and Leonard's documentary projects. Lacking clear explicative captions, the archives are characterised by an ambivalence symptomatic of a certain resistance to didacticism – a resistance that dovetails with the widespread idea that art, in order to be truly emancipatory and democratic, should resist simple and direct signification, allowing the spectators to construct their own readings.[73] This reluctance to provide contextual information may give these artists' projects the appearance of ambiguity and complexity that is the quality most valued in art today. This, in turn, sufficiently differentiates them from the naive immediacy and unsophisticated quality of much populist art, but the resulting ambivalence may paradoxically engender a similar effect: to suggest a vague populism which can serve opposite political projects and agendas.

NOTES

1   For a general account of the conceptualisation of the archive in post-World War II

art, see Sven Spieker, *The Big Archive: Art from Bureaucracy* (Cambridge: MIT Press, 2008).
2   Benjamin Buchloh, 'Gerhard Richter's *Atlas*: The Anomic Archive', *October*, no. 88 (1999), p. 134.
3   See Allan Sekula, 'Reading an Archive: Photography between Labour and Capital', in Jessica Evans and Stuart Hall, eds, *Visual Culture: A Reader* (London: Sage, 1999), pp. 181–92; Allan Sekula, 'The Traffic in Photographs', *Art Journal*, no. 41 (1981), pp. 15–25; John Tagg, *The Burden of Representation: Essays on Photographies and Histories* (Amherst: University of Massachusetts Press, 1988); John Tagg, *The Disciplinary Frame: Photographic Truths and the Capture of Meaning* (Minneapolis, MN: University of Minnesota Press, 2009).
4   Allan Sekula, 'Reading an Archive: Photography between Labour and Capital', p. 183.
5   See Karl Marx, *Das Kapital: A Critique of Political Economy* (1867) (London: Regnery, 2009), pp. 52–3. Ultimately, what is at stake is the possibility of a revolutionary transformation of society: for Marxists like Georg Lukács, it was only by reversing reification or the amnesia produced by commodity culture that a socialist revolution could take place. See György Lukács, 'Reification and Class Consciousness' (1923), in *History and Class Consciousness: Studies in Marxist Dialectic* (London: Merlin Press, 1971), pp. 83–209.
6   Marita Sturken, 'Memory, Consumerism, and Media: Reflections on the Emergence of the Field', *Memory Studies*, no. 1 (2008), p. 78.
7   See Fredric Jameson, 'Varieties of the Utopian', in *Archaeologies of the Future: The Desire Called Utopia and Other Science Fictions* (London: Verso, 2007), pp. 1–10.
8   Fredric Jameson, 'Utopia as Method, or the Uses of the Future', in Michael D. Gordin, Helen Tilley and Gyan Prakash, eds, *Utopia/Dystopia: Conditions of Historical Possibility* (Princeton, NJ: Princeton University Press, 2010), pp. 25–6.
9   *Ibid.*, p. 26.
10 See Rosalyn Deutsche and Cara Gendel Ryan, 'The Fine Art of Gentrification', *October*, no. 31 (1984); and Deutsche, *Evictions: Art and Spatial Politics* (Cambridge, MA: MIT Press, 1996). The authors also expose the complicity of art galleries and the art press in accelerating the gentrification of the area, which has been celebrated for years as the site of an artistic renaissance.
11 Zoe Leonard, 'Out of Time', *October*, no. 100 (2002), p. 88.
12 For all these interpretations see Mark Godfrey, 'Mirror Displacements', *Artforum* vol. 46, no. 8 , (2008), pp. 293–301; Helen Molesworth, 'Zoe Leonard: Analogue, 1998–2007', in Terry Smith, Okwui Enwezor and Nancy Condee, eds, *Antinomies of Art and Culture: Modernity, Postmodernity, Contemporaneity* (Durham, NC: Duke University Press, 2008), pp. 187–203; Svetlana Alpers, 'Zoe Leonard: Analogue', in Urs Stahel, ed., *Zoe Leonard* (Gottingen: Steidl/Zurich: Fotomuseum Winterthur, 2008), pp. 219–23; George Baker, 'Lateness and Longing', in Daniel Birnbaum, ed., *50 Moons of Saturn: T2 Torino Triennial* (Milan: Skira, 2008); Margaret Iversen, 'Analogue: On Zoe Leonard and Tacita Dean', *Critical Inquiry*, vol. 38, no. 4 (2012), pp. 796–818; Jenny Sorkin, 'Finding the Right Darkness', *Frieze*, no. 113 (2008), pp. 136–41.
13 I am here quoting Meyer Shapiro's famous critique of Heidegger's romantic interpretation of Van Gogh's depictions of worn-out peasant shoes: 'Heidegger indeed

imagined everything and projected it into the painting'; Meyer Shapiro, 'The Still Life as a Personal Object: A Note on Heidegger and Van Gogh', in *Theory and Philosophy of Art: Style, Artist, and Society, Selected Papers 4* (New York: George Braziller, 1994), p. 138.

14 The animation of objects is no novelty in Leonard's practice. One could look, for example, at her photographic series of wax anatomical models (1990–93) in order to find similar strategies.

15 The range of references to the history of photography that critics have attributed to *Analogue* is certainly impressive. The project has been compared to many diverse photographic traditions: from Atget to Berenice Abbot, from Walker Evans to Douglas Heubler, from Bernd and Hilla Becher to Hans Haacke and Martha Rosler. For a concise discussion of some of these references, see Sophie Berrebi, 'Goats, Lamb, Veal, Breasts: Strategies of Organisation in Zoe Leonard's *Analogue*', *Afterall*, no. 25 (2010), pp. 31–7.

16 Tom McDonough, 'The Photographer of Urban Waste: Zoe Leonard, Photographer as Rag-Picker', *Afterall*, no. 25 (2010), p. 29.

17 Ibid.

18 Arjun Appadurai, 'Introduction: Commodities and the Politics of Value', in Appadurai, ed., *The Social Life of Things: Commodities in Cultural Perspective* (Cambridge: Cambridge University Press, 1986), p. 5.

19 McDonough's model of 'criticality' can be traced back to the thinking of Louis Althusser and Pierre Bourdieu. For these theorists the task of the critical sociologist and artist is to unveil knowledge to those who don't have it. For a discussion of this conceptual framework and its problems, see Vereid Maimon, 'The Third Citizen: On Models of Criticality in Contemporary Artistic Practices', *October*, no. 129 (2009), pp. 85–112.

20 Zoe Leonard as quoted in Anna Blume, 'Zoe Leonard Interviewed by Anna Blume', in Kathrin Rhomberg, ed., *Zoe Leonard*, exhibition catalogue (Vienna: Secession, 1997), p. 13.

21 See Martha Gever, 'Video Politics: Early Feminist Projects', in Douglas Kahn and Diane Neumaier, eds, *Cultures in Contention* (Seattle: The Real Comet Press, 1985), pp. 92–101; Dianne Waldman and Janet Walker, eds, *Feminism and Documentary* (Minneapolis, MN: University of Minneapolis Press, 1999).

22 Karen Tranberg Hansen, *Salaula: The World of Second-Hand Clothing and Zambia* (Chicago: University of Chicago Press, 2000), p. 15.

23 As Catherine Wood has observed, Koons's work conveys a pervasive narrative of being born again. See Wood, 'Capitalist Realness', in Jack Bankowsky, Alison Gingeras and Catherin Wood, eds, *Pop Life: Art in a Material World*, exhibition catalogue (London: Tate, 2009). See also Max Hollein and Christoph Grunenberg, eds, *Shopping: A Century of Art and Consumer Culture* (Ostfildern-Ruit: Hatje Cantz, 2002); Y. Bois, ed., *Endgame: Reference and Simulation in Recent American Painting and Sculpture* (Boston: Institute of Contemporary Arts, 1986).

24 Zoe Leonard, 'Out of Time', p. 91.

25 John Kelsey, 'Sculpture in an Abandoned Field', in *Rachel Harrison: If I Did It* (Zurich: JRP Ringier, 2007), p. 122.

26 The chaotic assemblage of Harrison's proteiform sculptures recalls the experience of

surfing the web. As Matthew Jesse Jackson has written, 'Harrison's sculptures traverse a Googled universe'; M. J. Jackson, 'New Work: Rachel Harrison', *CAA Reviews* (2005), http://www.caareviews.org/reviews/741.

27 As Brian Sholis has remarked, 'her forced pairs, minimalism and pop art, sculpture and photography, sculpture and "display", volumetric space and representational space, the hand-made and the ready made, form and meaning, coexist without cancelling each other out'; Brian Sholis, 'Two into One', *Afterall*, 11 (2005), p. 36.

28 On Steinbach's art, see Johanna Burton, Tom Eccles and Giorgio Verzotti, *Once Again the World Is Flat* (Annadale-on-Hudson, NY: CCS Bard Hessel Museum of Art, 2013); Linda Weintraub, Arthur Danto, and Thomas McEvilley, *Art on the Edge and Over: Searching for Art's Meaning in Contemporary Society, 1970s–1990s* (Litchfield, CT: Art Insights, 1996); Germano Celant, Jean-Louis Froment, Elisabeth Lebovici and John Miller, *Haim Steinbach: Recent Works* (Bordeaux: Museum of Contemporary Art, 1988).

29 John Kelsey, 'Sculpture in an Abandoned Field', p. 120. Also highlighting the deceptive nature of Harrison's practice is Helen Molesworth: 'And what of the verbs in Harrison's work: to baffle, to trick, to believe, to deceive, to have faith?'; Molesworth, 'Rachel Harrison at Greene Naftali Gallery', *Documents*, no. 21 (2002), p. 51.

30 The title of the work has since changed to *Voyage of the Beagle, Two* (2008) and it was first shown in the exhibition *Lay of the Land*, curated by Franck Gautherot in Le Consortium, Dijon (6 July to 21 September 2008). There is also a third version of the work, *Voyage of the Beagle, Three* (2010) first exhibited in Harrison's 2010 solo exhibition at Regen Projects: *ASDFJKL* (Regen Projects, Los Angeles, 27 May to 10 July 2010).

31 Rachel Harrison as quoted in 'Rachel Harrison and Nayland Blake', *Bomb*, no. 105 (2008); http://bombmagazine.org/article/3178/.

32 'Despite the fact that each contributes to animating the others,' wrote Ina Bloom, 'every one of the weird and wonderful portrait-things chosen by Harrison is, in a sense, returned to its own idiotic singularity'; Ina Bloom, 'All Dressed Up', *Parkett*, no. 82 (2008), p. 136.

33 See Alison M. Gingeras, '(Un)Natural Selection', *Parkett*, no. 82 (2008), pp. 156–9.

34 David Joselit, 'Touch to Begin', in Iwona Blazwick, ed., *Museum with Walls* (London: Whitechapel Gallery, 2010), pp. 186–98.

35 Hal Foster, 'Dada Mime', *October*, no. 105 (Summer 2003), pp. 166–76.

36 Charles Darwin, *Charles Darwin's Beagle Diary* (1839), ed. Richard Darwin Keynes (Cambridge: Cambridge University Press, 1988), p. 124.

37 Mikhail Bakhtin, *Rabelais and His World* (1968), trans. Helene Iswolsky (Bloomington, IN: Indiana University Press, 1984), pp. 316–18.

38 *Ibid.*, p. 19.

39 *Ibid.*, p. 48.

40 Terry Eagleton, *Walter Benjamin, or, Towards a Revolutionary Criticism* (London: Verso, 1981), p. 149.

41 Moulène quoted in François Piron, 'A Serious Farce', *Kaleidoscope*, no. 9 (2010), p. 142.

42 For a survey of the performance work of Michel Journiac, see Vincent Labaume, *Le Tombeau de Michel Journiac* (Marseille: Al Dante, 1998). The catalogue also

contains a testimony written by Moulène. See also Sarah Wilson, 'Michel Journiac's Masquerades: Incest, Drag and the Anti-Oedipus', in Claudia Benthien and Inge Stephan, eds, *Mannlichkeit als Maskerade* (Köln: Böhlau Verlag, 2003), pp. 128–53.

43 Jean-Luc Moulène as quoted by Briony Fer, 'Each Any', in Jean-Pierre Criqui, Yve-Alain Bois and Briony Fer, eds, *Jean-Luc Moulène* (Cologne: König, 2009), p. 138.

44 Moulène's interest in the strike objects dates back as far as the end of the 1980s, when the artist began to privately collect them. In 2003 the artist donated his own collection to the Archive National du Monde du Travail in Roubaix, a museum specialising in the history of industries and trade unions, which has exhibited some of them. Moulène's photographs, in turn, were acquired by the Musée National d'Art Moderne at the Centre Pompidou in Paris. The initial version of the project – exhibited for the first time at the Galerie Noisy-le-Sec (Seine-Saint-Denis) from 20 May to 13 July 1999 – included 24 objects. In 2000 a new extended version – comprising 39 objects – was presented by Moulène at the Musée du Bassin Houiller Lorrain, La Petite-Rosselle, in Forbach (Moselle). The series of 24 objects was published in *Les Cahiers du Musée National d'Art Moderne*, no. 71 (2000), and then as a special extra supplement for the periodical of the trade union CGT with the title *Quarante objets de grève présentés par Jean-Luc Moulène* (NVO, no. 3057, 2003).

45 On the history of the strike objects, see Noëlle Gérôme, *Les Productions Symboliques des Travailleurs à l'Entreprise* (Paris: Ministère de La Culture, 1984); Noëlle Gérôme, *Archives Sensibles, Images et Objets du Monde Industriel et Ouvrier* (Cachan: Editions de l'ENS-Cachan, 1995); Véronique Moulinié, 'Des "oeuvriers" ordinaires, lorsque l'ouvrier fait le/du beau', *Terrain*, no. 32 (1999), pp. 37–54; Jean-Charles Leyris, 'Objets de Grève, un Patrimoine Militant', *In Situ*, no. 8 (2007), np.

46 Laurie Attias, 'Jean-Luc Moulène', *Frieze*, no. 47 (1999), p. 121.

47 Translation from Jean-Luc Moulène, *Jean-Luc Moulène: Opus 1995–2007, Documents 1999–2007* (Lisbon: Culturgest, 2007), p. 109.

48 Yve-Alain Bois, 'The Inventory of Solitudes', in Jean-Pierre Criqui, Yve-Alain Bois and Briony Fer, eds, *Jean-Luc Moulène* (Cologne: König, 2009), p. 100.

49 Sophie Duplaix, 'Objets de grève/objets de réflexion. À propos des 24 Objets de Grève présentés par Jean-Luc Moulène', *Les Cahiers du Musée National d'Art Moderne*, no. 71 (2000), p. 50.

50 Brian Rigby, *Popular Culture in Modern France: A Study of Cultural Discourse* (New York: Routledge, 1991), p. 156. On situationist détournement see Guy Debord, *The Society of the Spectacle* (1967) (New York: Zone Books, 1994); Raoul Vaneigem, *The Revolution of Everyday Life* (London: Left Bank Books/Rebel Press, 1983).

51 Michel De Certeau, *The Practice of Everyday Life* (Berkeley, CA: University of California Press, 1984).

52 Jean-Luc Moulène as cited in Sophie Duplaix, 'Objets de grève/objets de réflexion', p. 49.

53 Jean-Luc Moulène as cited in Jean-Max Colard, 'Jean-Luc Mouléne: La Reprise', *Les Inrockuptibles*, no. 198 (1999), p. 88.

54 Jacques Rancière as cited in Fulvia Carnevale and John Kelsey, 'Art of the Possible: An Interview with Jacques Rancière', *Artforum*, no. 7 (2007), p. 259.

55 Jacques Rancière, *The Ignorant School Master: Five Lessons in Intellectual Emancipation* (1987) (Stanford, CA: Stanford University Press, 1991).

56 Jacques Rancière, *The Nights of Labor: The Worker's Dream in Nineteenth-Century France* (1981) (Philadelphia, PA: Temple University Press, 1989).
57 Jacques Rancière, 'Good Times or Pleasure at the Barricades', in Adrian Rifkin and Roger Thomas, eds, *Voices of the People: The Politics and Life of 'La Sociale' at the End of the Second Empire* (London: Routledge & Kegan Paul, 1987), p. 50.
58 See Jacques Rancière, *The Politics of Aesthetics: The Distribution of the Sensible* (London: Continuum, 2004); Jacques Rancière, *The Emancipated Spectator* (London: Verso, 2009).
59 Jacques Rancière, *Aesthetics and Its Discontents* (Cambridge: Polity Press, 2009), p. 24.
60 Stephen Wright, 'Jean-Luc Moulène', *Contemporary*, no. 67 (2004), p. 65.
61 *Ibid.*
62 Stewart Martin, 'The Absolute Artwork Meets the Absolute Commodity', *Radical Philosophy*, no. 146 (2007), p. 18.
63 Hans Magnus Enzenzberger, 'Constituents of a Theory of the Media', *New Left Review*, no. 64 (1970), p. 25.
64 *Ibid.*
65 Terry Eagleton, 'Utopia and Its Opposites', *Socialist Register*, vol. 36 (2000), p. 34.
66 Terry Eagleton, *Walter Benjamin, or, Towards a Revolutionary Criticism*, p. 149.
67 Ernesto Laclau, 'Populism: What's in a Name?', in Lars Bang Larsen, Cristina Ricupero and Nicholas Schafhausen, eds, *The Populism Reader* (New York: Lukas & Sternberg, 2005), p. 107.
68 Fredric Jameson, *Postmodernism or, the Cultural Logic of Late Capitalism* (London: Verso, 1991), p. 2.
69 For this definition I am indebted to Julian Stallabrass. See Stallabrass, 'Elite Art in an Age of Populism', in Alexander Dumbadze and Suzanne Hudson, eds, *Contemporary Art: 1989 to the Present* (Oxford: John Wiley & Sons, 2013), pp. 39–49.
70 Ernesto Laclau, *On Populist Reason* (London: Verso, 2005), p. 246.
71 Ernst Bloch, *The Principle of Hope*, trans. Neville Plaice, Stephen Plaice and Paul Knight, vol. 1 (Oxford: Basil Blackwell, 1986), p. 33.
72 *Ibid.*, p. 5.
73 This can be found in Rancière's bias against those documentary and activist practices that rely on informational clarity and the transmission of a 'message'. Rancière seems to uphold a view of the documentary that reduces it to the pedagogical and the sociological, understood as univocal expression of power. As he explained: 'Political art cannot work in the simple form of a meaningful spectacle that would lead to an "awareness" of the state of the world. Suitable political art would ensure, at one and the same time, the production of a double effect: the readability of a political signification and a sensible or perceptual shock caused, conversely, by the uncanny, by that which resists signification.' J. Rancière, *The Politics of Aesthetics: The Distribution of the Sensible* (London: Continuum, 2004), p. 63.

CHAPTER FOUR
Digital Utopia in the Post-Internet Age

'Try polite differentiation, coolness and refreshed nostalgia.' So recommends Jaakko Pallasvuo's fake instructional video *How To / Internet* (2011).[1] Offering career tips to would-be digital artists, the video shows an anonymous Internet user surfing through a myriad of garish webpages and YouTube animations while an exhilarating remix of TLC's famous hit 'Waterfalls' can be heard in the background. 'Binge on 90s Pop Culture and HTML5', reads another of Pallasvuo's ironic slides. The video is an entertaining satire of how the imitation of the graphic style of 1990s Internet websites has become a trite strategy in the field of digital art.[2] The fascination for the primitive gif animations and midi music files of the early World Wide Web is not merely a fad, as the popularity of hacker groups such as the Archive Team demonstrates.[3] Defining themselves as 'a loose collective of rogue archivists, programmers, writers and loudmouths dedicated to saving our digital heritage', the team, founded in 2009, has preserved millions of webpages that were going to be erased from the web by their owners – usually, large media corporations such as Apple, Google or Yahoo![4] This phenomenon demands critical attention: why remember the times in which digital technology was still a slow and imperfect medium? Does this nostalgic impulse imply a critique of the present uses of communication technologies and dissatisfaction with our society's lack of democracy? Or, alternatively, does it excessively idealise the early development of the Internet, forgetting how the 1990s rhetoric about the 'information superhighways' was deeply enmeshed with the flourishing of neoliberalism?

The 1990s was certainly a crucial decade in the development of the Internet. It was the time when the network went public and was opened to commercial uses and large business investments.[5] It was also the time of the rise of Net art: a new heterogeneous field of art practices that was bound inextricably to the development of the Internet itself and borrowed from the language of conceptualism, video art, situationist détournement and appropriation art.[6] Less a coherent movement than a loose group of artists, activists, designers and social critics from various geographical contexts who shared an interest in exploring the possibilities of the emerging communication technologies, Net-based art remained for some years a specialised and highly discursive field, whose works and manifestos circulated online through mailing lists and websites, at a time when access to the Internet was still limited to a minority. Some of its early practitioners deployed strategies of détournement and hacked corporate websites. Consider, for instance, Vuk Kosic's *Net.art per se* (1996), a fake CNN site commemorating a meeting of Net artists and theorists in Trieste, Italy, in 1996, or *MOMA Tank, from Life* (1997), a digitally manipulated documentary photograph of a war tank patrolling a street with the inscription 'MOMA' on its side; or, consider RTMark spoof sites that stylistically mirrored official organisations such as the World Trade Organization (WTO) but loaded pages with radical content. Because of these tactics, Net art came to symbolise 'a subversive and anti-institutional attitude' and seemed to offer the promise of a new dematerialised, de-authored and unmarketable reality of collective, collaborative and participatory culture.[7] Commenting on the email forums of Net artists, Julian Stallabrass wrote: 'such forums for discussion and exhibition are open, disputatious, democratic and egalitarian, and permit a glimpse of a culture that is founded less on broadcast by celebrities than dialogue among equals'.[8] Enthusiastic statements about the digital revolution could also be found in the declarations of influential curators. Pieter Weibel, the director of the prestigious Center for Art and Media in Karlsruhe, was one of the most active promoters of electronic art at the time. In the introduction to the 1999 exhibition 'Net Condition: Art and Global Media', held in Karlsruhe, Barcelona and Tokyo, Weibel emphatically welcomed the advent of the digital revolution and commended the avant-garde and emancipatory potential of Net art.

> The global Net is the driving force behind a radical economical, social and cultural revolution at the beginning of the next millennium, the outer lines of which become visible in this exhibition for the first time. [...] Net art ranging from physically existing local installations to worldwide interlinked computer games has become the forum in which many of the liberating hopes of the historic avant-garde are expressed in new terms. Web art, net-based installations not only present the most topical phase of net art, which dominates the discourse on media after the video based sculpture of the 1980s and the computer based interactive installations of the 1990s, but also the form of

art, to which the highest political hopes are linked. The socially revolutionary utopias of the historic avant-garde, movements of enlightenment, such as freedom of contract, equal opportunities and intercultural emancipation are now to be implemented by technology.[9]

These statements paralleled the boosterism of the digital media of journalists and pundits. For the writers of the influential Californian magazine *Wired*, the 'digital revolution' was inescapable but, nevertheless, its trajectory led to favourable destinations; for best-seller authors and 'digital gurus' such as MIT professor Nicholas Negroponte, the Internet was supposed to 'flatten organizations, globalize society, decentralize control, and harmonize people'.[10] utopia, in other words, was at hand. The technologically deterministic discourse surrounding the rise of digital media bought into the neoliberal view that the market is a natural force that, if left unbridled or deregulated, is capable of bringing progress for all. Promoted in magazines, books, TV programmes and Net conferences, the ideology of the digital revolution promiscuously combined, in Richard Barbrook and Andy Cameron's words, 'the free-wheeling spirit of the hippies and the entrepreneurial zeal of the yuppies'. They concluded: 'This amalgamation of opposites has been achieved through a profound faith in the emancipatory potential of the new information technologies. In the digital utopia, everybody will be both hip and rich.'[11] In his book *The Holy Fools: A Critique of the Avant-Garde in the Age of the Net* (1998), Barbrook extended the critique of the ideology of digital utopianism to Net art's practices.[12] Net artists' celebration of new media and the World Wide Web as a radical, free and autonomous realm offered an experiential, aesthetic homology to the sanctification of free-market capitalism that permeated vernacular discourse. For Barbrook, Net art's celebration of new media was the other side of the same coin: the conservative and pernicious individualism of the 'Californian' ideology.

Barbrook has a point in saying that Net art's construction of cyberspace as an alternate *space* – as a new world rather than as a way of dealing with the existing one – dovetailed with the rugged individualism of neoliberal ideology and the myth of the digital frontier, another great construct of American capitalism. Indeed, one of the reasons for the 1990s Net art boom within galleries and museums in the USA in particular was that the institutions hoped for pecuniary aid from the emerging IT sector – aid which they partly received.[13] Yet his critique might sound too acerbic and sweeping, conflating a broad and nuanced spectrum of diverse practices into a single unitary artistic movement. Only a couple of years since Barbrook's famous indictment, the utopian rhetoric around the digital utopia soon appeared to be light in substance, as the catastrophic burst of the dot.com bubble laid bare the hollow promises and hype of the Internet revolution. Fast-forward from 2000 to the present, and buoyant claims about the digital revolution such as those made by Negroponte and Weibel appear naive to say the least. Internet and digital media are not the novelties they used to be, but constitute the quotidian landscape of our everyday experience. In addition, events such as the Wikileaks scandal and Edward Snowden's revelations about the US government's eavesdropping operations have somehow laid bare the geopolitical and economic structures of power governing the Internet.[14] The technology seems less and less an empowering and revolutionary tool than an instrument entirely controlled by businesses and national security agencies; less a platform for aspiring artists and talented amateurs than an outlet for celebrities to promote themselves through Twitter or Facebook.

Likewise, the art world has not been shaken by the rise of Net art; rather, it has absorbed and tamed the critical elements of this heterogeneous practice. Until the late 1990s, most Internet art circulated exclusively on websites and free online platforms, thriving within the enclave space of a still esoteric medium. Arguably, this allowed its practitioners to maintain their anti-establishment attitude and autonomy. However, very quickly Net-based art began to circulate within the mainstream art world; its history became a pop history or a pantheon, integrationist rather than transgressive, and its pioneers compared with illustrious precedents (e.g. Marcel Duchamp, Nam June Paik). As Rachel Greene, one of the first Internet art historians, remarked in 2000, 'originally conceived as an alternative social field where art and everyday life were merged, net.art may now seem threatened by its own success – that is, likely to cede a degree of its freewheeling, antiestablishment spirit as it is further brought into the institutional field'.[15] The incorporation of Net art in the art world has continued unabated, putting the category itself under severe pressure. Some of its practitioners now claim that the term 'Internet art' should be applied to digital works that appear both online and offline. 'I think it's important to address the impacts of the internet on culture at large,' says, for instance, Marisa Olsen, 'and this can be done well on networks but can and should also exist offline.'[16] To distinguish contemporary digital art from its early format, the term 'post-Internet' has been coined: in the words of one critic, 'Post-Internet could be understood as a term that represents the digitization and decentralization of all contemporary art via the internet as well as the abandonment of all New Media specificities'.[17] The glorious days of Net art are over: we are living in a 'post-Internet' age.[18]

The problematic expansion of the category of Internet art is symptomatic of three phenomena. Firstly, it reflects the ubiquitous nature of the digital revolution: in today's world online and digital media do not represent the future any more but have become ingrained in all aspects of social, cultural and economic life; secondly, the original distinction between high art and new media art is becoming increasingly blurred as more digital art appears in galleries and museums; and, thirdly, the divide between the Internet and the world of mass produced and commercial culture has also become less and less sharp. Art critic Gene McHugh captures well the disappointment provoked by the growing expansion and commodification of the Internet. Speaking about the post-Internet 'turn', he writes:

> So, what changed? What about what we mean when we say 'Internet' changed so drastically that we can speak of 'post-Internet' with a straight face? [sic] On some general level, the rise of social networking and the professionalization of web design reduced the technical nature of the network, shifting the Internet from a specialized world for nerds and the technologically-minded, to a mainstream world for nerds, the technologically-minded, and grandmas and sports fans and business people and painters and everyone else. Here comes everybody. Furthermore, any hope for the Internet to make things easier, *to reduce the anxiety of my existence*, was simply over – it failed – and it was just another thing to deal with it. What we mean when we say 'Internet' became not a thing in the world to escape into, but rather *the world one sought to escape from*... sigh... It became the place where business was conducted, and bills paid. It became the place where people tracked you down.[19]

In less than a decade, the 'new' media has shifted from novelty to banality: the new technology has ceased to be the embodiment of the utopian dream of an 'elsewhere' and a 'not-yet' and has become the 'here' and 'now'. Given the disillusionment of the hopes raised by the digital revolution, the nostalgic tendency to look back at the 1990s as a golden age could be better understood. The nostalgic impulse so pervasive in contemporary digital art and visual culture reflects the widespread perception that the Internet is now an ossified technology.

This chapter does not provide an ontological inquiry into the essential nature of digital media, nor does it attempt to replace the utopian rhetoric of the Internet with the rhetoric of crisis and catastrophe which has dominated theoretical discourse in the field of film, media and urban studies for a long time;[20] rather, it is an effort to articulate something about the meaning of digital and online media for contemporary artists today. The chapter is premised on the idea that technologies are complex 'material social practices' that are called into being through the conflicting needs and desires of corporations, states and social groups. These diverse needs and desires are articulated in public discourses and theories – including the writings of academics, pundits, bloggers, activists and (last but not least) artistic practices that reflect on technological change. Culture plays and has played a significant role in shaping the construction of the Internet, as Thomas Streeter has remarked in his study of the development of the technology in the USA. Historically, utopian or dystopian visions of the Internet have shaped policy-makers' decisions and design choices, determining its uses and effects. While utopian and dystopian constructions often tell us more about the political orientation of the claimants than they do about the nature of a technology, the way the Internet is built and organised, Streeter suggests, is 'inseparable from the *way* builders imagine it, even if they do imagine it partially or inaccurately'.[21]

Artists' utopian or dystopian fantasies, therefore, should not be quickly dismissed. Instead of presenting a general survey, I want to consider the work of just four artists, Richard Vijgen, Thomson and Craighead, and Hito Steyerl. Their writings and installations share the awareness of the transition to the post-Internet age and its broad negative implications for digital utopianism; nevertheless, their approaches to the transformation of the Internet are different and manifest different levels of critical awareness. While a certain nostalgia characterises Vijgen's and Thomson and Craighead's installations, Steyerl's films seem to be more about the 'revolutionary' power of the medium and avoid looking back at the 1990s as a golden age of the Internet. Despite the dissimilar tones of their approaches and the distinct temporality evoked by their works, they all face the same dilemma: that of celebrating the alternative, utopian possibilities offered by the new technology without hypostatising it as an autonomous force, independent from capitalism. In other words, how can the utopia of the Internet be reinvented without falling into the uncritical boosterism that, as we have seen, was typical of certain Net art discourse and unconsciously chimed with the celebration of individualism and *laissez faire* economics of neoliberalism? This is the key question framing this chapter.

* * *

Included in the database of the magazine *Rhizome*, one of the most prominent journals in the field of digital art, the computer installation *The Deleted City* (2011) is introduced as an act of 'digital archaeology' by its author, Dutch designer and artist Richard Vijgen. The project was intended to be a touch-screen installation which would be exhibited in a gallery setting.[22] It is based on a graphic interface programmed and designed by Vijgen that allows viewers to explore Geocities, a now abandoned web-hosting service – and, according to the artist, a powerful symbol of the utopian potential of the 1990s Internet. Launched in 1994, Geocities became the third most visited website by 1999, when it was bought by the multimedia company Yahoo! for $3.57 billion. A decade later, Yahoo! decided to shut down Geocities, after most of its users had moved to other platforms. Vijgen used a back-up file of the website to produce an interactive video that visualises the dismantled online community as the map of an imaginary city.

In the artist's own words, the work aims 'to revisit a previous incarnation of the Internet and allows you to see how the technology, the aesthetics, the metaphors, and the values that underpin it have changed'.[23] *The Deleted City* thus aims to avoid the sentimentality of contemporary websites that simply recycle the kitschy graphic elements from early homepages. Unlike many of them, it does not show endless photographs of funny kittens, cute babies and adorable grannies but provides the viewer with contextual information about Geocities' history through captions and texts. However, as we will see, although the project may reveal some of the consequences of the technology's increasing commodification, this digital archaeology is not immune from criticism insofar as it unduly aggrandises the democratic, utopian nature of Geocities and the kind of do-it-yourself mythology surrounding the 1990s Internet.

Geocities allowed its users to produce and design independent homepages which were arranged according to 'neighbourhoods' (named 'Hollywood' for homepages about movies or, say, 'Athens' for pages on Greek mythology). At its peak, Geocities had twenty-nine neighbourhoods for all its homesteaders to congregate in. Vijgen devised a computer programme that translated each neighbourhood into phosphorescent squares whose size depends on the number of homepages it contained. As a consequence, the old online community appears as a labyrinthic structure composed of green squares on a black background. By using drag and pinch gestures on a multi-touch screen, the viewer can navigate around the city in a manner reminiscent of Google Maps. Starting with a zoomed-out view, the entire city emerges as an abstract image, a constellation of large squares surrounded by small dots and large empty areas. Zooming in on a neighbourhood, the computer slowly reveals the sub-neighbourhoods, blocks and individual homepages of Geocities. Zooming in even further reveals more and more detail: individual HTML pages and the images they contain become gradually visible, and, like a ghostly echo of times gone by, nearby MIDI files are played as you browse.

The Deleted City possesses significant affinities with Vuk Cosić's well-known intervention *Documenta Done* (1997). A pioneering work in Net art, this was a mirror of the website of Documenta X – the prominent international exhibition held in Kassel every five years, claiming to present state-of-the-art contemporary art to a wide public.[24] Documenta X was also the first important event where Internet art was showcased. When the organisers announced that the website was going to be shut down and sold as a CD-rom, Cosić created a pirate copy and spammed a counter-announcement saying that the website was still available. *Documenta Done* can be interpreted as a statement about the importance of keeping digital art accessible and free from institutional mediations. It aimed to return Net art to its authentic location, that is, 'cyberspace': a communal,

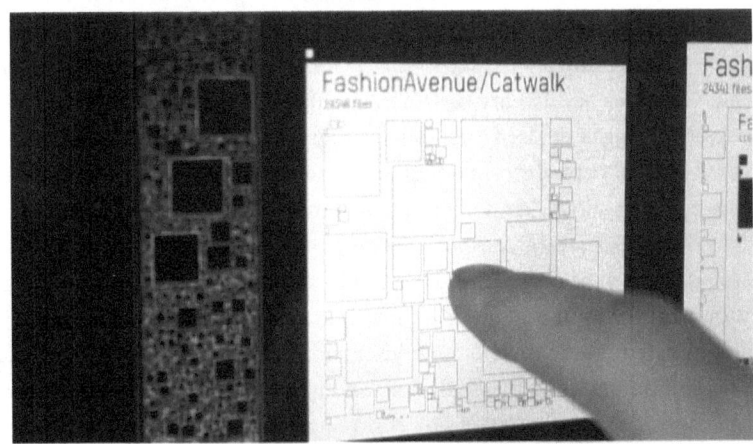

Figs. 41, 42, 43. Richard Vijgen, *The Deleted City*, 2012, interactive data visualization (Courtesy Richard Vijgen)

equalitarian space, antagonistic to the market and the mainstream art world. Vijgen's work seems animated by the same spirit of Cosić's famous project: *The Deleted City* is not only an act of digital archaeology but also a gesture of defiance against large business's decision to wipe down Geocities. But why, we may wonder, preserve Geocities and not another website? In other words, why would Geocities today represent a model for an alternative Internet?

As Vijgen explains, Geocities was shaped according to the model of the public library. This model does not pertain any more to the Internet. Unlike its contemporary counterparts such as Facebook and MySpace, Geocities seemed much more focused on hosting actual content than on allowing the exchange of personal and biographical information between its users. It offered a wealth of information on a variety of topics, which were not controlled by the service provider and which were not previously accessible to users. In a sense, Geocities was closer to Wikipedia than Facebook: its aim was less the expression of a narcissist and exhibitionist culture than the free sharing of information. Furthermore, unlike contemporary social media, Geocities did not posit rigid limitations on the format and content of the users' homepages. The lack of conventions allowed for the possibility of experimentation with different designs. 'Home-page culture', Vijgen says, 'developed in tandem with the medium itself, incorporating new technical possibilities (audio, moving images) as they became available.'[25] Thus, he argues, the 'under construction' sign so typical of Geocities homepages was not simply an index of the shabbiness of webmasters but instead a powerful symbol of the Internet's flux and radical incompleteness. The same remarks have been made by important Net art pioneers such as the Russian-born Olia Lialina.[26] Lialina's recollections of 1990s Internet do well to capture the sense of excitement triggered by the new medium and allow us to understand the widespread nostalgia for the 1990s:

> Ordinary people came with their tools and used the chance to build their own roads and junctions, work was everywhere and everywhere there was something that wasn't ready. The Internet was the future, it was bringing us into new dimensions, closer to other galaxies. So the look of the internet had to be an appropriate one like in Star Crash or Galaga. It had to be like the inside of a computer or somewhere out there. Space wallpapers made the Internet look special. This was obviously a space with a mission that other media could never accomplish.[27]

Both Vijgen and Lialina lament the privileging of high production values in today's web design; they praise the amateurial status of the early Internet. 'Geocities', Vijgen explains, 'provided a page wizard that allowed you to get started quickly using configurable templates, but many decided to build their home pages by hand using html.'[28] 'What do we mean by the web of the mid-1990s and when did it end?', Lialina writes. 'One could say it was the web of the indigenous ... or the barbarians. [...] it was a web of amateurs soon to be washed away by dot. com ambitions, professional authoring tools and guidelines designed by usability experts.'[29] For contemporary artists, the 1990s represents the time when the Internet was still a pure, esoteric medium, untainted by the logic of the capitalist market. 'The space that we've researched as a new medium, for the last ten years has turned into the most mass medium of them all.'[30]

The obsolescence of the Internet is thus invested with utopian connotations in both Lialina's and Vijgen's works. Interestingly, their discourse has significant resonances with important precedents in the history of avant-garde cinema and photography. Consider, for instance, the fascination for the first decade of cinema history of 1970s experimental filmmakers such as Ken Jacobs, Ernie Gehr and Michael Snow (as well as contemporary artists such as Matthew Buckingham, whose work is discussed in chapter one). Commenting on that fascination, Tom Gunning pointed out that one of the reasons for avant-garde artists' interest in the history of early cinema is that this represented, and continues to represent, an alternative to mainstream film production and aesthetics. 'Early cinema', he remarked, 'offers a numbers of roads not taken, ambiguities not absorbed in commercial narrative cinema.'[31] Gunning insisted that the avant-garde's archival impulse was not to be seen as a melancholic dead end. For experimental filmmakers, he concluded, the exploration of early cinema could provide 'inspirations for new understandings of tradition and for new films'.[32] Another well-known celebration of medium obsolescence is Walter Benjamin's *Little History of Photography*.[33] Writing at the beginning of the 1930s, at a time when photography was not a new medium any more and was beginning to be accepted as an art, Benjamin extolled the 1840s as photography's best period. He described photography's history as one of rapid and inexorable decline, due to the rapid commodification and professionalisation of the medium. In Benjamin's view, the first decade of photography's history operated as 'a kind of promise folded within its medium of an openness and invention before the rigidification of the image as commodity'.[34] According to Benjamin, the flowering of photography happened in its first decade, 'that is the decade which preceded its industrialization' and in which 'the peddlers and the charlatans had not gotten hold of the new technology and turned it to profit'.[35] Borrowing from Benjamin's theory, in the past ten years, art historians such as Rosalind Krauss and George Baker, editors of the influential art journal *October*, have championed an aesthetic of obsolescence that involves a simultaneous retrieval and reinvention of analogue media conventions and strategies.[36] In their writings, the rapid emergence of digital photography is interpreted as the symptom of the last stage of capitalist amnesia and abstraction, defined as 'that violent decontextualization, voiding, and recoding of objects endemic to the principles of capitalistic modernity'.[37]

Nostalgic projections onto outmoded media continue to have traction among artists and cultural critics today, and, ironically, they permeate even the discourse surrounding recent technological inventions such as the Internet. Despite its high-tech touch-screen software, Vijgen's computer installation mimics the simple design of early computer interfaces: the monochrome lines and squares that delineate the thematic neighbourhoods and sub-neighbourhoods of Geocities are reminiscent of old computer screens. Vijgen's nostalgia for the 1990s demonstrates the incredibly fast evolution of digital media. While it would be easy to deconstruct it as a naive fantasy, it nevertheless must be considered as a symptom of a wider dissatisfaction with contemporary society's modes of cultural production. The nostalgic cult of obsolescence implies a critique of modernity, but, interestingly, it seems to consider technology as both the cause *and* the solution to the problem – be that capitalistic reification, social inequality or lack of freedom. In fact, *The Deleted City*'s emphasis on the DIY quality of the 1990s Internet seems to suggest that the amateurial embrace of tools and technologies could *per se* guarantee the kind of personal and political liberation that it is missing; and this perhaps marks one of the main limits of Vijgen's project.

The artist's glorification of Geocities' 'homesteaders' as creative amateurs possesses striking affinities with the rhetoric of making and tinkering of the Arts and Crafts movement. Inspired by British socialist William Morris and particularly strong in Europe and the USA in the late nineteenth century, the movement fostered free access to tools, organised craft exhibitions and advocated the home-making of objects as a path toward self-fulfilment. It was characterised by a marked resistance against mechanisation and saw technological progress as a threat to the moral strength and autonomous will of individuals. In the movement's view, one of the reasons for the decline of the human race was the degrading and de-humanising quality of mechanised factory work. The movement thus advocated a return to simple rural life and praised the figure of the medieval craftsman. While Vijgen claims to be interested in recuperating the now obsolete spatial metaphors of the Internet as a public library and the city, his description of Geocities evokes early cyberspace less as a city than as a village. Geocities members, he writes, were 'homesteaders' who 'could get a free piece of land' to build their digital homes, and 'Heartland' was the largest neighbourhood – 'a neighbourhood for all things rural'.[38] The artist's language strikingly recalls the romanticisation of rural life of the Arts and Crafts movement.

The parallel between Vijgen's celebration of Geocities and the Arts and Crafts movement is less farfetched than it may seem at first. Indeed, there are significant similarities between the ideology of 'making' of the Arts and Crafts movement and the utopian discourse around cyber-culture that emerged in the counterculture of the 1960s. With its celebration of simplicity, its endorsement of savvy consumerism as a form of political activism and its glorification of the figure of the hacker, the counterculture appropriated and reinvented some of the motifs, strategies and critiques of the Arts and Crafts movement. One of the protagonists of the San Francisco's counterculture was artist-cum-entrepreneur Stewart Brand, who later became a friend of Apple founders Steve Jobs and Steve Wozniak and one of the most active promoters of the personal computer. Brand's articles, speeches and forums were crucial to the construction of the myth of cyberspace and the invention of the computer hacker as romantic hero, which constitutes a central element of the myth.[39] The term 'hacking' had long been in use to refer to hobbyist-tinkerers who worked with gadgetry for fun. Brand gave this figure a rebellious twist: he described the hacker as an imaginative individual, a brilliant problem-solver and an outlaw. A similar tendency to romanticise the practices of computer users pervades Vijgen's account of Geocities members. While the artist avoids the rhetorical emphasis of Brand's articles, he nevertheless presents early Internet users as highly creative and entrepreneurial individuals who built the Internet from scratch with their own 'hands'.

Vijgen's work seems to extend a long anti-modernist tradition that goes as far back as the late nineteenth century. Unfortunately, however, it may also share some of its problematic and contradictory elements. As historian T. J. Jackson Lears's study of the American Arts and Crafts movement demonstrates, the movement did not tackle the real problem that plagued its society: that is, alienated labour and the separation of individuals from the collective means of production. While it expressed dissatisfaction with the conditions of modern capitalism and mechanised production, he argues, the Arts and Crafts movement provided yet another therapeutic escape from more fundamental social and political problems. The rhetoric of do-it-yourself making and craftsmanship inadvertently fostered adaptation to bourgeois culture and technological progress, becoming 'less a critique of modern culture than a means of reaffirming it'.[40] The ideology and fate of the Arts and Crafts movement bear more than superficial affinities to the ideology and fate of the counterculture celebration of computer hacking. As the movement ended up turning craft into a pleasurable hobby for the affluent, the counterculture's embrace of hacking and home computing overlapped with the neoliberal conception of digital media that dominated public discourse around the digital revolution in the 1980s and 1990s. Within this discourse, the figure of the hacker as creative tinkerer, capable of thinking 'outside the box', came to resemble the myth of the individual as self-employed entrepreneur, moving flexibly from place to place, building his knowledge bases in a process of constant self-education – in other words, it underwrote the ideology of work 'flexibility', self-employment and individualism that have been brilliantly discussed by Luc Boltanski and Ève Chiappello in their book *The New Spirit of Capitalism*.[41] In his study of the rise of digital utopianism in America since the 1960s, Fred Turner has well captured the ambivalent relation of the counterculture to conservative politics. 'As they turned away from agonistic politics and toward technology, consciousness, and entrepreneurship as the principles of a new society,' Turner writes, 'the communards of the 1960s developed a utopian vision that was in many ways quite congenial to the insurgent Republicans of the 1990s.'[42]

Like Brand's hackers, the members of Geocities celebrated by Vijgen appear less as radical revolutionaries, who used technology to 'smash the system', than as innocuous amateurs, who deployed the new technology in the pursuit of their personal and idiosyncratic interests and hobbies. Browsing through Vijgen's software installation, one realises that the kind of knowledge circulating through Geocities was not as subversive as the artist suggests in his account: photographs of fashion catwalks, trips to Paris, cemeteries and graveyards, and websites selling old guidebooks about United States coins are the objects buried under each of the squared blocks of the Geocities virtual map. Like the archival projects of Lialina and the Archive Team, Vijgen's *The Deleted City* draws its criticality from the noble aim of preserving popular memory against the destructiveness of the culture industry. As Michel Foucault reminded us a long time ago, popular memory is a very important factor in political struggle. Folk songs, festivals and oral storytelling retain and transmit the knowledge of past social conflicts and their achievements, energising the oppressed, giving them an identity, a direction and hope for future change. 'If one controls people's memory, one controls their dynamism,' declared Foucault, 'and one also controls their experience, their knowledge of previous struggles.'[43] Now, does the heterogeneous content of Geocities qualify as popular memory? And if so, does Vijgen's computer interface allow for popular memory to coalesce into a clear and overarching narrative? I would say 'no'. Viewers of the installation need to zoom in through the interface to find the millions of individual homepages contained in Geocities. Ultimately, they are plunged into an immersive digital waterfall and exposed to the pleasures of the data sublime, that is, the unthinking immersion in a chaotically complex and immensely large configuration of data.[44] More importantly, there is a fundamental disparity between Vijgen's evocative language – presenting Geocities as a collective space – and the individualistic and mundane nature of its information. Indeed, there seems to be no 'agora' in Geocities' virtual city, no centre where political life and discussion could take centre stage. Instead, the city appears as a chaotic constellation of individual homes. If anything, Vijgen's visualisation reveals the atomisation of popular, collective memory and the relentless privatisation of the American public sphere. Instead of being the model of a more democratic use of the Internet, as the artist would suggest, *The Deleted City* might inadvertently represent a record of the individualistic ideology of the hegemonic digital utopianism of the 1990s.

* * *

As in Vijgen's archaeological project, an undercurrent of nostalgia pervades Thomson and Craighead's installations. Yet irony and an absurdist tone distinguish them from the works of other contemporary artists. Consider, for instance, their *Dot-Store* (2002), which for me exemplifies the essential humour of Thomson and Craighead's practice. The website is an actual online website selling a variety of objects modelled upon cheesy Internet aesthetics: tea towels displaying Google search results of emotive phrases; old tapes of mobile phone conversations scanned using surveillance equipment; a playable version of Atari's *Breakout* where 'you must escape an obsolete version of the Netscape browser'; a sheet of eleven 'Under Construction' gif decorative temporary tattoos, 'made in the USA to the highest quality' ('Each gif', the item description in the website reads, 'has been sought out then plucked from the web by the tireless dot-store research team, so now you too can be, "under construction" either literally or metaphorically').[45] Ironic works such as *Dot-Store* seem to mock and criticise the superficial and faddish nature of much contemporary nostalgia for the early Internet; what is more, this work acknowledges the willing participation of users in the online mall experience and the importance of market forces in the development of the digital network – a fact, as we have seen, often forgotten by artists and designers who idealise 1990s Internet aesthetics.[46]

Among the pioneers of Net art in the UK, Jon Thomson and Alison Craighead have produced a large body of work that explores how the network shapes our experience and knowledge of the world. A central strategy of their practice is the appropriation and manipulation of information drawn from the Internet. The artists have appropriated graphic elements from the web (*CNN Interactive Just Got More Interactive* [1998]; *Weightless* [1998]), news feeds (*Decorative Newsfeeds* [2006]), weather data (*Weather Gauge* [2003–5]), web-cams (*Horizon* [2009]; *Six Years of Monday* [2013]), online videos (*Several Interruptions* [2009]; *October* [2012]; *Belief* [2012]), Flickr photographs (*A Short Film about War* [2009]; *My_Contacts* [2008]) and Twitter posts (*London Wall* [2010–11]). Captioning, subtitling, repetition and split-screens are among some of the devices used by Thomson and Craighead to bestow a high degree of self-reflexivity on their practice. Instead of using digital media as a transparent recording technology, they highlight the mediated, manipulated nature of information and acknowledge the material quality of digital networks against the commonplace trope of cyberspace as a virtual, disembodied and imaginary world. Thomson and Craighead's detached analysis of our electronic landscape has thus been praised by critics for its capacity to eschew exaggerated claims about new media's alterity and capacity to transcend the real. 'Thomson and Craighead's interest in data as material', argues Michael Archer, 'stands against the romantic, would-be revolutionary view of the internet that can be referred to as *cyber-idealism*.'[47] Nevertheless, I think we should not put the matter to rest so quickly: I would argue, against the reading of Thomson and Craighead as sceptical 'structural-materialist' filmmakers, that there is an element of romantic 'techno-idealism' within their practice, despite its ironic and self-reflexive tone. Thomson and Craighead's work does not fit comfortably within either the camp of theorists and artists that consider digital technology as inextricably linked to late capitalism and power, or the camp of the ultra-optimistic cyber-idealists who treat the Internet as an idyllic space of becoming immune from the contradictions and limitations of 'meatspace', that is, the world outside the Net. The ambivalence of Thomson and Craighead's video installations is evidenced by the coexistence of apparently opposite themes and aesthetics. On the one hand, the artists adopt the language of conceptualism with its emphasis on seriality, repetition, systems and rules; this language could be interpreted, among other things, as a nod to the idea of technology as a homogenising and alienating tool, which constrains and oppresses subjectivity.[48] On the other, Thomson and Craighead insist on the trope of the sublime, the infinite and the contingent, that is to say, on themes that are typically associated with romanticism and the valorisation of individual expression and subjectivity.

To illustrate my argument further I want to discuss their recent gallery installation *A Live Portrait of Tim Berners-Lee (An Early Warning System)* (2012). The work was commissioned by the National Media Museum in the UK, on the occasion of the 2012 exhibition 'open source', which examined the importance of sharing and equal access in the regulation of the Internet and the World Wide Web.[49] It is dedicated to computer engineer Tim Berners-Lee, who is widely considered as the 'inventor' of the World Wide Web. Yet *A Live Portrait...* is not a documentary about Berners-Lee's life and genius; rather, the work is a computer installation which contains many of the components common to Thomson and Craighead's practice: the emphasis on the geographically displaced quality of Internet information, temporal simultaneity and liveness, and, last but not least, the tension between chance and repetition, control and unpredictability. Occupying an entire wall of the gallery, the work consists of a gigantic silent screen projection divided into multiple windows. On the left side, a large black-and-white drawing of Berners-Lee faces the viewer; a highly pixelated image, the portrait recalls the low-tech aesthetic of early computers and thus hints at the current widespread nostalgia for the early days of digital technology; the right

Fig. 44. Jon Thomson and Alison Craighead, *A Live Portrait of Tim Berners-Lee (An Early Warning System)*, 2012, digital projection from online sources (Courtesy Thomson & Craighead; Carroll / Fletcher Gallery, London)

side of the screen comprises two quadrants that show live feeds from two webcams located on opposite sides of the world and eleven time zones apart. The first one, occupying the top-right corner of the projection, monitors the tarmac of an airport; the second camera, occupying the bottom-right corner, offers a bird's-eye-view of a coastline of a nondescript location. Captions and digital clocks indicating the exact time and date of the two places where the live video feeds are recorded appear under each camera feed. For its use of Internet webcams, the installation may recall one of Thomson and Craighead's most frequently cited works: *Short Films about Flying*. The film was built from live online feeds from a camera on the perimeter of Boston's Logan Airport and intertitles generated from random results of Google searches alternately using the terms 'He said' and 'She said'. The result was a series of short inconclusive and fragmentary scenes showing airplane landings on the tarmac and hangars viewed from afar; in *Short Films about Flying* the live quality of the clips, the muzak and the intertitles helped to dramatise otherwise banal and repetitive visual material. *A Live Portrait...* takes the minimalist style of *Short Films about Flying* to an extreme: the absence of textual supplements and sound completely evacuates the screen of any narrative content. Therefore, the work demands a patient viewer and an existentialist, almost Heideggerian attitude of being open towards the world. *A Live Portrait...* evokes the same feeling of boredom mixed with entrancement described by Robert Smithson in relation to experimental cinema. 'The longer we look through a camera or watch a projected image, the remoter the world becomes, yet we begin to understand that remoteness more',[50] Robert Smithson wrote in 1971, pointing to the defamiliarising effect of cinematic perception. In Thomson and Craighead's projection, however, the hypnotic experience of boredom is enhanced by the presence of multiple screens. But why place the web-cams next to the drawing of Berners-Lee? And why is the work entitled *A Live Portrait of Tim Berners-Lee (An Early Warning System)*? Indeed, if one keeps watching, one notices that the image updates every sixty seconds, changing its luminosity slightly. One also notices that the three elements in the installation are connected. Through a computer programme, the artists linked half of the image's pixels to one webcam and the other half to the other. As the earth rotates and orbits the sun and night becomes day in one camera and day becomes night in the other; every twelve hours the picture inverts tonality. After a cycle of twenty-four hours the image resumes its original composition. The portrait of Berners-Lee is indeed 'live' – but not because it is a real-time recording of the engineer's face but because it acts as an *interface* between the two widely remote webcams.

Originally borrowed from chemistry – where it means 'a surface forming a common boundary of two bodies, spaces, phases' – the term 'interface' is now widely used in computing and denotes a device that links software and hardware to each other and allows users to dialogue with computers and other individuals through digital networks.[51] Since the mid-1990s new media artists and art museums have deployed sophisticated computer interfaces in order to promote a benignly inclusive aesthetic of audience involvement.[52] One of the consequences of the celebration of new media interactivity has been the simplistic conflation of technical interaction with equality and democracy. As the interface devised by the artists does not enable viewers to control any of the elements in the installation, *A Live Portrait...* shies away from too facile a celebration of human/computer interaction. For its implicit critique of the dream of interactivity, *A Live Portrait...* may recall Bruce Nauman's dark live-taped video corridors of the 1970s. In her engaging analysis of the American artist's seminal body of work, Janet Kraynak has suggested that Nauman's environmental sculptures simultaneously beseeched and thwarted viewers, evoking a form of 'programmed' and 'constrained' interaction.[53] More importantly, Kraynak explains, Nauman's unsettling environments staged a dialectic of participation and control that resonated with contemporary discussions around the increasingly bureaucratic and technocratic nature of post-industrial societies. First introduced by sociologist Alain Touraine in the 1970s, the concept of 'technocratic society' evoked the image of modernity where technology and reason were being used to systematically control the freedom of individuals rather than to enhance it. 'Ours is a society of alienation,' Touraine wrote, 'not because it reduces people to misery or because it imposes police restriction, but because it seduces, manipulates and enforces conformism.'[54]

Writing at the same confluence of accelerated technocracy and structuralism were George Perec and the members of literary movement Oulipo, which is often mentioned by the artists as one of the major cultural references that influenced their practice. An acronym for 'Ouvroir de Litterature Potentielle', meaning 'Workshop for Potential Literature', the movement was founded in 1960 in France and included novelists and poets such as Raymond Queneau, George Perec, Harry Mathews and Italo Calvino.[55] The group predicated a method of writing based on a set of rigorous rules, inspired by mathematics and cybernetics. They experimented with lipogrammatic forms. A lipogram is a text that omits a particular letter of the alphabet: one of the Oulipo's most famous lipograms was Perec's well-known 1969 novel *La Disparition/The Void*, written entirely without the letter 'e'. Another machinery of regulation that was devised by the members of Oulipo was the notorious N + 7 device, whereby the writer takes a poem already in existence and replaces each of the poem's substantive nouns with the noun appearing seven nouns away in the dictionary. The Oulipo is usually discussed as an anti-chance literary movement whose goal was to neutralise the subjectivity of the author and to tame randomness (Perec famously described the rules of his *La Vie mode d'emploie/Life: A User's Manual* as 'a programming of chance').[56] However, such interpretation has come under pressure most recently from the publications of literary scholars such Alison James, who have pointed out that the philosophical issue of chance was central to the writings of many of the members of the group. Perec, for example, used constrained compositional techniques to play with contingency and court the imponderable and the unpredictable. 'The creativity of Oulipian constraints', she has remarked, 'depends precisely on this capacity to generate the accidental and the unexpected – to enable the writer to take chances – at the same time pointing the way to order and aesthetic closure.'[57] A similar dialectical exploration of chance and necessity is at the heart of Thomson and Craighead's practice. In their installations, the artists deploy the automatic quality of computer interfaces as regulatory systems or a set of instructions in a way that resembles the literary experiments of the Oulipo's writers. The embracement of computer interfaces involves the partial abdication of authorial control, in favour of accident, chance and unforeseen circumstances: computers are treated as devices that make something happen rather than describing or imposing a given state of affairs and subject position. The outcome of the artists' use of the Internet information network is less the evocation of a suffocating, technocratic and bureaucratic universe than the construction of a space where technology acts as a springboard for chance.

A Live Portrait... exemplifies Thomson and Craighead's Oulipian method: here, the rigorously simple, almost 'binary' image of Berners-Lee is linked to webcams whose purpose is to monitor ephemeral and unforeseeable entities such as the weather and the highly regulated but nevertheless ever-changing space of the airport. The transience of these feeds contrasts with the rigorous impersonality and timeless quality of the interface. The use of low-resolution images can also be read as another self-imposed 'rule' or 'constraint' that further enhances the sense of contingency of the representation. New media art historian Kris Paulsen has suggested that interfaces, 'be they representational, like television screens or webcam feeds, or abstract, like radar and tracking equipment, are both mediated and indexical. [...] The interface may be virtual,' Paulsen continues to explain, 'but the represented events and any actions one takes via the interface and its controls are real; the images are mediated and indirect, but they, like the photograph, are existentially connected to the world'.[58] In this regard, Paulsen's reading appears valid for Thomson and Craighead's work as well. *A Live Portrait...* challenges the myth that analogue mediums – in virtue of their superior 'indexicality' – are marked by a privileged relation to the contingent and the real, as opposed to digital media.[59]

The Oulipo's emphasis on rules and impersonal techniques was part of a wider critique of the romantic notion of the author as innate genius that was prominent among French intellectuals, including Foucault and Barthes, in the 1960s. The use of arbitrary constraints tended to foreground the role of language and the reader in the construction of the text against conventional readings that reduced meaning to the expression of the author's inner self and his or her unique vision of the world. However, despite the absence of clear stylistic marks of individual authorship, the Oulipian text did not empty the work of expressive elements. Instead of purely self-reflexive devices, the rules shaping the form of the Oulipo's literary experiments could have been interpreted metaphorically. Thus, for example, one of Mathews' lipograms in 'e' – written shortly after Perec's death – 'offers a fitting form both for lamenting Perec's absence (made particularly poignant by the impossibility of writing his name in this text) and for paying homage to that author's literary virtuosity'.[60] The same can be argued in regard to Thomson and Craighead's constrained appropriation techniques. The degraded quality of Berners-Lee image as well as the blurriness and low speed of the live video feeds may suggest the prospect of an imminent breakdown or interruption of the Internet connection. This low-tech aesthetic may be read both as a formal constraint *and* as the expression of the 'provisional quality' of the Internet. In an interview the artists have declared that the low-tech aesthetic of *A Live Portrait...* reflects the imminent dangers to the survival of the Internet due to the possible elimination of the principle of Net neutrality and the relentless commodification of the medium over the last decade.[61] In addition, Thomson and Craighead's aesthetics of noise and error may suggest the blurring of the boundaries between the human and the machinic. Commenting on the expressive function of the computer glitch, new media theorists Olga Goriunova and Alexei Shulgin have written: 'Dysfunctional machines are not only those that are broken, they are also those that do not comply with the general logic of machines, by acting irrationally and sometimes even turning into humans.'[62] To be clear: I am not suggesting that Thomson and Craighead deploy a low-tech Internet aesthetic to 'humanise' the computer interface. Rather, I want to propose that Thomson and Craighead's playful aleatory poetics challenge Frankfurt School-inspired images of progress and technology as the expression of modern instrumental reason gone wrong. *A Live Portrait...* stages the Internet as a tool for play and enjoyment, rather than de-humanising control and surveillance. By linking the changes of Berners-Lee's picture to the changes of daylight of the web-cam feeds and therefore the natural rotation of the earth, the installation invokes the image of a mediated, technologically complex world that seems to flow together and become a kind of organic whole.

Thomson and Craighead's work appeals to a broader fascination with information technology, viewing it as an instrument of liberation from dominant rationalist and utilitarian notions of human behaviour. The artists' penchant for the elusiveness of information networks echoes some of the aspects of the computer romanticism of the 1960s counterculture, which has been discussed by Thomas Streeter in *Net Effects: Romanticism, Capitalism and the Internet* (2011). Streeter points out – against the commonplace notion of romanticism as a backward-looking and nostalgic philosophy opposed to industrialisation and mechanisation – that romantic ideas played a crucial role in the development and promotion of computer technologies and cybernetics in the post-World War II era. Romantic tropes could be found, for instance, in the ecstatic and visionary language of pioneers of human/computer interactions such as scientist Joseph Licklider. Head of the US administration's Advanced Research Project Agency for much of the 1960s, Licklider helped to fund the research that laid the foundation for the Internet; he famously spoke about the 'self-motivating exhilaration that accompanies truly effective interaction with information through a good console and a good computer network'.[63] Once developed by other scientists, designers and cyber-enthusiasts – from Douglas Engelbart to Ted Nelson and the already mentioned Stewart Brand – Licklider's benevolent theory of human-computer interaction paved the way for the celebration of cyber-culture of the following decades. More importantly, central to certain aspects of the counter-culture imagination was the idea that computers could be harnessed to explore the fortuitous and unpredictable. Streeter explains:

> Used interactively, computers can become in a specific way, unpredictable machines. [...] The experience of drifting while interacting with a computer offers an experiential homology to the romantic sense of exploration, an experience of a self-shaping process that unfolds according to its own logic, that cannot be mapped to some external grid. That homology becomes particularly active socially, however, when it is mapped on to resistance or skepticism towards efforts to predict, rationalize, and control human behavior.[64]

Within the discourse of the 1960s counterculture, the unpredictability of human/computer interaction carried with it a critique of (and embodied an escape from) the regimented way of life of contemporary post-industrial societies. Streeter warns the reader to be careful of placing too much agency in the romanticism of vernacular theory: ultimately, economic and political forces played a significant part in the development of the Internet. Yet, he suggests, the romantic discourse about cyber-culture that originated in the 1960s and 1970s gave legitimacy to the spread and triumph of the 'personal' computer, supporting the Internet's explosion of the following decades. What is more, this discourse helped establish expectations about the medium and, among them, the idea that the Internet should be a space of free exchange beyond regulation. The emphasis on chance and unpredictability in human/computer interaction has often gone hand in hand with libertarian notions of the global network. However, technological romanticism has fed into the popular fascination with entrepreneurial success stories and an ideology of rugged individualism. The glorification of the superficially anti-conformist figure of the computer-geek-cum-successful-entrepreneur – epitomised by extremely popular media celebrities such as Apple's founder Steve Jobs and, more recently, Facebook's inventor Mark Zuckerberg – has been an offshoot of the counterculture romanticisation of computer technology. Despite its countercultural origins, Streeter remarks, romantic discourse has worked in concert with capitalistic expansion and the dominance of a neoliberal ideology since the 1980s of Ronald Reagan and Margaret Thatcher.

Thompson and Craighead's aesthetics of chance may imply a defence of the democratic freedom of the Internet and the need to preserve it from government and corporate attempts to constrain and regulate its power. However – and this truly marks one of the major limits of their artistic practice – the artists' ambivalent works could also evoke that selfish individualism at the heart of much romantic discourse surrounding new media. Nowhere is this more evident, and more ironically so, than in *A Live Portrait...*. The artists define the project as a tribute to Berners-Lee's democratic concept of the Internet; however, the monumental size of Berners-Lee's picture in the installation seems to underwrite the romantic myth of the solitary inventor and to forget the importance of institutions and society in the development of technologies. Moreover, rather than erasing authorial expression, the ingenious quality of their interface may function as a marker of authorship; that is to say, as much as an homage to Berners-Lee, the work can be read as an allegory of the Net artist as a brilliant and uniquely talented hacker. But is there a kind of Internet romanticism that can be mobilised to promote collectivity instead of unbridled individualism? In other words, does Internet romanticism always pull in a capitalist direction? Hito Steyerl's work represents an attempt to answer this troubling question.

***

Where in Thomson and Craighead's installations low-tech aesthetics serve to enhance the unpredictable quality of information flows and the openness of the work to chance, in Steyerl's practice the figure of the compressed, low-resolution digital picture – or what she calls the 'poor image' – is invested with connotations of class. Steyerl has argued that highly pixelated images circulating on platforms such as YouTube, UBU Web or pirated DVDs should be viewed as the 'avatars' of the anonymous and transnational collectivity of subaltern and potentially revolutionary subjects who are exploited by capitalism.[65] As she explained in her 2009 essay 'In Defense of the Poor Image':

> The poor image is a rag or a rip; an AVI or a JPEG, a lumpen proletarian in the class society of appearances, ranked and valued according to its resolution. [...] Poor images are poor because they are not assigned any value within the class society of Images. [...] It is a complete mystification to think of the digital image as a shiny immortal clone of itself. On the contrary, not even the digital image is outside history. It bears the bruises of its crashes with politics and violence. [...] The bruises of images are its glitches and artefacts, the traces of its rips and transfers.[66]

The artist's politically committed approach to digital media represents a salutary antidote to the Internet romanticism that can be found to different degrees in Vijgen's and Thomson and Craighead's installations. As we have seen, in these artists' works, the great accomplishment of cyberspace emerges more as the triumph of the self than as the triumph of the social. Vijgen's and Thomson and Craighead's art seems to construct computing as an alternative space – as a new world rather than as a way of dealing with the existing one; in contrast, Steyerl insists on the necessity, even the urgent necessity, to consider the Internet and the everyday as coterminous worlds. This proposition does not imply, however, that we need to surrender to the fact that the Internet has been completely subsumed by the capitalist machinery of power and control. In fact, Steyerl advocates a dialectical approach to technology – one which allows for the possibility of transgressive and subversive uses of digital media to exist.

A filmmaker and a writer, the artist has tackled the recent debate on the 'end of the Internet' in an article published on the pages of the influential contemporary art journal *e-flux* in 2013. 'Is the internet dead?' begins Steyerl's essay; 'this is not a metaphorical question. It asks what happened to the internet after it stopped being a possibility.'[67] About twenty-five years since the medium went public, the digital network is, in fact, not a novelty any more but deeply enmeshed in reality, or as Steyerl claims, it has started 'moving offline'. The technology has been commodified and subjected to the control of corporate and state power, and yet, Steyerl argues, its 'revolutionary' potential has not diminished. What is actually over is the trope of the Internet as an ideal, alternative transcendental sphere – a trope which was extremely popular in the 1990s. But the widespread ubiquity and popularity of the medium should not be seen as a drawback, as indeed contemporary artists such as Vijgen and Lialina seem to imply, but as an opportunity. According to Steyerl, the mobility and malleability of digital media – their capability to be re-appropriated and circulated ad infinitum – might reflect back on reality, showing how 'unstable' and 'fragile' the capitalistic system is. 'If images can be shared and circulated [through the Internet], why can't everything else be too?' declares Steyerl. 'If copyright can be dodged and called into question, why can't private property?'[68] For the artist, capitalism is not a seamless indestructible monolith but, rather, a very precarious and vulnerable social and historical configuration. Steyerl thus intimates that to confuse the question of the formidable power of capitalism with the question of its stability is to fail to grasp that in one sense the system is as unstable as it is precisely because of its power. This philosophy, as we will see, recalls Deleuze and Guattari's 'accelerationist' theory of capitalism. To demonstrate this argument I want to discuss one of Steyerl's experimental films in which the artist's notions of digital media and capitalism and their overlaps emerge more fully: *In Free Fall* (2010). Importantly, this experimental documentary was conceived and produced in the aftermath of the 2008 financial meltdown, which, for many, sounded the death knell for thirty years of hubristic neoliberal capitalism.[69]

In Free Fall is a thirty-minute single-channel video divided into three chapters, entitled respectively 'After the Crash', 'Before the Crash' and 'Crash'. It departs from mainstream cinematic representations of the 2008 crisis insofar as the video does not indulge in the kind of pathos of the personal and the familial typical of European and American films about this event.[70] The plot is not centred on the figure of an individual hero, beset by economic difficulties. In contrast, Steyerl follows in the steps of Sergei Tretyakov's 'biography of the object'.[71] This was a slogan coined in 1929 by the Russian avant-garde writer for a new revolutionary literary form that would have been opposed to the idealism of the nineteenth-century bourgeois novel. As Devin Fore observes, Tretyakov's method 'was not just a matter of enthroning objects at the center of the novel where the hero once was'; rather, it was about taking 'the points of intensity concentrated by the novel's intrigue in the hero's emotional biography and distribut[ing] them among a plurality of actants over the entire work'.[72] Steyerl's video recalls Tretyakov's method in that it is structured upon numerous tangled narrative threads that coalesce around the figure of an object, a Boeing airplane.

The work begins with shots of a junkyard in the Mojave Desert. Carcasses of passenger airplanes lie on the ground while the owner of the place, a bearded man in a wheelchair called Mike Potter, explains that airlines tend to abandon their aircraft during periods of economic downturn as it becomes unprofitable to fly them. However, the life of these airplanes does not end there. Surprisingly, profit is made out of the scrap: the discarded carcasses are sold to Chinese companies that then recycle their aluminium to manufacture DVDs. Money is also made by renting the objects to the Hollywood industry. In fact, the conclusive scene of the famous blockbuster movie *Speed* (Jan de Bont, 1994) was shot in Potter's airplane graveyard. This scene – replayed over and over in the video – portrays the collision of an abandoned Boeing with a moving bus on tarmac.

Steyerl then interviews her cameraman, Kevan Jenson. A freelance worker for the Hollywood industry, Jenson has found it harder and harder to find a job since the financial crisis of 2008. He explains that, because of the crisis, his house was repossessed. The proliferation of digital technologies further aggravated Jenson's difficult financial conditions. Digital software enabled the spread of film piracy and consequently decreased the revenues of the Hollywood studios, which in turn squeezed labour and led to the sacking of many freelancers like Jenson. His story is juxtaposed with the tale of aviation pioneer Howard Hughes. Hughes, the founder of Trans World Airlines (TWA), began his career as a Hollywood film producer and director. His most expensive and famous production, *Hell's Angels* (1930), narrates the aerial adventures of English and German pilots during World War I. The film caused controversy for the accidental deaths of several pilots and for its inflated budget. Steyerl shows us a clip from the film, portraying an airplane crashing on the ground. Finally, the video follows the story of how the Boeing airplanes owned by Hughes's airline became a key weapon for the Israeli military forces in the 1970s. This narrative is told by an 'expert', played by actor Imri Kahn, who relates that a batch of TWA airplanes was bought by the Israeli government in the late 1960s and used for various military operations such as 1976's famous Operation Entebbe. Meanwhile, clips from various hijacking films inspired by this actual event appear on screen. One of these is *Operation Thunderbolt* (Menahem Golan, 1977), starring the charismatic Klaus Kinski and the gorgeous Sybil Danning as German radical terrorists. In one particularly amusing scene, Kinski extracts a grenade from a bottle of champagne and proceeds to hijack the plane. The video then shows Steyerl and Kahn dressed up as flight attendants and performing a seatbelt safety demonstration. Instead of belts and oxygen masks, they hold DVDs in their hands in front of a backdrop of windmills superimposed onto a blue screen. *In Free Fall* concludes with a freeze-frame shot of a parachutist falling from a plane over a clear blue sky.

Steyerl does not linger over the painful effects of the economic crash. Instead, she portrays the crisis as a process that disrupts conventional boundaries between reality and fiction. All the interviewees relate the experience of the crash as a sudden descent into the unreal. Retired pilot Mike Potter exclaims, addressing the abandoned airplanes: 'And I said to myself, is this for real? These planes are all ghosts.' Similarly, Jenson describes his stupor when his house was repossessed during the crisis: 'I felt like the captain of a plane and I was unable to land it. It is a little amazing … this descent from something that felt so real into another place.' Steyerl's montage elicits a similar sense of bewilderment. The testimonies of Potter and Jenson are interspersed with clips from Hollywood movies. The explosion sequence from *Speed* is replayed, slowed down and reversed several times. The 1970s history of terrorist hijacking is presented through the overdramatised form of movies such as *Operation Thunderbolt*. Documentary and fictional images are constantly jumbled up so that the crash, and by extension the economic crisis, is transformed into an oneiric and hallucinatory experience in which the boundaries between fact and fiction, reality and fantasy, have collapsed.

The effect recalls the condition of schizophrenia as described by Fredric Jameson in his theory of postmodernism. Borrowing from Lacan, Jameson defines the schizophrenic experience as one in which 'isolated, disconnected, discontinuous material signifiers … fail to link up into a coherent sequence', whereby the world appears 'with heightened intensity, bearing a mysterious and oppressive charge of affect, glowing with hallucinatory energy'.[73] Importantly, Jameson associates the attributes of schizophrenia with late capitalism since, he argues, mass culture of the late twentieth century simulates schizoid experience. Writing in the 1980s, at the time of the rise of MTV, Jameson alludes to the fragmented and rapid montage of music clips, movie trailers and television advertisements. Steyerl's work resembles this form through its fast-paced editing. The interviews are frequently chopped so that *In Free Fall* ultimately looks more like a long movie trailer than a finished work. In light of Jameson's theory, then, the video can be said to express and perhaps even exacerbate the schizophrenic conditions of late capitalist culture.

Yet the video also reconfigures these conditions in less pathological terms. In fact, the soundtrack, composed of melodic pop tunes such as Nancy Sinatra's 'My

Beautiful Balloon', puts the viewer in such a lighthearted mood that the figure of the airplane crash becomes less a synonym for a schizophrenic disconnection from reality than an expression of pleasurable weightlessness and even exhilaration. As she explains, the experience of falling and, by extension, the collapse of the financial system should be viewed as a process of liberation that is capable of opening new horizons. 'While falling, people may sense themselves as being things, while things may sense that they are people. Traditional modes of seeing and feeling are shattered. Any sense of balance is disrupted. Perspectives are twisted and multiplied. New types of visuality arise.'[74] Therefore, if Steyerl's work simulates schizophrenic disorder, it also reinvents it and invests it with generative and revolutionary potential. Similarly, Gilles Deleuze and Félix Guattari long ago suggested that the only possible way out from capitalism is, indeed, to exploit and exacerbate its 'schizophrenic' logic.[75]

According to Deleuze and Guattari, schizophrenia and capitalism are related categories in that capitalism should be considered as a profoundly irrational social system. As they claim, the apparent rigor of economic sciences cloaks the profound delirium at the heart of this historical formation. Against the Weberian line of thought that sees modernity as a process of relentless de-enchantment, Deleuze and Guattari argue that unconscious and irrational desires should be seen as constitutive and propulsive elements of capitalism. As they remarked, 'the true history is the history of desire'.[76] But what is the desire driving capitalism? This system is animated by the urge to disrupt social codes and barriers, and thrives on the destruction of previous technologies, economies and configurations of power. Capitalism dismantles all existing social and cultural structures, norms and models of the sacred.

> But in every respect, capitalism has a very particular character: its lines of flight are not just difficulties that arise, they are the conditions of its own operation. It is constituted by a generalized decoding of all flux, fluctuations of wealth, fluctuations of work, fluctuations of language, fluctuations of art, etc. [...] It ligatures the points of escape and leaps forward. It expands its own boundaries endlessly and finds itself having to seal new leaks at every limit. It doesn't resolve any of its fundamental problems, it can't even foresee the monetary increase in a country over a single year. It never stops crossing its own limits, which keep reappearing farther away. It puts itself in alarming situations with respect to its own production, its social life, its demographics, its borders with the Third World, its internal regions, etc. Its gaps are everywhere, forever giving rise to the displaced limits of capitalism.[77]

According to these theorists, there is something intrinsically creative in the capitalistic obsession with production and the accumulation of wealth. If capitalism is a repressive system, it is because the bourgeoisie has historically been able to manipulate, control and channel the social energies underpinning this economy in its own interests. But what is the relation between capitalism and schizophrenia? Like capitalism, schizophrenia is systematically attracted to chaos. It is a pathology that is characterised, according to Deleuze and Guattari, by the irresistible need to cross over epistemological and normative boundaries. 'The schizophrenic', they remarked, 'is a person who, for whatever reason, has been touched off by a desiring flow which threatens the social order.'[78] Indeed, they wrote, 'schizophrenia is the exterior limit of capitalism itself or the conclusion of its deepest tendency [...] but that capitalism only functions on condition that it inhibit this tendency, or that it push back or displace this limit'.[79]

Having said that, the implications of Deleuze and Guattari's theory are significant with respect to the notion of a critically engaged art. According to their hypothesis, a revolutionary art should not rely on a systematic and dispassionate ideological critique. As one cannot completely resolve the drives of the unconscious – they argue – one can never completely demystify the irrational desires which drive individuals under capitalism and constitute their myths and beliefs. The sphere of the economic and the sphere of the imaginary cannot ultimately be disentangled. Therefore, according to Deleuze and Guattari, critiquing ideology is ultimately a futile endeavour; a more fruitful approach would be to seize on the schizophrenic impulses of capital, to exacerbate its energies and direct them for revolutionary purposes.

> But which is the revolutionary path? Is there one? – To withdraw from the world market, as Samir Amin advises Third World countries to do, in a curious revival of the fascist 'economic solution'? Or might it be to go in the opposite direction? To go still further, that is, in the movement of the market, of decoding and deterritorialization? For perhaps the flows are not yet deterritorialized enough, not decoded enough, from the viewpoint of a theory and a practice of a highly schizophrenic character. Not to withdraw from the process, but to go further, to 'accelerate the process,' as Nietzsche put it: in this matter, the truth is that we haven't seen anything yet.[80]

In *In Free Fall*, Steyerl seems to embrace Deleuze and Guattari's project. She appropriates spectacular clips from commodified culture as if they were a reservoir of untapped energies. Her fast-paced and delirious montage suggests that capitalism, with its tendency towards cycles of boom and bust, is a contingent and fragile order and that its inherent flux can escape the control of the elites.[81] In Steyerl's video this notion of a 'capitalist excess' is conveyed not only through

Fig. 45. Hito Steyerl, *In Free Fall*, 2010, single channel video HD, sound, 32 minutes (Courtesy Hito Steyerl)

the image of the airplane falling but through a variety of other techniques. Consider, for instance, the way in which the filmmaker uses the blue screen. This device is not deployed to reduce the visibility of the technological apparatus, as in mainstream Hollywood cinema. Rather, the blue screen foregrounds the fluid and constructed quality of the *mise-en-scène*. Moreover, throughout the video, there is an emphasis on the dynamics of movement: Steyerl's editing selects action-packed shots of airplanes and machines frantically moving. The moments of stillness are extremely rare: most of the scenes have been filmed through panning or zooming shots. At some point even the steady-cam used to record the airplane graveyard appears precarious: Jenson is accidentally hit by the demolition truck and he consequently loses control of the camera. The editing and shooting techniques deployed by Steyerl ultimately suggest that, like the airplane crashing, images are also constantly at risk of collapsing and morphing into something else.

The notion of excess is also symbolised by the figure of the DVD, which, in my view, is central to the understanding of the video. In this sequence we witness the resurrection of the crashed airplanes into DVDs on which the video will be recorded. Melted aluminium from the decommissioned airplanes is poured into circular moulds using various high-tech machines. An animation depicts a DVD spinning around the earth, as if the airplane had metamorphosed into it and had resumed flying.[82] The soundtrack – sampled from a Michael Jackson songs – links the diverse images of this fast-paced montage together, crossing each cut and melding them continuously. In the meantime Steyerl recites this text:

Matter lives on in different forms
Matter loves on
Matter lives on in different forms
(It is so recyclable)
Matter loves
Matter lives
Matter lives on
Matter continues to exist in different forms

Delivering the vision of kinetic, fluid matter, morphing in and out of images, this sequence evokes a world where destruction is generative and where the human subject is ultimately resilient.[83] Matter lives on, in spite of the meltdown of the financial market. The sheer exuberance of the DVDs moving, as well as the frenetic action of the machines, energised by the rhythmic pop music, evokes the flow of desire animating capitalism discussed by Deleuze and Guattari. Like the notion of schizophrenia and excess, the mercurial figure of the DVD represents the idea that capitalistic oppression is never definitive and that destruction can generate new lines of flight.[84] In this sequence Steyerl intimates that there is life and creativity in modernity and that there is hope for a better future.

Instead of providing viewers with a dry and rational unmasking of the fraudulent mechanisms of financial capital, Steyerl appropriates Hollywood cinema to represent our economy as a system inclined to self-destruction. She suggests that embracing and exacerbating this tendency could lead, paradoxically, to creating an alternative form of social belonging. As the artist points out, the figure of the Boeing airplane, which is at the centre of *In Free Fall*, represents less the past than the future. 'The idea [behind *In Free Fall*] is', she declared, 'to follow the object [the Boeing airplane or the DVD] to find out about the reality that creates it. In this case, it might be: follow it into the future, not into its history.'[85]

But if Steyerl's approach is informed by a nuanced optimism, the overloaded aesthetics of her video could be considered as a double-edged sword. Her

Figs. 46, 47. Hito Steyerl, *In Free Fall*, 2010, single channel video HD, sound, 32 minutes (Courtesy Hito Steyerl)

Digital Utopia in the Post-Internet Age

Fig. 48. Hito Steyerl, *In Free Fall*, 2010, single channel video HD, sound, 32 minutes (Courtesy Hito Steyerl)

mimicry of commodity culture hints at a 'politics of accelerationism', which has been taken to task by a number of theorists. A term coined by Noys, 'accelerationism' designates a philosophical strand of post-1968 radical thought based on the notion that a socialist revolution will be possible only by exacerbating the contradictions inherent in the dominant economic system. Epitomised by Deleuze and Guattari's notion of schizophrenia, 'accelerationism,' writes Noys, is 'an exotic variant of the *politique du pire*'; it argues that 'if capitalism generates its own forces of dissolution then the necessity is to radicalize capitalism itself: the worse the better' (emphasis in the original).[86] Emerging from the ashes of 1960s French radicalism, this political thought has not been borne out: indeed, since the times of Margaret Thatcher and Ronald Reagan, capitalism has actively promoted the radicalisation of its own destructive forces, surviving its periodic crises and even taking advantage from them. As Steven Shaviro has remarked,

> the problem with accelerationism as a political strategy has to do with the fact that – like it or not – we are all accelerationists now. It has become increasingly clear that crises and contradictions do not lead to the demise of capitalism. Rather, they actually work to promote and advance capitalism, by providing it with its fuel. Crises do not endanger the capitalist order; rather, they are occasions for the dramas of 'creative destruction' by means of which, phoenix-like, capitalism repeatedly renews itself. We are all caught within this loop. And accelerationism in philosophy or political economy offers us, at best, an exacerbated awareness of how we are trapped.[87]

Similarly to Noys, Shaviro argues that, as a radical politics, accelerationism has failed in that it has placed too much hope in the immanent transformation of capitalism. Yet its programme continues to exert great fascination for contemporary political theorists, critics and even artists. In fact, Shaviro argues, an accelerationist aesthetics is emerging in some recent cinematic works; films such as Mark Neveldine and Brian Taylor's *Gamer* (2009) and Alex Cox's *I'm a Juvenile Delinquent, Jail Me!* (2004) embrace an accelerationist aesthetic, for they indulge in the delirious and excessive redeployments of pop culture.[88] According to him, accelerationism in art can only provide viewers with the recognition of our impotence in front of the current socio-economic order. However, unlike accelerationist politics, Shaviro remarks, accelerationist aesthetics has the merit of not offering us 'the false hope that piling on the worst that neoliberal capitalism has to offer will somehow help to lead us beyond it'.[89] In other words, the criticality of these films lies in the cynical enlightenment they provide.

But can we distinguish between, on the one hand, an accelerationist aesthetic that cynically indulges in the pleasures of nihilism and, on the other, one that prompts critical awareness and some hope for the future? Thinking back to Steyerl's practice in light of Shaviro's reflections, we may conceive the artist's hypertrophic mimicry of commodity culture as another example of accelerationist aesthetics. Nevertheless, Steyerl's accelerationism should be seen less as a gesture of enlightened cynicism than as an attempt at representing the complex reality of late capitalism. Indeed, a pedagogical impulse can be traced throughout *In Free Fall*, and, despite its complex narrative structure and visual excess, the video never gives way to total confusion and negativity. For this pedagogical impulse, Steyerl's work recalls the notion of 'cognitive mapping' tentatively sketched out by Jameson.[90] An art of cognitive mapping – Jameson suggests – would have the task of making viewers aware of their positions within capitalism's global system and would be an integral part of a socialist politics. Whether Steyerl succeeds or not in representing global capital remains an open question. Yet her focus on the life of the Boeing airplane gives us a sense of the complex constellations of social forces driving capitalism. Importantly, Jameson suggested that cognitive mapping could draw on a homeopathic use of the strategies, techniques and elements of consumer culture, 'To undo postmodernism homoeopathically by the methods of postmodernism,' he declared, 'to work at dissolving the pastiche by using all the instruments of pastiche itself, to reconquer some genuine historical sense by using the instruments of what I have called substitutes for history'.[91] Steyerl's kaleidoscopic mimicry of popular culture could be seen as an instance of just such a homeopathic method.

NOTES

1 The video is available at https://vimeo.com/32839686 (last accessed 28 May 2014).
2 Consider, for instance, websites like *Geocities-izer*: according to its slogan, *Geocities-izer* allows users 'to make any webpage look like it was made by a thirteen-year-old in 1996'. The website is available at http://www.wonder-tonic.com/geocitiesizer/.
3 Here as elsewhere I am using the words 'World Wide Web' and 'Internet' as synonyms for convenience, although I am aware that they are different technical concepts.
4 From the website of the Archive Team, available at http://archiveteam.org/; 'History is our Future', reads the title of the homepage.
5 As with other media, it is difficult to determine in a clear-cut way when the Internet was invented. A first experimental but not public version of the Internet went online in 1969 and was called ARPANET, after the Advance Research Projects Agency of the US Department of Defense, which funded much of the research on the new technology. However, other web historians consider 1989 as the year of the creation of the Internet. It was in that year that computer scientist Tim Berners-Lee declared the invention of HTTP and HTML (the name 'WorldWideWeb' was coined in October 1990, when the first web server and the first webpage were launched). For an engaging and accessible account of the invention of the Internet, see James Gillies and Robert Cailliau, *How the Web Was Born: The Story of the World Wide Web* (Oxford and New York: Oxford University Press, 2000). For an overview of existing literature on the history of the web, see Niels Brügger, ed., *Web History* (New York: Peter Lang, 2010).
6 The different terms that have been used to indicate this artistic field – from 'Net art' to 'Net.art', and from 'digital art' to 'new media art' – reflect its protean form. On the problems of defining Internet art, see Josephine Bosma, *Nettitudes: Let's Talk Net Art* (Amsterdam: Institute of Network Cultures/Nai Publishers, 2011).
7 See Josephine Bosma, *Nettitudes*, pp. 128–9.
8 Julian Stallabrass, 'The Aesthetics of Net.Art', *Qui Parle*, vol. 14, no. 1 (2003), p. 59. In a recent article, Stallabrass reiterates his beliefs in the inherent utopian, that is to say socialist, quality of digital art. See Julian Stallabrass, 'Why Digital Art Is Red', *Leonardo Electronic Almanac*, special issue: 'Red Art: New Utopias in Data Capitalism', vol. 20, no. 1 (2014), pp. 18–19. See also Julian Stallabrass, *Internet Art: The Online Clash of Culture and Commerce* (London: Tate, 2003).
9 Peter Weibel, 'The Project', in Peter Weibel and Timothy Druckery, eds, *Net Conditions* (Cambridge, MA: MIT Press, 2000), p. 18
10 Nicholas Negroponte, 'Being Digital – A Book (P)review', *Wired*, 3.02 (1995), p. 182.
11 Richard Barbrook and Andy Cameron, 'The Californian Ideology', *Science as Culture*, vol. 6, no. 1 (1996), p. 44.
12 Richard Barbrook, *The Holy Fools: A Critique of the Avant-Garde in the Age of the Net* (London: Hypermedia Research Centre, University of Westminster, 1998).
13 For an informative account of the rise and sudden collapse of Internet art, see Verena Kuni, 'Why I Never Became a Net-Art Historian', in Dieter Daniels and Gunther Reisinger, eds, *Net Pioneers 1.0: Contextualizing Early Net-Based Art* (Berlin: Sternberg Press, 2009), pp. 181–98.
14 For a clear account of the reasons for the failure of Julian Assange's revolutionary online platform Wikileaks, see Benedetta Brevini, Arne Hintz and Patrick McCurdy,

eds, *Beyond WikiLeaks: Implications for the Future of Communications, Journalism and Society* (Basingstoke: Palgrave Macmillan, 2013).

15 Rachel Greene, 'Web Work: A History of Internet Art', *Artforum*, vol. 38, no. 9 (2000), p. 167.
16 Marisa Olsen as cited in Lauren Cornell, 'Net Results: Closing the Gap between Art and Life Online', *Time Out New York*, 9 February 2006.
17 Artie Vierkant, 'The Image-Object Post Internet' (2010); http://jstchillin.org/artie/vierkant.html (accessed 10 June 2014).
18 For an alternative understanding of the term 'post-Internet', see Marisa Olson, 'Post-Internet', *Foam Magazine*, no. 29 (2012), pp. 59–63. See also Jennifer Chan, 'Notes on Post-Internet', in Omar Kholeif, ed., *You Are Here: Art after the Internet* (Manchester: Cornerhouse Books, 2014), pp. 106–23.
19 Gene McHugh, *Post-Internet* (Brescia: Link Editions, 2011), p. 5.
20 Perhaps as a reaction against the bland boosterism of vernacular theory, during the 1990s scholars interpreted the digital as the signal of an epochal loss of perception, materiality, memory and even reality itself, and as the symptom of a catastrophic historical rupture. As Paul Virilio famously remarked, the rise of the digital image is 'a catastrophic event, and if we don't take it into account, every hope will be lost'; Paul Virilio, *The Accident of Art*, trans. Michael Taormina (New York: Semiotext(e), 2005), p. 67. For similar rhetoric of crisis and catastrophe, see Jean Baudrillard, *Why Hasn't Everything Already Disappeared?*, trans. Chris Turner (London: Seagull, 2009); Mary Ann Doane, 'Information, Crisis, Catastrophe', in Wendy Hui Kyong Chun and Thomas Keenan, eds, *New Media, Old Media: A History and Theory Reader* (New York and London: Routledge, 2006), pp. 251–64; Jonathan Crary, *Techniques of the Observer* (Cambridge: MIT Press, 1992); Vivian Sobchack, 'The Scene of the Screen: Envisioning Cinematic and Electronic "Presence"' (1995), in Robert Stam and Toby Miller, eds, *Film and Theory: An Anthology* (Malden: Blackwell, 2000), pp. 67–84.
21 Thomas Streeter, *The Net Effect: Romanticism, Capitalism, and the Internet* (New York: New York University Press, 2011), p. 9.
22 Vijgen's work in *Rhizome*'s art database is available at http://rhizome.org/artbase/artwork/53493/. The installation has been shown in contemporary art museums and new media art festivals such as the Los Angeles County Museum of Art (LACMA) (2013), the 'Digital Revolution' exhibition at the Barbican Gallery in London (2014), the Festival Cultura Digital de Rio de Janeiro (2011) and the Screengrab International New Media Arts Prize in Townsville, Australia (2013).
23 Richard Vijgen, 'The Deleted City: A Digital Archaeology', *Parsons Journal for Information Mapping*, vol. 5, no. 2 (2013), p. 6.
24 See http://www.ljudmila.org/~vuk/dx/ (last accessed 2 August 2014).
25 Richard Vijgen, 'The Deleted City', p. 2.
26 Lialina has produced an extensive archaeological work on early Internet homepages. See Olia Lialina and Dragan Espenschied, eds, *Digital Folklore* (Stuttgart: Merz & Solitude, 2009).
27 Olia Lialina, 'A Vernacular Web', talk at the Decade of Web Design Conference, Amsterdam, January 2005; http://art.teleportacia.org/observation/vernacular/ (accessed 14 July 2014).
28 Richard Vijgen, 'The Deleted City', p. 2.

29 Olia Lialina, 'A Vernacular Web', np.
30 Olia Lialina, 'A Vernacular Web 2', *Contemporary Home Computing*, July 2010, np; http://contemporary-home-computing.org/vernacular-web-2/ (accessed 14 July 2014).
31 On the avant-garde's fascination for early cinema, see also Tom Gunning, 'An Unseen Energy Swallows Space: The Space in Early Film and Its Relation to American Avant-Garde Film', in John L. Fell, ed., *Film Before Griffith* (Berkeley, CA: University of California Press, 1983), p. 366.
32 *Ibid.*
33 Walter Benjamin, 'Little History of Photography', in Michael W. Jennings, Howard Eiland and Gary Smith, eds, *Selected Writings/Walter Benjamin Volume 2 (1927–1934)*, trans. Rodney Livingstone and others (Cambridge, MA: The Belknap Press of Harvard University, 1999).
34 Rosalind Krauss, 'Reinventing the Medium', *Critical Inquiry*, vol. 25, no. 2 (1999), p. 304.
35 Walter Benjamin, 'Little History of Photography', p. 519.
36 See Rosalind Krauss, *'A Voyage on the North Sea': Art in the Age of Post-Medium Condition* (London: Thames and Hudson, 2000); and Krauss, *Under the Blue Cup* (Cambridge, MA: MIT Press, 2011); on the idea of obsolescence as a site of resistance, see also *October*'s special issue on obsolescence edited by George Baker, 'Artist Questionnaire: 21 Responses', *October*, no. 100 (2002), pp. 6–98. *October* made some timid forays in the world of digital film but, nevertheless, it limited its scope to practices that are still indebted to the experimental language and concerns of the 1960s structural cinema. See Malcolm Turvey, 'Ken Jacobs: Digital Revelationist', *October*, no. 137 (2011), pp. 107–24; and John Powers, 'Darkness on the Edge of Town: Film Meets Digital in Phil Solomon's In Memoriam (Mark LaPore)', *October*, no. 137 (2011), pp. 84–100.
37 George Baker, 'Photography and Abstraction', in Charlotte Cotton and Alex Klein, eds, *Words without Pictures* (Los Angeles: Wallis Annenberg Photography Department, Los Angeles County Museum of Art, 2009), p. 359.
38 Richard Vijgen, 'The Deleted City', p. 1.
39 A founder of the widely popular magazine *Wired*, Brand contributed significantly to the emergence of the home computer industry through popular publications such as the *Whole Earth Catalog* (1968) and the *Whole Earth Software Catalog* (1983). Brand's initiatives provided a forum for entrepreneurs, politicians and computer engineers to meet and discuss the shape of the emerging world of digital media. For a clear and accessible account of Brand's fascinating life and his role in promoting the 'digital revolution', see Fred Turner, *From Counterculture to Cyberculture: Stewart Brand, the Whole Earth Network, and the Rise of Digital Utopianism* (Chicago: University of Chicago Press, 2006).
40 T. J. Jackson Lears, *No Place of Grace: Antimodernism and the Transformation of American Culture* (Chicago: Chicago University Press, 1981), p. 93.
41 Luc Boltanski and Ève Chiapello, *The New Spirit of Capitalism* (London: Verso, 2007).
42 Fred Turner, *From Counterculture to Cyberculture*, p. 8.
43 Michel Foucault, 'Film in Popular Memory: An Interview with Michel Foucault (1974)',

in Jeffrey K. Olick, Vered Vinitzky-Seroussi and Daniel Levy, eds, *The Collective Memory Reader* (New York: Oxford University Press, 2011), p. 253. For the notion of counter-memory, see also Michel Foucault, *Language, Counter-Memory, Practice: Selected Essays and Interviews*, trans. Donald F. Bouchard and Sherry Simon (Oxford: Blackwell, 1977).

44 For this fascination for the information sublime, Vijgen's work recalls a significant strand of Net art (e.g. Matthew Fuller's web browser, *I/O/D 4* [1997], Mark Hansen and Ben Rubin's *Listening Post* [2004], and Charles Sandison's *Utopia* [2006]) that aims to visualise the complexity of Internet structure and ends by overwhelming viewers with a mesmerising flow of data.

45 The work is available at http://www.ucl.ac.uk/slade/slide/dotstore/system/index.html (last accessed 14 August 2014).

46 For an alternative reading of this work and the relation of Thomson and Craighead's practice to commercial culture and high art, see Julian Stallabrass, 'Reasons to Hate Thomson and Craighead', in Steven Bode and Nina Ernst, eds, *Thomson and Craighead* (London: Film and Video Umbrella, 2005).

47 Michael Archer, 'er... stolen', in Steven Bode and Nina Ernst, eds, *Thomson and Craighead* (London: Film and Video Umbrella, 2005), p. 11.

48 For an essay that frames Thomson and Craighead's work in relation to the history of information art and conceptualism, see Sarah Cook, 'Far Out! Distance and Location in the Work of Thomson & Craighead', in Steve Rushton, Clive Gillman and Sarah Cook, eds, *Thomson and Craighead: Flat Earth* (Memmingen/Dundee: MEWO Kunsthalle/ Dundee Contemporary Arts, 2013), pp. 8–25.

49 The idea for the show arose from recent threats to the telecommunication principle of 'Net neutrality', or the notion that everything on the web should be treated equally regardless of the type of content or who produced it. Net neutrality is currently under attack in the USA and Europe due to proposed legislations that would allow Internet service providers the right to build special lanes with faster connection speeds for companies and 'special' customers. For a definition of the principle of 'Net neutrality', see Tim Wu, 'Network Neutrality, Broadband Discrimination', *Journal of Telecommunications and High Technology Law*, vol. 2 (2003), pp. 141–79.

50 Robert Smithson, 'A Cinematic Atopia', in Jack Flam, ed., *Robert Smithson: The Collected Writings* (Berkeley, CA: University of California Press, 1996), p. 141.

51 Florian Cramer, 'Interface', in Matthew Fuller, ed., *Software Studies: A Lexicon* (Cambridge, MA: MIT Press, 2008), p. 149.

52 George Legrady's *Pockets Full of Memory* (2001) is a paradigmatic example of this tendency to equate technical interactivity to equality and democracy. The work consisted of a data collection station where the public could deposit an image of an object of personal value through a phalanx of scanners. Users could also access and add information to the continually evolving database from their homes, uploading images from their computers via the Internet. Mark Poster commented on this work emphatically: 'The clear separation of artist and audience, subject and object, is broken in a new relation of aesthetics and politics'; Mark Poster, 'The Aesthetic of Distracting Media', *Culture Machine*, vol. 4 (2002); http://www.culturemachine.net/ (last accessed 14 April 2014).

53 Janet Kraynak, 'Dependent Participation: Bruce Nauman's Environments', in Tanya

Leighton, ed., *Art and The Moving Image: A Critical Reader* (London: Tate/Afterall Books, 2008), pp. 228–45.

54 Alain Touraine, *The Post-Industrial Society, Tomorrow's Social History: Classes, Conflicts and Culture in the Programmed Society*, trans. Leonard F. X. Mayhew (New York: Random House, 1971), p. 9.

55 'What we like about the "Ouvroir de Literature Potentielle"', the artists have declared in an interview, 'is how they shift emphasis from what is being written to how it is being written, and in doing so they remind us how much the architectures and the conventions of society inform what things mean and also how they control us'; Thomson and Craighead as cited in Diana Stevenson, 'Hypnosis as Data Retrieval and Web Searches as Railway Signs', *The Creators Project*, 20 May 2013, np; http://thecreatorsproject.vice.com/ (last accessed 14 June 2014).

56 Monographs on the Oulipo includes Peter Consenstein, *Literary Memory, Consciousness, and the Group Oulipo* (Amsterdam: Rodopi, 2002); and Hervé Le Tellier, *Esthétique de l'Oulipo* (Bordeaux: Le Castor Astral, 2006).

57 Alison James, *Constraining Chance: Georges Perec and the Oulipo* (Evanston, IL: Northwestern University Press, 2009), p. 131.

58 Kris Paulsen, 'The Index and the Interface', *Representations*, vol. 122, no. 1 (2013), p. 101.

59 Margaret Iversen defines analogue media as more open to chance and reality than digital media in her analysis of Tacita Dean's and Zoe Leonard's photography. This evaluation, in my view, tends to hypostatise old and new media and reiterate reductive notions of indexicality based on the materiality of a medium. See Iversen, 'Analogue: On Zoe Leonard and Tacita Dean', *Critical Inquiry*, vol. 38, no. 4 (2012), pp. 796–818.

60 Alison James, 'Automatism, Arbitrariness and the Oulipian Author', *French Forum*, vol. 31, no. 2 (2006), p. 121.

61 See the video interview released for their retrospective exhibition at Dundee Contemporary Arts in 2014; https://www.youtube.com/watch?v=y8eAgxDNAKc (accessed 14 June 2014).

62 Olga Goriunova and Alexei Shulgin, 'Glitch', in Matthew Fuller, ed., *Software Studies: A Lexicon* (Cambridge, MA: MIT Press, 2008), p. 114.

63 Katie Hafner and Matthew Lyon, *Where Wizards Stay Up Late: The Origins of the Internet* (New York: Simon and Shuster, 1996), p. 34.

64 Thomas Streeter, *The Net Effect*, p. 172.

65 Steyerl takes issue against the commonplace argument that digital images are immaterial and therefore eternal, which can be found, for example, in the writings of film theorist and historian Mary Ann Doane. For Doane the capability of a medium to convey memory and history depends on its physical degradation and this degradation, in turn, is a property that is only specific to analogue cinema. As Doane declared, 'because [analogue] cinema has a material base that can be touched, manipulated, and also scarred, degraded, eroded, it becomes the repository of a historical (and to some extent a personal) memory'; Mary Ann Doane, 'Imaging Contingency: An Interview with Mary Ann Doane', *Parallax*, vol. 13, no. 4 (2007), p. 18.

66 Hito Steyerl, 'In Defense of the Poor Image', *e-flux*, no. 10 (2009), np.

67 Hito Steyerl, 'Too Much World: Is the Internet Dead?', *e-flux*, no. 49 (2013), np.

68　*Ibid.*

69　See, for instance, the optimistic declarations of German cultural historian Joseph Vogl after the financial crisis. The crisis, Vogl remarked enthusiastically, 'is the *epochē* of the financial economy' and a 'stroke of epistemological luck'; Joseph Vogl, 'Taming Time: Media of Financialization', trans. Christopher Reid, *Grey Room* no. 46 (2012), p. 82; and Vogl, 'Capital and Money Are Profane Gods', *The European*, 20 November 2011; http://www.theeuropean-magazine.com/joseph-vogl--2/6646-the-spectre-of-capital (accessed 12 April 2013).

70　In a tentative survey of these films, Jeff Kinkle and Alberto Toscano have argued that mainstream cinema tended to reduce the 2008 financial crisis to an inevitable personal catastrophe. In so doing, they claim, filmmakers ended up overshadowing the systemic and political responsibilities for the crisis. Jeff Kinkle and Alberto Toscano, 'Filming the Crisis: A Survey', *Film Quarterly*, vol. 65, no. 1 (2011), pp. 39–51.

71　Sergei Tretyakov, 'The Biography of the Object', *October*, no. 118 (2006), pp. 57–62.

72　Devin Fore's introduction to Tretyakov, 'The Biography of the Object', p. 58

73　Fredric Jameson, 'Postmodernism and Consumer Society', in Hal Foster, ed., *Postmodern Culture* (London: Pluto Press, 1985), p. 120.

74　Hito Steyerl, 'In Free Fall: A Thought Experiment on Vertical Perspective', *e-flux*, no. 14 (2011), p. 8.

75　See Gilles Deleuze and Félix Guattari, *Anti-Oedipus: Capitalism and Schizophrenia* (Minneapolis, MN: University of Minnesota Press, 1983).

76　Gilles Deleuze and Félix Guattari, 'Capitalism: A Very Special Delirium', in Silvère Lotringer, ed., *Chaosophy*, trans. David L. Sweet, Jarred Becker and Taylor Adkins (Cambridge, MA: MIT Press, 2009), p. 36.

77　*Ibid.*, p. 47.

78　*Ibid.*, p. 152.

79　*Ibid.*, p. 246.

80　*Ibid.*, pp. 239–40.

81　In an interview Steyerl has referred to this notion of capitalist excess: 'Whilst Capital, for sure, is moving, this doesn't necessarily mean that every movement is fully captured by Capital. Movement … can also constitute a flight from labour or other capital-based relations (of course these evasions are immediately recaptured, but again not fully). Capital is not able to fully come to terms with evasion, resistance, distraction, irritation, sleepiness'; Steyerl as cited in Rosemarie Heather, 'Hito Steyerl Speaks to Rosemarie Heather', *Apengine*, 22 September; http://www.apengine.org/2010/09/hito-steyerl-speaks-to-rosemary-heather/ (accessed 24 May 2013).

82　The image of pristine windmills in the desert that forms the background of Steyerl and Kahn's perfectly synchronized safety-instruction sequence can also be read as the prefiguration of a utopian world. 'The windmills', David Riff observes, 'indicate the possibility for a new stage of post-Fordist rationalization involving smart energy, knowledge production, and other new sources of income for a nicer, softer capitalism with a post-human face'; David Riff, 'Is This for Real? A Close Reading of *In Free Fall* by Hito Steyerl', *eipicp* (2011); available at http://eipcp.net/transversal/0311/riff/en (accessed 25 February 2011).

83　This conception of commodities as a reservoir of transformative desires recalls Walter

Benjamin's approach to popular culture. See Susan Buck-Morss, *The Dialectics of Seeing: Walter Benjamin and the Arcades Project* (Cambridge, MA: MIT Press, 1989).

84 The figure of the DVD in *In Free Fall* recalls the uncontrollable and revolutionary excess of capitalism described by Toni Negri in relation to the postmodern city. 'The picture [of the contemporary city]', he writes, 'is one of a circulation of commodities, webs of information, continuous movements, and radical nomadism of labour, and the ferocious exploitation of these dynamics'. And yet, the picture is also one 'of constant and inexhaustible *excess*, of the biopolitical power of the multitude and of its excess with regard to the structural controlling ability of dominant institutions'; Toni Negri, 'On Rem Koolhaas', *Radical Philosophy*, no. 154 (2009), p. 49.

85 Steyerl as cited by Francesca Boenzi, 'Do You Speak Spasmoc?', *Mousse Contemporary Art Magazine*, no. 23 (2010), np; http://moussemagazine.it/articolo.mm?id=540 (accessed 3 September 2012).

86 Benjamin Noys, *The Persistence of the Negative: A Critique of Contemporary Continental Theory* (Edinburgh: Edinburgh University Press, 2010), p. 5.

87 Steven Shaviro, 'Accelerationist Aesthetics: Necessary Inefficiency in Times of Real Subsumption', *e-flux*, no. 46 (2013), np.

88 For an analysis of these films, see Steven Shaviro, *Post-cinematic Affect* (Winchester, UK: Zero Books, 2010).

89 Steven Shaviro, 'Accelerationist Aesthetics', np.

90 See Fredric Jameson, 'Cognitive Mapping', in Cary Nelson and Lawrence Grossberg, eds, *Marxism and the Interpretation of Culture* (Urbana, IL: University of Illinois Press, 1988), pp. 347–60.

91 Fredric Jameson, 'Interview with Anders Stephanson', in Ian Buchanan, ed., *Jameson on Jameson: Conversations on Cultural Marxism* (Durham, NC: Duke University Press, 2007), p. 59.

EPILOGUE
Utopia Now

Not long after being declared dead at the end of the twentieth century, utopia resurfaced in the guise of an archipelago in the map of the 2009 Tate Triennial. Entitled *Altermodern* and curated by prominent French critic Nicolas Bourriaud, the exhibition included several of the artists that have been examined in this book. Central to *Altermodern* was the image of a cluster of islands. Can we view

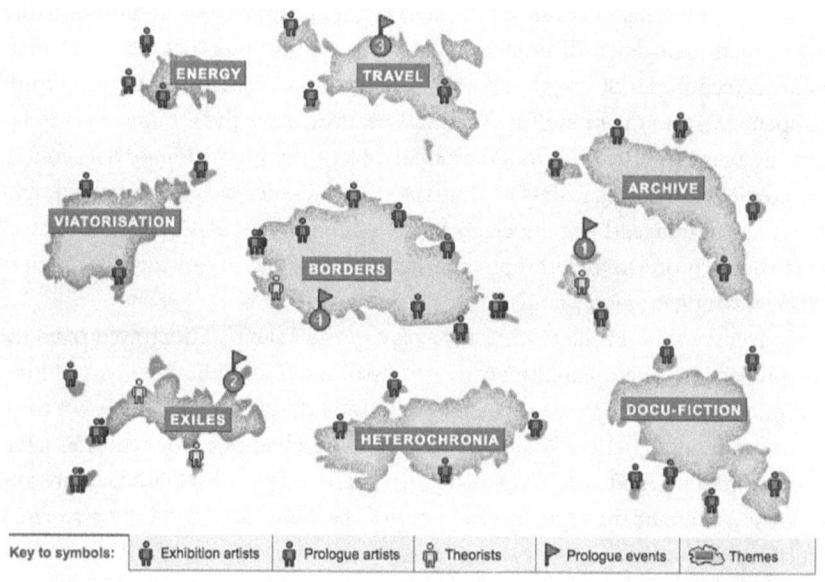

Fig. 49. 'Explore Altermodern', exhibition map from the website of the Fourth Tate Triennal at Tate Britain, 3 February–26 April 2009

161

Bourriaud's archipelago as a 'no place' reminiscent of More's utopia? I would say 'yes and no'. The altermodern recalls its sixteenth-century precedent insofar as it embodies difference. However, it departs from More's Utopia in its fundamental lack of closure. Where in early Renaissance illustrations of More's novel the island of Utopia is dotted by fortified settlements – evoking the closed and exclusionary nature of many modernist utopian visions – Bourriaud's archipelago appears open and accessible to foreigners. Instead of castles and walls, tiny and identical human figures inhabit the isles forming the 'altermodern', each representing a different contemporary artist showcased in the exhibition.

Yet the map is not an allegory of modernity gone wrong or in indictment of utopia. Indeed Bourriaud's archipelago does not resemble Walter Benjamin's Angel of History, swiped by the storm of progress; rather, it epitomises a constellation of multiple centres from which various trajectories and possibilities may unfold or, to use the curator's words, it intimates 'a positive vision of chaos and complexity'. In other words, in proposing the figure of the archipelago as the shorthand through which to discuss the exhibition, Bourriaud does not relinquish utopian aspirations. In fact, the archipelago is the harbinger, according to him, the birth of a new and happier cultural era, namely the 'altermodern', characterised by heterochrony, dislocation and nomadism. 'The archipelago,' he claimed in a buoyant tone, 'functions here as a model representing the multiplicity of global cultures.' The curator's optimism can be understood in light of the specific circumstances in which the Triennial came about. In autumn 2008 the sudden melt-down of numerous financial institutions thought to be rock-solid revived hopes of social and political change, suggesting that cracks could be opened within the monolith of capitalism. Presenting the economic crisis as a turning point in history, *Altermodern* partook of the spirit of hope triggered by the credit crunch. Regardless of Bourriaud's reluctance to use the term utopia, his use of an image, the archipelago, vaguely reminiscent of More's novel as well his insistence on the heterotopic and heterocronic quality of the altermodern betray a strong utopian impulse.

Indeed, several of the works on display in the Triennial borrowed from the large repertoire of utopian literature. As Bourriaud himself noted, many of films and photographic projects in the exhibition took the form of a journey – a trope central to utopian fiction. 'From the time of More's book and for centuries later,' Louis Marin pointed out, 'utopias tend to begin with a travel, a departure and a journey, most of the time by sea, most of the time interrupted by a storm, a catastrophe that is the sublime way to open a neutral space, one that is absolutely different.' As we have seen, the theme of the voyage also characterises the works by Dean, Koester, Buckingham, Harrison and Leonard which have been discussed in this study. Often, in the experimental documentaries of the artists at issue here, the journey takes the form of an exploration of the blind spots on the maps of the past, showing how porous the boundaries between nostalgia and utopia are.

On the other hand, the elusive figure of Bourriaud's archipelago symbolises the challenge faced by contemporary practices that aim to engage with utopian thinking today. This is the risk of diluting the concept of utopia into a poetic celebration of indeterminacy and desire for its own sake. The contours of Bourriaud's archipelago are blurry and his discussion of pluralism as one of the main features of the altermodern remains on an abstract level. Consider for instance this passage which in my view exemplifies the critic's cautious attitude: 'just as alterglobalisation does not seek cumulative solutions to the steamrollering effect of economic globalisation,' Bourriaud argues, 'altermodern has no desire to substitute for postmodern relativism a new universalism, rather a networked "archipelago" form of modernity.' It is hard to understand what he means by this statement. Furthermore, we might claim that, *contra* Bourriaud, proclamations of multiplicity are not enough if they are not leading to 'cumulative' or 'universal' solutions to global capitalism. In other words, can utopia be effective and even survive without a clear-cut and prescriptive vision of what the alternative to the status quo should and could be?

More than a decade ago Ruth Levitas lamented the political costs paid by utopian thinking as it was increasingly being dissected and transformed by post-1968 critical theorists. For Levitas, authors such as Jean-François Lyotard, Gilles Deleuze and Félix Guattari (and we might add to the list Louis Marin and Fredric Jameson) tended to relegate the function of utopia to the critique of ideology and to desire – often indeterminate and inconclusive. While responding to some of the problematic contradictions of utopian thinking, namely its historical complicity with totalitarianism and authoritarianism, these philosophers ended up reducing utopia to the sublime and the negative (for example, in the writings of Marin and Jameson) or overtly emphasized desire and emotion (in Deleuze and Guattari). As a consequence, they jeopardised one of the most important tasks of utopian thinking: the imagination of an alternative world. 'Perhaps forms of utopian thought which are more than expressive of desire,' Levitas pointed out, 'are intrinsically holistic, totalising and evaluative. Perhaps prescription is necessary.' By forsaking the consideration of utopia in terms of its ability to portray an alternative in favour of its critical and deconstructive function, we are seemingly left with only its negative and critical dimension. What is at stake in the postmodern reinvention of utopia, according to Levitas, is its transformative function. 'The transformative function of utopia,' she concluded, 'requires the disruption of the structural closure of the present, and it requires us to imagine both what this might mean and how it might be possible, in order that we might be able to hope.'

Shunning the task of imagining the future, Bourriaud's altermodern lacks persuasiveness, leaving us with too many unresolved questions. Some of them are even mentioned by the critic himself in a final passage of his introductory essay:

> The movement [of the altermodern] is also taking shape under the urgent pressure to answer very basic questions: how do we live in this world that we are told is becoming 'global', but which seems to be buttressed on particular interests or tensed behind the barricades of fundamentalism – when not upholding icons of mass culture as role models? How to represent a power that is becoming ever more furtive as it slips into bed with economics? How, finally, to make art anything but a secondary type of merchandise in a system of values entirely oriented towards this 'general and abstract equivalent' that is money, and how can it bear witness against 'economic horror' without reducing itself to sheer militancy?

Unfortunately, the critic does not offer a response to these crucial issues. Bourriaud's archipelago – like the works of many of the experimental filmmakers and photographers examined in this book – is certainly a much needed paean for pluralism and the multiplicity of global cultures under threat by the homogenising force of globalisation. But can it reach a different audience with images of, with the look and feel and shape and experiences of what an alternative society might and could actually be?

BIBLIOGRAPHY

Alpers, S. (2008) 'Zoe Leonard: Analogue', in Urs Stahel (ed.) *Zoe Leonard*. Gottingen: Steidl/Zurich: Fotomuseum Winterthur, 219–23.
Alter, N. (2007) 'Translating the Essay into Film and Installation', *Journal of Visual Culture*, 6, 1, 44–57.
Anderson, T. (1995) 'Why Stalinist Musicals?', *Discourse*, 17, 3, 38–48.
Appadurai, A. (1986) 'Introduction: Commodities and the Politics of Value', in A. Appadurai (ed.) *The Social Life of Things: Commodities in Cultural Perspective*. Cambridge: Cambridge University Press, 3–63.
Archer, M. (2005) 'er... stolen', in S. Bode and N. Ernst (eds) *Thomson and Craighead*. London: Film and Video Umbrella, 6–14.
Attias, L. (1999) 'Jean-Luc Moulène', *Frieze*, 47; http://www.frieze.com/issue/review/jean_luc_moulene/ (accessed 6 March 2011).
Baker, G. (2002) 'Artist Questionnaire: 21 Responses', *October*, 100, 6–98.
____ (2008) 'Lateness and Longing', in D. Birnbaum (ed.) *50 Moons of Saturn: T2 Torino Triennial*. Milan: Skira.
____ (2009) 'Photography and Abstraction', in C. Cotton and A. Klein (eds) *Words without Pictures*. Los Angeles: Wallis Annenberg Photography Department, Los Angeles County Museum of Art, 358–78.
Bakhtin, M. (1984) *Rabelais and His World*, trans. Helene Iswolsky. Bloomington, IN: Indiana University Press.
Balasopoulos, A. (2011) 'Anti-Utopia and Dystopia: Rethinking the Generic Field', in V. Vlastaras (ed.) *Utopia Project Archive, 2006–2010*. Athens: School of Fine Arts, 59–67.
Barbrook, R. (1998) *The Holy Fools: A Critique of the Avant-Garde in the Age of the Net*. London: Hypermedia Research Centre, University of Westminster.
Barbrook, R. and A. Cameron (1996) 'The Californian Ideology', *Science as Culture*, 6, 1, 44–72.
Baudrlllard, J. (1994) *The Illusion of the End*. Cambridge: Polity Press.
____ (2009) *Why Hasn't Everything Already Disappeared?*, trans. Chris Turner. London: Seagull.
Bauman, Z. (2003) 'Utopia with No Topos', *History of the Human Sciences*, 16, 1, 11–25.
Bazin, A. (1967a) 'The Ontology of the Photographic Image', in *What Is Cinema?*. Berkeley, CA: University of California Press, 9–16.

____ (1967b) 'Theater and Cinema', in *What Is Cinema?*. Berkeley, CA: University of California Press, 76–124.
Bazin, A. (1967) *What Is Cinema?*. Berkeley, CA: University of California Press.
Belting, H. (1987) *The End of the History of Art?* trans. Christopher S. Wood. Chicago: University of Chicago Press.
Benjamin, W. (1999) 'Little History of Photography', in M. W. Jennings, H. Eiland and G. Smith (eds) *Selected Writings/Walter Benjamin Volume 2 (1927–1934)*. Cambridge, MA: The Belknap Press of Harvard University.
Bentley, J. (1982) *Between Marx and Christ: The Dialogue in German Speaking Europe: 1870–1970*. London: Verso.
Berrebi, S. (2010) 'Goats, Lamb, Veal, Breasts: Strategies of Organisation in Zoe Leonard's Analogue', *Afterall: A Journal of Art, Context, and Enquiry*, 25, 31–7.
Bishop, C. (2013) 'Monumental Bling', *Still Searching: An On-Line Discourse on Photography*, 24 September 2013; http://blog.fotomuseum.ch/2013/09/2-monumental-bling/ (accessed 12 November 2013).
Blatt, A. J. (2011) 'Thinking Photography in Film, or the Suspended Cinema of Agnès Varda and Jean Eustache', *French Forum*, 36, 2–3, 181–200.
Bloch, E. (1986) *The Principle of Hope*, trans. N. Plaice, S. Plaice and P. Knight, three volumes. Oxford: Basil Blackwell.
____ (1991) *Heritage of Our Times*. Berkeley, CA: University of California Press.
____ (2000) *The Spirit of Utopia*. Stanford, CA: Stanford University Press.
Bloom, I. (2008) 'All Dressed Up', *Parkett*, 82, 130–6.
Blume, A. (1997) 'Zoe Leonard Interviewed by Anna Blume', in K. Rhomberg (ed.) *Zoe Leonard*. Vienna: Secession.
Boenzi, F. (2010) 'Do You Speak Spasmoc?', *Mousse Contemporary Art Magazine*, 23, 10 March; http://moussemagazine.it/articolo.mm?id=540 (accessed 3 September 2012).
Bois, Y. (ed.) (1986) *Endgame: Reference and Simulation in Recent American Painting and Sculpture*. Boston: Institute of Contemporary Arts.
____ (2009) 'The Inventory of Solitudes', in J. Criqui, Y. Bois and B. Fer (eds) *Jean-Luc Moulène*. Cologne: König.
Boltanski, C. and C. Esche (1997) *Pentimenti*. Milano: Charta.
Boltanski, L. and È. Chiapello (2007) *The New Spirit of Capitalism*. London: Verso.
Bosma, J. (2011) *Nettitudes: Let's Talk Net Art*. Amsterdam: Institute of Network Cultures/Nai Publishers.
Bourriaud, N. (2009) 'Altermodern', in N. Bourriaud (ed.) *Altermodern: Tate Triennial*. London: Tate, 11–23.
Boym, S. (2001) *The Future of Nostalgia*. New York: Basic Books.
____ (2008) 'On Diasporic Intimacy: Ilya Kabakov's Installations and Immigrant Homes', *Critical Inquiry*, 24, 2, 498–524.
Brevini, B., A. Hintz and P. McCurdy (eds) (2013) *Beyond WikiLeaks: Implications for the Future of Communications, Journalism and Society*. Basingstoke: Palgrave Macmillan.
Brügger, N. (ed.) (2010) *Web History*. New York: Peter Lang.
Buchloh, B. (1981) 'Figures of Authority, Ciphers of Regression: Notes on the Return of Representation in European Painting', *October*, 16, 39–68.
____ (1999) 'Gerhard Richter's Atlas: The Anomic Archive', *October*, 88, 117–45.
Buckingham, M. (2000) 'Archives Are Where You Find Them'; http://www.

matthewbuckingham.net/PT%20ArchivesACCText.html (accessed 9 April 2013).

____ (2003) 'Round Table: The Projected Image in Contemporary Art', *October*, 104, 71–96.

Buckingham, M. and J. Koester (2002) 'Points of Suspension', *October*, 100, 55–63.

Buck-Morss, S. (1989) *The Dialectics of Seeing: Walter Benjamin and the Arcades Project*. Cambridge, MA: MIT Press.

Burton, J., T. Eccles and G. Verzotti (2013) *Once Again the World Is Flat*. Annadale-on-Hudson, NY: CCS Bard Hessel Museum of Art.

Carnevale, F. and J. Kelsey (2007) 'Art of the Possible: An Interview with Jacques Rancière', *Artforum*, 45, 7, 256–69.

Carruthers, M. (2010) 'How to Make a Composition: Memory Craft in Antiquity and in the Middle Ages', in B. Schwarz and S. Radstone (eds) *Memory: Histories, Theories, Debates*. New York: Fordham University Press, 15–29.

Casey, E. S. (1987) 'The World of Nostalgia', *Man and World*, 20, 4, 361–84.

Celant, G., J. Froment, E. Lebovici and J. Miller (1988) *Haim Steinbach: Recent Works*. Bordeaux: Museum of Contemporary Art.

Chan, J. (2014) 'Notes on Post-Internet', in O. Kholeif (ed.) *You Are Here: Art After the Internet*. Manchester: Cornerhouse Books, 106–23.

Claeys, G. (2011) *Searching for Utopia: The History of an Idea*. London: Thames & Hudson.

Colard, J. (1999) 'Jean-Luc Mouléne: La Reprise', *Les Inrockuptibles*, 198, 88.

Combs, J. (1993) *The Reagan Range: The Nostalgic Myth of American Politics*. Bowling Green, OH: Bowling Green State University Popular Press.

Consenstein, P. (2002) *Literary Memory, Consciousness, and the Group Oulipo*. Amsterdam: Rodopi.

Cook, P. (2004) *Screening the Past: Memory and Nostalgia in Cinema*. London: Routledge.

Cook, S. (2013) 'Far Out! Distance and Location in the Work of Thomson & Craighead', in S. Rushton, C. Gillman and S. Cook (eds) *Thomson and Craighead: Flat Earth*. Memmingen/Dundee: MEWO Kunsthalle/Dundee Contemporary Arts, 8–25.

Cornell, L. (2006) 'Net Results: Closing the Gap between Art and Life Online', *Time Out New York*, 9 February; http://www.timeout.com/newyork/art/net-results (accessed 12 May 2013).

Cramer, F. (2008) 'Interface', in M. Fuller (ed.) *Software Studies: A Lexicon*. Cambridge, MA: MIT Press, 149–53.

Crary, J. (1992) *Techniques of the Observer*. Cambridge: MIT Press.

Crimp, D. (1979) 'Pictures', *October*, 8, 75–88.

Danto, A. (1997) *After the End of Art: Contemporary Art and the Pale of History*. Princeton: Princeton University Press.

Darwin, C. ([1839] 1988) *Charles Darwin's Beagle Diary*. Cambridge: Cambridge University Press.

Dean, T. (2001) 'Bubble House', in R. Groenenboom (ed.) *Tacita Dean*. Barcelona: Museum of Contemporary Art, 52–3.

____ (2001) 'Once Upon a Different Sort of Time: The Story of Donald Crownhurst', in R. Groenenboom (ed.) *Tacita Dean*. Barcelona: Museum of Contemporary Art, 34–41.

Debord, G. ([1967] 1984) *The Society of the Spectacle*. New York: Zone Books.

De Certeau, M. ([1980] 1984) *The Practice of Everyday Life*. Berkeley, CA: University of California Press.

Defert, D. (1997) 'Foucault, Space and the Architects', in *Politics/Poetics: Documenta X – The Book*. Ostfilder-Ruit: Cantx Verlag, 274–83.

Deleuze, G. and F. Guattari (1983) *Anti-Oedipus: Capitalism and Schizophrenia*. Minneapolis, MN: University of Minnesota Press.

____ (1986) *Kafka: Toward a Minor Literature*. Minneapolis, MN: University of Minnesota Press.

____ (2009) 'Capitalism: A Very Special Delirium', in S. Lotringer (ed.) *Chaosophy*. Cambridge, MA: MIT Press, 35–52.

Derrida, J. (2005) 'Not Utopia, the Im-possible', in J. Derrida, *Paper Machine*. Stanford: Stanford University Press, 121–35.

Deutsche, R. (1996) *Evictions: Art and Spatial Politics*. Cambridge, MA: MIT Press.

Deutsche, R. and C. Gendel Ryan (1984) 'The Fine Art of Gentrification', *October*, 31, 91–111.

Díaz, E. (2013) 'Under the Dome: Architectures of Networked Engagement from Drop City to Rockaway Beach', *Rhizome*, 25 July.

Dillon, B. (2011) *Ruins*. London: Whitechapel Gallery.

Doane, M. A. (2006) 'Information, Crisis, Catastrophe', in W. H. Kyong Chun and T. Keenan (eds) *New Media, Old Media: A History and Theory Reader*. London: Routledge, 251–64.

____ (2007) 'Imaging Contingency: An Interview with Mary Ann Doane', *Parallax*, 13, 4, 16–25.

Dobrenko, E. (2007) *Political Economy of Socialist Realism*, trans. Jesse M. Savage. New Haven, CT: Yale University Press.

Duplaix, S. (2000) 'Objets de grève/objets de réflexion. À propos des 24 Objets de Grève présentés par Jean-Luc Moulène', *Les Cahiers du Musée National d'Art Moderne*, 71, 46–79.

Dyer, R. (1992) *Only Entertainment*. New York: Routledge.

Eagleton, T. (1981) *Walter Benjamin, or, Towards a Revolutionary Criticism*. London: Verso.

____ (2000) 'Utopia and Its Opposites', *Socialist Register*, 36, 31–40.

Edensor, T. (2005) *Industrial Ruins: Spaces, Aesthetics, and Materiality*. New York: Berg.

Enns, A. (2007) 'The Politics of Ostalgie: Post-Socialist Nostalgia in Recent German Film', *Screen*, 48, 4, 475–91.

Enzenzberger, H. M. (1970) 'Constituents of a Theory of the Media', *New Left Review*, 64, 13–36.

____ (1993) '"We were born to turn a fairy tale into reality": Grigori Alexandrov's *The Radiant Path*', in R. Taylor and D. Spring (eds) *Stalinism and Soviet Cinema*. New York: Routledge, 97–108.

Epstein, M. (2010) 'The Philosophical Implications of Russian Conceptualism', *Journal of Eurasian Studies*, 1, 64–71.

Farber, H. (1983) 'Das Unentdeckte Kino', in A. Kluge (ed.) *Bestandsaufnahme: Utopie Film*. Frankfurt am Main: Zweitausendeins.

Farocki, H. and K. Silverman (eds) (1998) *Speaking about Godard*. New York: New York University Press.

Faubion, J. D. (2008) 'Heterotopia: An Ecology', in M. Dehaene and L. De Cauter (eds) *Heterotopia and the City: Public Space in a Postcivil Society*. London: Routledge, 31–40.

Fer, B. (2009) 'Each Any', in J. Criqui, Y. Bois and B. Fer (eds) *Jean-Luc Moulène*. Cologne: König.

Finoki, B. (2009) 'The Anatomy of Ruins', *Triple Canopy*, 7.
Fisher, M. (2009) *Capitalist Realism: Is There No Alternative?*. Winchester: Zero Books.
Foster, H. (2003) 'Dada Mime', *October*, 105, 166–76.
____ (2004) 'An Archival Impulse', *October*, 110, 3–22.
____ (2006) 'Blind Spots: The Art of Joachim Koester', *Artforum*, 44, 8, 212–17, 266, 274.
Foucault, M. (1977) *Language, Counter-Memory, Practice: Selected Essays and Interviews*. Oxford: Blackwell.
____ (1988) 'Truth, Power, Self: An Interview with Michel Foucault', in L. H. Martin, H. Gutman and P. H. Hutton (eds) *Technologies of the Self*. Amherst, MA: University of Massachusetts Press, 9–15.
____ (1994) *The Order of Things: An Archaeology of the Human Sciences*. New York: Vintage.
____ ([1967] 2008) 'Of Other Spaces', in M. Dehaene and L. De Cauter (eds) *Heterotopia and the City: Public Space in a Postcivil Society*. New York: Routledge, 13–30.
____ (2011) 'Film in Popular Memory: An Interview with Michel Foucault', in J. K. Olick, V. Vinitzky-Seroussi and D. Levy (eds) *The Collective Memory Reader*. New York: Oxford University Press, 252–3.
Fukuyama, F. (1989) 'The End of History?', *The National Interest*, 16, 3–18.
____ (1992) *The End of History and the Last Man*. New York: Free Press.
Genocchio, B. (1995) 'Discourse, Discontinuity, Difference: The Question of Other Spaces', in S. Watson and K. Gibson (eds) *Postmodern Cities and Spaces*. Cambridge: Blackwell, 35–46.
Gérôme, N. (1984) *Les Productions Symboliques des Travailleurs à l'Entreprise*. Paris: Ministère de La Culture.
____ (1995) *Archives Sensibles, Images et Objets du Monde Industriel et Ouvrier*. Cachan: Editions de l'ENS-Cachan.
Gerverau, L. (2000) 'Symbolic Collapse: Utopia Challenged by Its Representations', in R. Schaer, G. Claeys and L. T. Sargent (eds) *Utopia: The Search for the Ideal Society in the Western World*. New York: New York Public Library.
Gever, M. (1985) 'Video Politics: Early Feminist Projects', in D. Kahn and D. Neumaier (eds) *Cultures in Contention*. Seattle: The Real Comet Press, 92–101.
Gillick, L. (2006) *'Now I See*, One Work by Anri Sala', in M. Godfrey, L. Gillick and H. U. Obrist (eds) *Anri Sala*. London: Phaidon, 103–10.
Gillies, J. and R. Cailliau (2000) *How the Web Was Born: The Story of the World Wide Web*. Oxford and New York: Oxford University Press.
Gingeras, A. M. (2008) '(Un)Natural Selection', *Parkett*, 82, 156–9.
Gioni, M. and M. Robecchi (2001) 'Anri Sala: Unfinished Histories', *Flash Art*, 214, 104–7.
Godfrey, M. (2006) 'Articulate Enigma: The Works of Anri Sala', in M. Godfrey, L. Gillick and H. U. Obrist (eds) *Anri Sala*. London: Phaidon, 33–102.
____ (2007) 'The Artist as Historian', *October*, 120, 140–72.
____ (2008) 'Mirror Displacements', *Artforum*, 46, 8, 293–301.
Goriunova, O. and A. Shulgin (2008) 'Glitch', in M. Fuller (ed.) *Software Studies: A Lexicon*. Cambridge, MA: MIT Press, 110–19.
Goulding, D. (2002) *Liberated Cinema: The Yugoslav Experience, 1945–2001*. Bloomington, IN: Indiana University Press.
Greene, R. (2000) 'Web Work: A History of Internet Art', *Artforum*, 38, 9, 162–9, 190.
Groenenboom, R. (2001) 'A Conversation with Tacita Dean', in R. Groenenboom (ed.) *Tacita Dean*. Barcelona: Museum of Contemporary Art, 93–7.

Groys, B. (2006) *Ilya Kabakov: The Man Who Flew into Space from His Apartment*. London: Afterall.

____ (2010) 'Ilya Kabakov: The Theatre of Authorship', in *History Becomes Form: Moscow Conceptualism*. Cambridge, MA: MIT Press, 105–23.

Gunning, T. (1983) 'An Unseen Energy Swallows Space: The Space in Early Film and Its Relation to American Avant-Garde Film', in J. L. Fell (ed.) *Film Before Griffith*. Berkeley, CA: University of California Press, 355–66.

____ (1990) 'Cinema of Attractions: Early Cinema, Its Spectator and the Avant-Garde', in T. Elsaesser (ed.) *Early Cinema: Space, Frame, Narrative*. London: British Film Institute, 56–62.

____ (2007) 'Moving away from the Index: Cinema and the Impression of Reality', *Differences*, 8, 1, 29–52.

Hafner, K. and M. Lyon (1996) *Where Wizards Stay Up Late: The Origins of the Internet*. New York: Simon and Shuster.

Hansen, M. (1991) *Babel and Babylon: Spectatorship in American Silent Film*. Cambridge, MA: Harvard University Press.

____ (1993) 'Early Cinema, Late Cinema: Permutations of the Public Sphere', *Screen*, 34, 3, 197–210.

Harrison, R. and N. Blake (2008) 'Rachel Harrison and Nayland Blake', *Bomb*, 105; http://bombmagazine.org/article/3178/ (accessed 1 April 2010).

Havránek, V. (2008) 'The Documentary Ontology of Forms in Transforming Countries', in M. Lind and H. Steyerl (eds) *The Green Room*. Berlin: Sternberg Press, 128–43.

Heather, R. (2010) 'Hito Steyerl Speaks to Rosemarie Heather', *Apengine*, 22 September; available at http://www.apengine.org/2010/09/hito-steyerl-speaks-to-rosemary-heather/ (accessed 24 May 2013).

Hell, J. and A. Schönle (eds) (2010a) *Ruins of Modernity*. Durham, NC: Duke University Press.

____ (2010) 'Introduction', in Julia Hell and Andreas Schönle (eds) *Ruins of Modernity*. Durham, NC: Duke University Press, pp. 1–14.

Hewison, R. (1987) *The Heritage Industry: Britain in a Climate of Decline*. London: Methuen.

Hight, C. and Roscoe J. (2001) *Faking It: Mock-Documentary and the Subversion of Factuality*. Manchester: Manchester University Press.

Higson, A. (2006) 'Re-presenting the National Past: Nostalgia and Pastiche in the Heritage Films', in L. D. Friedman (ed.) *British Cinema and Thatcherism: Fires Were Started*. London: University College London, 91–109.

Hofer, J. (1934) 'Medical Dissertation on Nostalgia', *Bulletin of the History of Medicine*, 2, 376–91.

Hollein, M. and C. Grunenberg (eds) (2002) *Shopping: A Century of Art and Consumer Culture*. Ostfildern-Ruit: Hatje Cantz.

Huser, R. (1999) 'Nine Minutes in the Yard: A Conversation with Harun Farocki', *Senses of Cinema*, 21, np.

Hutcheon, L. (2000) 'Irony, Nostalgia, and the Postmodern', in Raymond Vervliet and Annemarie Estor (eds) *Methods for the Study of Literature as Cultural Memory*. Amsterdam: Rodopi, 189–207.

Huyssen, A. (1995) 'Memories of Utopia', in *Twilight Memories: Marking Time in a Culture of Amnesia*. New York: Routledge, 85–101.

____ (2003) 'Present Pasts: Media, Politics, Amnesia', in A. Huyssen, *Present Pasts: Urban Palimpsests and the Politics of Memory*. Stanford: Stanford University Press, 11–29.

____ (2006) 'Nostalgia for Ruins', *Grey Room*, 23, 6–21.
Iles, C. (2001) *Into the Light: The Projected Image in American Art 1964–1977*. New York: Whitney Museum.
Iversen, M. (2012) 'Analogue: On Zoe Leonard and Tacita Dean', *Critical Inquiry*, 38, 4, 796–818.
Jackson, M. J. (2005) 'New Work: Rachel Harrison', *CAA Reviews*; http://www.caareviews.org/reviews/741 (accessed 12 May 2014).
____ (2010) *The Experimental Group: Ilya Kabakov, Moscow Conceptualism, Soviet Avant-Gardes*. Chicago: University of Chicago Press.
James, A. (2006) 'Automatism, Arbitrariness and the Oulipian Author', *French Forum*, 31, 2, 111–25.
____ (2009) *Constraining Chance: Georges Perec and the Oulipo*. Evanston, IL.: Northwestern University Press.
Jameson, F. (1985) 'Postmodernism and Consumer Society', in Hal Foster (ed.) *Postmodern Culture*. London: Pluto Press, 111–25.
____ (1988) 'Cognitive Mapping', in C. Nelson and L. Grossberg (eds) *Marxism and the Interpretation of Culture*. Urbana, IL: University of Illinois Press, 347–60.
____ (1991a) *Postmodernism, or, The Cultural Logic of Late Capitalism*. London: Verso.
____ (1991b) 'Video: Surrealism without the Unconscious', in *Postmodernism, or, The Cultural Logic of Late Capitalism*. London: Verso, pp. 1–10.
____ (1998) 'Postmodernism and Consumer Society', in F. Jameson, *The Cultural Turn: Selected Writings on the Postmodern: 1983–1998*. London: Verso, 1–20.
____ (1999) 'Notes on Globalization as a Philosophical Issue', in F. Jameson and M. Miyoshi (eds) *The Cultures of Globalization*. Durham, NC: Duke University Press, 54–77.
____ (2004) 'The Politics of Utopia', *New Left Review*, 25, 35–53.
____ (2007a) *Archaeologies of the Future: The Desire Called Utopia and Other Science Fictions*. London: Verso.
____ (2007b) 'Varieties of the Utopian', in *Archaeologies of the Future: The Desire Called Utopia and Other Science Fictions*. London: Verso pp. 1–9.
____ (2007c) 'Interview with Anders Stephanson', in I. Buchanan (ed.) *Jameson on Jameson: Conversations on Cultural Marxism*. Durham, NC: Duke University Press, 44–73.
____ (2010) 'Utopia as Method, or the Uses of the Future', in Michael D. Gordin, H. Tilley and G. Prakash (eds) *Utopia/Dystopia: Conditions of Historical Possibility*. Princeton, NJ: Princeton University Press, 21–44.
Jay, M. (2000) 'The Trouble with Nowhere', *London Review of Books*, 1 June, 23–4.
Joselit, D. (2010) 'Touch to Begin', in I. Blazwick (ed.) *Museum with Walls*. London: Whitechapel Gallery, 186–98.
Juhasz, A. and J. Lerner (2006) 'Introduction: Phony Definitions and Troubling Taxonomies of the Fake Documentary', in A. Juhasz and J. Lerner (eds) *F Is for Phony: Fake Documentary and Truth's Undoing*. Minneapolis, MN: University of Minnesota Press, 1–38.
Kabakov, I. and E. Kabakov (2001) *Dvorets Proektov/Der Palast der Projekte/The Palace of Projects*. Essen: Kokerei Zollverein.
Kantor, S. G. (2002) *Alfred H. Barr, Jr. and the Intellectual Origins of the Museum of Modern Art*. Cambridge, MA: MIT Press.
Kellner, D. (1997) 'Ernst Bloch, Utopia and Ideology Critique', in J. Owen Daniel and T. Moylan (eds) *Not Yet: Reconsidering Ernst Bloch*. London: Verso, 80–95.

Kelly, M. (2009) *The Political Philosophy of Michel Foucault*. London: Routledge.

Kelsey, J. (2007) 'Sculpture in an Abandoned Field', in *Rachel Harrison: If I Did It*. Zurich: JRP Ringier, 120–5.

Kinkle, J. and A. Toscano (2011) 'Filming the Crisis: A Survey', *Film Quarterly*, 65, 1, 39–51.

Koester, J. (2006) 'Morning of the Magicians', in A. Kreuger (ed.) *Messages from the Unseen: Joachim Koester*. Lund: Veenman.

Kracauer, S. (1960) *Theory of Film: The Redemption of Physical Reality*. Princeton, NJ; Chichester: Princeton University Press.

____ (1987) 'Cult of Distraction: On Berlin's Picture Palaces', *New German Critique*, 40, 91–6.

____ ([1993] 1995) 'Photography', in *The Mass Ornament*. Cambridge, MA: Harvard University Press, 47–63.

Krauss, R. (1999) 'Reinventing the Medium', *Critical Inquiry*, 25, 2, 289–305.

____ (2000) *'A Voyage on the North Sea': Art in the Age of Post-Medium Condition*. London: Thames and Hudson.

____ (2011) *Under the Blue Cup*. Cambridge, MA: MIT Press.

Kraynak, J. (2008) 'Dependent Participation: Bruce Nauman's Environments', in T. Leighton (ed.) *Art and the Moving Image: A Critical Reader*. London: Tate/Afterall Books, 228–45.

Kuni, V. (2009) 'Why I Never Became a Net-Art Historian', in D. Daniels and G. Reisinger (eds) *Net Pioneers 1.0: Contextualizing Early Net-Based Art*. Berlin: Sternberg Press, 181–98.

Labaume, V. (1998) *Le Tombeau de Michel Journiac*. Marseille: Al Dante.

Laclau, E. (2005a) 'Populism: What's in a Name?', in L. B. Larsen, C. Ricupero and N. Schafhausen (eds) *The Populism Reader*. New York: Lukas & Sternberg, 101–11.

____ (2005b) *On Populist Reason*. London: Verso.

Lambert-Beatty, C. (2009) 'Parafiction Make Believe: Parafiction and Plausibility', *October*, 129, 51–84.

Lane, A. (2004) *Yugoslavia: When Ideals Collide*. Basingstoke: Palgrave.

Lears, T. J. J. (1981) *No Place of Grace: Antimodernism and the Transformation of American Culture*. Chicago: Chicago University Press.

Leary, J. P. (2011) 'Detroitism', *Guernica: A Magazine of Arts and Politics*, 15 January.

Lebow, A. (2007) 'Strategic Sentimentality: Nostalgia and the Work of Eleanor Antin', *Camera Obscura*, 22, 3, 129–67.

Leonard, Z. (2002) 'Out of Time', *October*, 100, 88–97.

Le Tellier, H. (2006) *Esthétique de l'Oulipo*. Bordeaux: Le Castor Astral.

Levitas, R. (1990a) *The Concept of Utopia*. London: Philip Allan.

____ (1990b) 'Educated Hope: Ernst Bloch on Abstract and Concrete Utopia', *Utopian Studies*, 1, 2, 13–26.

____ (2000) 'For Utopia: The (Limits of the) Utopian Function in Late Capitalist Society', *Critical Review of International Social and Political Philosophy*, 3, 2–3, 25–43.

____ (2007) 'The Archive of the Feet: Memory, Place and Utopia', in M. J. Griffin and T. Moylan (eds) *Exploring the Utopian Impulse: Essays on Utopian Thought and Practice*. Oxford: Peter Lang, 19–42.

Leyris, J. (2007) 'Objets de Grève, un Patrimoine Militant', *In Situ*, 8; http://insitu.revues.org/3044 (accessed 13 March 2011).

Lialina, O. (2010) 'A Vernacular Web 2', *Contemporary Home Computing*, 12 July; http://contemporary-home-computing.org/vernacular-web-2/ (accessed 14 July 2013).

____ (2014) 'A Vernacular Web', Decade of Web Design Conference, Amsterdam, January 2005; http://art.teleportacia.org/observation/vernacular/ (accessed 14 July 2013).
Lialina, O. and D. Espenschied (eds) (2009) *Digital Folklore*. Stuttgart: Merz & Solitude.
Lind, M. and H. Steyerl (eds) (2008) *The Green Room*. Berlin: Sternberg Press.
Lowenthal, D. (1989) 'Nostalgia Tells It Like It Wasn't', in C. Shaw and M. Chase (eds) *The Imagined Past: History and Nostalgia*. Manchester: Manchester University Press, 18–32.
Lugon, O. (2008) 'Documentary: Authority and Ambiguities', in M. Lind and H. Steyerl (eds) *The Green Room*. Berlin: Sternberg Press, 28–37.
Lukács, G. (1971) 'Reification and Class Consciousness', in G. Lukács, *History and Class Consciousness: Studies in Marxist Dialectic*. London: Merlin Press, 83–209.
____ (1983) *The Historical Novel*. Lincoln, NE: University of Nebraska Press.
Lundqvist, C. (2009) 'Journal No. 1. An Artist's Impression'; available at http://www.modernamuseet.org/v4/templates/template1.asp?lang=Eng&id=3661 (accessed 9 June 2009).
MacDonald, S. (1989) *A Critical Cinema: Interviews with Independent Filmmakers*. Berkeley, CA: University of California Press, 16–54.
Maier, C. (1993) 'A Surfeit of Memory? Reflections on History, Melancholy and Denial', *History and Memory*, 5, 2, 136–52.
Maimon, V. (2009) 'The Third Citizen: On Models of Criticality in Contemporary Artistic Practices', *October*, 129, 85–112.
Makarius, M. (2004) *Ruins*. Paris: Flammarion.
Mannheim, K. (1979) *Ideology and Utopia*. London: Routledge and Kegan Paul.
Marchand, Y. and R. Meffre (2013) *The Ruins of Detroit*. Göttingen: Steidl.
Marin, L. (1984) *Utopics: The Semiological Play of Textual Spaces*, trans. Robert A. Vollrath. Atlantic Highlands, NJ: Humanities Press International.
____ (1993) 'Frontiers of Utopia: Past and Present', *Critical Inquiry*, 19, 3, 397–420.
Martin, S. (2007) 'The Absolute Artwork Meets the Absolute Commodity', *Radical Philosophy*, 146, 15–26.
Marx, K. ([1852] 1978) 'The Eighteenth Brumaire of Louis Bonaparte', in R. C. Tucker (ed.) *The Marx-Engels Reader*. New York: W. W. Norton.
____ ([1867] 2009) *Das Kapital: A Critique of Political Economy*. London: Regnery.
Matt, G. (2008) *Interviews: Vol. 2*. Köln: Walther König.
McDonough, T. (2007) 'Calling from the Inside: Filmic Topologies of the Everyday', *Grey Room*, 26, 6–29.
____ (2010) 'The Photographer of Urban Waste: Zoe Leonard, Photographer as Rag-Picker', *Afterall: A Journal of Art, Context, and Enquiry*, 25, 18–29.
McHugh, G. (2011) *Post-Internet*. Brescia: Link Editions.
Molesworth, H. (2002) 'Rachel Harrison at Greene Naftali Gallery', *Documents*, 21, 49–53.
____ (2008) 'Zoe Leonard: Analogue, 1998–2007', in T. Smith, O. Enwezor and N. Condee (eds) *Antinomies of Art and Culture: Modernity, Postmodernity, Contemporaneity*. Durham, NC: Duke University Press, 187–203.
More, T. (2012) *Utopia*. London: Penguin Books.
Moulène, J. (2007) *Jean-Luc Moulène: Opus 1995–2007 / Documents 1999–2007*. Lisbon: Culturgest.
Moulinié, V. (1999) 'Des oeuvriers ordinaires, lorsque l'ouvrier fait le/du beau', *Terrain*, 32, 37–54;

Mumford, L. (1967) 'Utopia, the City and the Machine', in F. E. Manuel (ed.) *Utopias and Utopian Thought*. Boston: Beacon, 3–24.

Negri, A. (1999) *Insurgencies: Constituent Power and the Modern State*. Minneapolis: University of Minnesota Press.

Negri, T. (2009) 'On Rem Koolhaas', *Radical Philosophy*, 154, 48–50.

Negroponte, N. (1995) 'Being Digital – A Book (P)review', *Wired.com*, 3.02; available at http://archive.wired.com/wired/archive/3.02/negroponte.html?pg=2&topic= (accessed 7 March 2012).

Nesbit, M., H. Obrist and R. Tiravanija (2003) 'What is a Station?', in F. Bonami (ed.) *Dreams and Conflicts: The Dictatorship of the Viewer*. Venice: La Biennale di Venezia.

Nichols, B. (2001) *Introduction to Documentary*. Bloomington, IN: Indiana University Press.

Nora, P. (1989) 'Between Memory and History: Les Lieux de Memoire', *Representations*, 26, 7–24.

_____ (1996) 'General Introduction: Between Memory and History', in P. Nora (ed.) *Realms of Memory: The Construction of the French Past*, vol. 1. New York: Columbia University Press, pp. 1–20.

_____ (ed.) (2006) *Rethinking France: Les Lieux de Mémoire*. Chicago: University of Chicago Press.

Novick, P. (1988) *That Noble Dream: The 'Objectivity Question' and the American Historical Profession*. Cambridge: Cambridge University Press.

Noys, B. (2010) *The Persistence of the Negative: A Critique of Contemporary Continental Theory*. Edinburgh: Edinburgh University Press.

Olson, M. (2012) 'Post-Internet', *Foam Magazine*, 29, 59–63.

Paulsen, K. (2013) 'The Index and the Interface', *Representations*, 122, 1, 83–109.

Pavkovic, A. (1997) *The Fragmentation of Yugoslavia: Nationalism in a Multinational State*. Basingstoke: Palgrave.

Pettifer, J. (2006) *The Albanian Question: Reshaping the Balkans*. London: I.B. Tauris.

Piron, F. (2010) 'A Serious Farce', *Kaleidoscope*, 9, 141–7.

Poster, M. (2002) 'The Aesthetic of Distracting Media', *Culture Machine*, 4; available at http://www.culturemachine.net/ (accessed 14 April 2014).

Powers, J. (2011) 'Darkness on the Edge of Town: Film Meets Digital in Phil Solomon's In Memoriam (Mark LaPore)', *October*, 137, 84–100.

Powrie, P. (1997) *French Cinema in the 1980s: Nostalgia and the Crisis of Masculinity*. Oxford: Oxford University Press.

Rancière, J. (1987) 'Good Times or Pleasure at the Barricades', in A. Rifkin and R. Thomas (eds) *Voices of the People: The Politics and Life of 'La Sociale' at the End of the Second Empire*. London: Routledge & Kegan Paul, 45–94.

_____ ([1981] 1989) *The Nights of Labor: The Worker's Dream in Nineteenth-Century France*. Philadelphia, PA: Temple University Press.

_____ ([1987] 1991) *The Ignorant School Master: Five Lessons in Intellectual Emancipation*. Stanford: Stanford University Press.

_____ (2004) *The Politics of Aesthetics: The Distribution of the Sensible*. London: Continuum.

_____ (2006) 'Documentary Fictions: Marker and the Fiction of Memory', in J. Rancière, *Film Fables*. Oxford: Berg, 157–70.

_____ (2009a) *The Emancipated Spectator*. London: Verso.

_____ (2009b) *Aesthetics and Its Discontents*. Cambridge: Polity Press.

Riff, D. (2011) 'Is This for Real? A Close Reading of *In Free Fall* by Hito Steyerl', *eipicp*; available at http://eipcp.net/transversal/0311/riff/en (accessed 25 February 2013).

Rigby, B. (1991) *Popular Culture in Modern France: A Study of Cultural Discourse*. New York: Routledge.

Rimgaila, S. (2003) *The Strange Afterlife of Stalinist Musical Films*. National Council for Eurasian and East European Studies; available at http://www.ucis.pitt.edu/nceeer/2003-817-08-Salys.pdf (accessed 21 April 2014).

Roberts, J. L. (2000) 'Landscapes of Indifference: Robert Smithson and John Lloyd Stephens in Yucatán', *Art Bulletin*, 82, 3, 544–67.

____ (2004) *Mirror-Travels: Robert Smithson and History*. New Haven, CT: Yale University Press.

Roelstraete, D. (2009a) 'The Way of the Shovel: On the Archaeological Imaginary in Art', *e-flux*, 3, np.

____ (2009b) 'After the Historiographic Turn: Current Findings', *e-flux*, 6, np.

Rosen, G. (1975) 'Nostalgia: A Forgotten Psychological Disorder', *Clio Medica*, 10, 1, 29–51.

Ross, C. (2014) *The Past Is the Present, It's the Future Too: The Temporal Turn in Contemporary Art*. London: Bloomsbury Academic.

Roth, M., C. Lyons and C. Merewether (1997) *Irresistible Decay: Ruins Reclaimed*. Los Angeles: Getty Research Institute for the History of Art and the Humanities.

Saltzman, L. (2006) *Making Memory Matter: Strategies of Remembrance in Contemporary Art*. Chicago: University of Chicago Press.

Salys, R. (2006) *The Strange Afterlife of Stalinist Musical Films*.Washington D. C: National Council for Eurasian and East European Studies.

Sargent, L. T. (2003) 'The Problem of the Flawed Utopia: A Note on the Costs of Eutopia', in Raffaella Baccolini and Tom Moylan (eds) *Dark Horizons: Science Fiction and the Dystopian Imagination*. New York: Routledge, 225–32.

Schwarz, B. (2010) 'Memory, Temporality, Modernity: *Les Lieux de Mémoire*', in B. Schwarz and S. Radstone (eds) *Memory: Histories, Theories, Debates*. New York: Fordham University Press, 41–58.

Scott, F. (2007) *Architecture or Techno-utopia: Politics after Modernism*. Cambridge, MA: MIT Press.

Scribner, C. (2003) *Requiem for Communism*. Cambridge, MA: MIT Press.

Sekula, A. (1981) 'The Traffic in Photographs', *Art Journal*, 41, 15–25.

____ ([1983] 1999) 'Reading an Archive: Photography between Labour and Capital', in J. Evans and S. Hall (eds) *Visual Culture: A Reader*. London: Sage, 181–92.

Shapiro, M. (1994) 'The Still Life as a Personal Object: A Note on Heidegger and Van Gogh', in M. Shapiro, *Theory and Philosophy of Art: Style, Artist, and Society, Selected Papers 4*. New York: George Braziller, 135–42.

Shaviro, S. (2010) *Post-cinematic Affect*. Winchester: Zero Books.

____ (2013) 'Accelerationist Aesthetics: Necessary Inefficiency in Times of Real Subsumption', *e-flux*, 46, np.

Shklar, J. (1998) 'The Political Theory of Utopia: From Melancholy to Nostalgia', in S. Hoffman (ed.) *Political Thought and Political Thinkers*. Chicago: Chicago University Press, 161–74.

Sholis, B. (2005) 'Two into One', *Afterall: A Journal of Art, Context, and Enquiry*, 11, 44–52.

Simmel, G. ([1911] 1965) 'The Ruin', in K. H. Wolff (ed.) *Essays on Sociology, Philosophy and Aesthetics*, trans. David Kettler. New York: Harper & Row, 259–66.

Sloterdijk, P. (2011) *Bubbles: Microspherology*. Cambridge, MA: MIT Press.
Smithson, R. (1995) 'Hotel Palenque', *Parkett*, 43, 117–32.
____ (1996a) 'A Tour of the Monuments of Passaic, New Jersey', in J. Flam (ed.) *Robert Smithson: The Collected Writings*. Berkeley, CA: University of California Press, 68–74.
____ (1996b) 'A Cinematic Atopia', in J. Flam (ed.) *Robert Smithson: The Collected Writings*. Berkeley, CA: University of California Press, 138–42.
Sobchack, V. (2000) 'The Scene of the Screen: Envisioning Cinematic and Electronic "Presence"', in R. Stam and T. Miller (eds) *Film and Theory: An Anthology*. Malden: Blackwell, 67–84.
Sorkin, J. (2008) 'Finding the Right Darkness', *Frieze*, 113, 136–41.
Spieker, S. (2008) *The Big Archive: Art from Bureaucracy*. Cambridge, MA: MIT Press.
Stallabrass, J. (2003a) 'The Aesthetics of Net.Art', *Qui Parle*, 14, 1, 49–72.
____ (2003b) *Internet Art: The Online Clash of Culture and Commerce*. London: Tate.
____ (2005) 'Reasons to Hate Thomson and Craighead', in S. Bode and N. Ernst (eds) *Thomson and Craighead*. London: Film and Video Umbrella, 15–21.
____ (2013) 'Elite Art in an Age of Populism', in A. Dumbadze and S. Hudson (eds) *Contemporary Art: 1989 to the Present*. Oxford: John Wiley & Sons, 39–49.
____ (2014) 'Why Digital Art Is Red', *Leonardo Electronic Almanac*, special issue: 'Red Art: New Utopias in Data Capitalism', 20, 1, 18–19.
Starobinsky, J. (1966) 'The Idea of Nostalgia', *Diogenes*, 14, 54, 81–103.
Stevenson, D. (2013) 'Hypnosis as Data Retrieval and Web Searches as Railway Signs', *The Creators Project*, 20 May; http://thecreatorsproject.vice.com/ (accessed 14 June 2014).
Stewart, S. (1993) *On Longing: Narratives of the Miniature, the Gigantic, the Souvenir, the Collection*. Durham, NC: Duke University Press.
Steyerl, H. (2007a) 'From Ethnicity to Ethics', in M. Lind and T. Zolghadr (eds) *A Fiesta of Tough Choices: Contemporary Art in the Wake of Cultural Policies*. Oslo: Torpedo, 58–70.
____ (2007b) 'Documentary Uncertainty', *A Prior*, 15, 304–6.
____ (2008) 'A Language of Practice', in M. Lind and H. Steyerl (eds) *The Green Room*. Berlin: Sternberg Press, 224–31.
____ (2009) 'In Defense of the Poor Image', *e-flux*, 10, np.
____ (2011) 'In Free Fall: A Thought Experiment on Vertical Perspective', *e-flux*, 14, np.
____ (2013) 'Too Much World: Is the Internet Dead?', *e-flux*, 49, np.
Stiegler, B. (1998) *Technics and Time: The Fault of Epimetheus*. Stanford: Stanford University Press.
Stites, R. (1992) *Russian Popular Culture*. Cambridge: Cambridge University Press.
Streeter, T. (2011) *The Net Effect: Romanticism, Capitalism, and the Internet*. New York: New York University Press.
Sturken, M. (2008) 'Memory, Consumerism, and Media: Reflections on the Emergence of the Field', *Memory Studies*, 1, 73–8.
Sutin, L. (2002) *Do What You Wilt: A Life of Alisteir Crowley*. New York: Godalming.
Tagg, J. (1988) *The Burden of Representation: Essays on Photographies and Histories*. Amherst: University of Massachusetts Press.
____ (2009) *The Disciplinary Frame: Photographic Truths and the Capture of Meaning*. Minneapolis, MN: University of Minnesota Press.
Tannock, S. (1995) 'Nostalgia Critique', *Cultural Studies*, 9, 3, 453–64.

Taylor, R. (1999) 'Singing on the Steppes for Stalin: Ivan Pyr'ev and the Kolkhoz Musical in Soviet Cinema', *Slavic Review*, 58, 1, 143–59.

——— (2003) '"But Eastward, Look, the Land Is Brighter"': Toward a Topography of the Utopia in the Stalinist Musical', in E. Dobrenko, *The Landscape of Stalinism: The Art and Ideology of Soviet Space*. Seattle: University of Washington Press, 201–15.

Terdiman, R. (1993) *Present Past: Modernity and the Memory Crisis*. Ithaca: Cornell University Press.

Thompson, E. P. (1977) *William Morris: Romantic to Revolutionary*. London: Merlin.

Thörn, H., C. Wasshede and T. Nilson (eds) (2011) *Space for Urban Alternatives? Christiania 1971–2011*. Goteborg: Gidlunds Förlag.

Tosh, J. (2006) *The Pursuit of History: Aims, Methods, and New Directions in The Study of Modern History*. Harlow: Longman.

Touraine, A. (1971) *The Post-Industrial Society, Tomorrow's Social History: Classes, Conflicts and Culture in the Programmed Society*, trans. Leonard F. X. Mayhew. New York: Random House.

Tranberg Hansen, K. (2000) *Salaula: The World of Second-Hand Clothing and Zambia*. Chicago: University of Chicago Press.

Tretyakov, S. (2006) 'The Biography of the Object', *October*, 118, 57–62.

Trodd, T. (ed.) (2011) *Screen/Space: The Projected Image in Contemporary Art*. Manchester: Manchester University Press.

Turner, F. (2006) *From Counterculture to Cyberculture: Stewart Brand, the Whole Earth Network, and the Rise of Digital Utopianism*. Chicago: University of Chicago Press.

Turovskaya, M. (1988) 'I. A. Pyr'ev i ego muzykal'nye komedii. K probleme zhanra' [I. A. Pyriev and His Musical Comedies: On the Problem of Genre], *Kino-vedcheskie zapiski* [Scholarly Film Notes], 1, 111–46.

Turvey, M. (2011) 'Ken Jacobs: Digital Revelationist', *October*, 137, 107–24.

Turvey, M., H. Foster, C. Iles, G. Baker, M. Buckingham, A. McCall (2003) 'Roundtable: The Projected Image in Contemporary Art', *October*, 104, 71–96.

Urban, H. B. (2006) *Magia Sexualis: Sex, Magic, and Liberation in Modern Western Esotericism*. Berkeley, CA: University of California.

Vaneigem, R. (1983) *The Revolution of Everyday Life*. London: Left Bank Books/Rebel Press.

Vattimo, G. (1992) 'Utopia, Counter-Utopia, Irony', in *The Transparent Society*. Baltimore, MD: Johns Hopkins University Press, 76–89.

Vickers, M. (1999) *The Albanians: A Modern History*. London: I.B. Tauris.

Vidolke, A. (2012) 'Interview with Ilya and Emilia Kabakov', in C. Esche and B. Groys (eds) *Utopia and Reality: El Lissitzky, Ilya and Emilia Kabakov*. Eindhoven: Van Abbemuseum, 29–39.

Viera, F. (2010) 'The Concept of Utopia', in Gregory Claeys (ed.) *The Cambridge Companion to Utopian Literature*. Cambridge: Cambridge University Press, 3–27.

Vierkant, A. (2010) 'The Image-Object Post Internet'; http://jstchillin.org/artie/vierkant.html (accessed 10 June 2014).

Vijgen, R. (2013) 'The Deleted City: A Digital Archaeology', *Parsons Journal for Information Mapping*, 5, 1–7.

Virilio, P. (2005) *The Accident of Art*, trans. Michael Taormina. New York: Semiotext(e).

Vogl, J. (2011) 'Capital and Money are Profane Gods', *The European*, 20 November; http://www.theeuropean-magazine.com/joseph-vogl--2/6646-the-spectre-of-capital (accessed 12 April 2013).

____ (2012) 'Taming Time: Media of Financialization', *Grey Room*, 46, 72–83.

Waldman, D. and J. Walker (eds) (1999) *Feminism and Documentary*. Minneapolis, MN: University of Minneapolis Press.

Warner, M. (2006) 'Interview', in J. Royoux, M. Warner and G. Greer, *Tacita Dean*. London: Phaidon.

Weibel, P. (2000) 'The Project', in P. Weibel and T. Druckery (eds) *Net Conditions: Art and Global Media*. Cambridge, MA: MIT Press, 8–19.

Weintraub, L., A. Danto and T. McEvilley (1996) *Art on the Edge and Over: Searching for Art's Meaning in Contemporary Society, 1970s–1990s*. Litchfield, CT: Art Insights.

White, H. (2007) 'The Future of Utopia in History', *Historein: A Review of the Past and Other Stories*, 7, 5–19.

Wilson, S. (20003) 'Michel Journiac's Masquerades: Incest, Drag and the Anti-Oedipus', in C. Benthien and I. Stephan (eds) *Mannlichkeit als Maskerade*, Köln: Böhlau Verlag, 128–53.

Winston, B. (1995) *Claiming the Real: The Griersonian Documentary and Its Legitimations*. London: British Film Institute.

Wood, C. (2009) 'Capitalist Realness', in J. Bankowsky, A. Gingeras and C. Wood (eds) *Pop Life: Art in a Material World*. London: Tate.

Wright, P. (1985) *On Living in an Old Country: The National Past in Contemporary Britain*. London: Verso.

Wright, S. (2004) 'Jean-Luc Moulène', *Contemporary*, 67, 62–5.

Wu, T. (2003) 'Network Neutrality, Broadband Discrimination', *Journal of Telecommunications and High Technology Law*, 2, 141–79.

Zickel, Raymond E. and Walter R. Iwaskiw (eds) (1994) *Albania: A Country Study*. Washington: US Government.

Zurbrugg, N. (1991) 'Jameson's Complaint: Video-Art and the Intertextual "Time-Wall"', *Screen*, 32, 1, 16–34.

INDEX

Abandoned Futures 30
Adorno, Theodor 16, 115
Albania 15, 54, 55–60, 81; *see also* Communism
Altermodern 161–4
amnesia 2, 5, 6, 7, 87–9, 95; capitalist 133; culture of 4; historical 58; narratives of 8; postmodern 7; social 4
Analogue 87, 89–99, 119n.15
Anger, Kenneth 32, 49n.23
Anna Karina 30
Appadurai, Arjun 95
Archaeologies of the Future 10, 89
archipelago 161–4; *see also* Bourriaud, Nicolas
Arts and Crafts movement 133–5
Atget, Eugène 94, 119n.15
Atlas 87–9, 101–2
avant-garde 39, 64, 77, 88, 124–5, 132

Bakhtin, Mikhail 98, 104–6
Baldessari, John 100
Balibar, Étienne 14, 26
Barbrook, Richard 17, 125
Barry Lyndon 4
Baselitz, Georg 1
Battle of Neretva, The 65–6
Bauman, Zygmunt 46–7
Belief 136
Benjamin, Walter 132, 162
Berners-Lee, Tim 137–9, 141–4, 154n.5
Bickerton, Ashley 97

Blade Runner 26, 44
Blindfold 57
Bloch, Ernst 11–12, 15–16, 57, 67, 79–80, 117
Blue Galouise Blues – 441 111
Bosnia 63–7, 81; and collective memory 64–6
Both Sides of Broadway 38
Bourriaud, Nicolas 161–4
Brand, Stewart 134–5, 142, 156n.39
Brauntuch, Troy 3
Brave New World 13, 26; *see also* anti-utopia
Bubble House 23–4, 36, 45, 46, 47
Buchloh, Benjamin 1, 8, 87–9,
Buckingham, Mattew 10, 15, 29–30, 37–47, 50n.n.32,33, 132, 162

capitalism 4–7, 13, 16, 17, 44–7, 58, 73, 87–90, 93, 95–6, 98, 102, 106, 110–11, 114–17, 125, 128, 132–7, 142–53, 159n.81, 160n.84, 162–3; and anti-capitalism 40
Carnevale, Fulvia 112
carnival 98, 104–6, 115; and utopia 106
Cefalù 31, 32, 36
Christiania 31, 40–3, 46–7
Chronique d'un Eté 60–2
cinéma vérité 55, 60–2
CNN Interactive Just Got More Interactive 136
Cold War 13, 48

Communism 14, 15, 17, 54–60, 68, 73, 75, 79; Communist Party 55, 58, 59, 63, 71, 76; disintegration of 81; utopia of 75; and propaganda 80; and Russia 15, 54, 56, 69, 77
Ćosić, Vuk 129, 131
counterculture 33, 35, 134–5, 142–3; American 45–6; architecture 45; discourse 17; movement of 33, 35; origins of 143
Craighead, Alison 16–17, 128, 136–44
Critique de la Séparation 61
Crowley, Aleister 31–7
cyber-culture 17, 134, 142–3
cyber-enthusiasts 142
cyber-idealism 137
cybernetics 140, 142
cyberspace 125, 129–30, 133–7, 144

Dada 102
Dammi I Colori 57
Day for Night Christiania 31
Dean, Tacita 2, 15, 23, 24, 36, 45, 158n.59
Debord, Guy 61, 110
Decorative Newsfeeds 136
DeLeeuw, Rudolph 38–9
Deleted City, The 128–31, 133, 135–6
Deleuze, Gilles 14, 145, 148–52, 163
Derrida, Jacques 14
détournement 110–11, 124
discourse: academic 44; architectural 44; of documentary 56; factual 56; formalist 88; media 124; pedagogical 36; memorial 9; Net art 128; public 127, 134; romantic 17, 143; theoretical 56, 127; vernacular 16, 125
DIY 133; *see* do-it-yourself
Dobrenko, Evgeny 75–
Documenta Done 129
documentaries 56, 57, 62, 68, 81; anti-documentary 61; experimental 78, 162; fake 56; mockumentary/mock-documentary 55–6, 78–9; reflexive documentary 56; *see also* mockumentary/mock-documentary

Documenta 12 90
Documenta X Project, Media Plan, Kassel 107
do-it-yourself 17, 129, 134
+ d'ordre, – d'ordre 112
Dot-Store 136
Do You Remember Dolly Bell? 66
Dyer, Richard 73
dystopia 16, 25–7, 43, 47, 53, 98, 128

Eagleton, Terry 16, 106, 115
Edensor, Tim 26
e-flux (journal) 145
Ein-heit 101
entropy 35, 44, 46; aesthetics of 46
Enzensberger, Hans Magnus 115–16
Every Building on the Sunset Strip 38
Eureka 39

Fae Richards Photo Archive, The 96
False Future 37–9
Farocki, Harun 55, 62, 65
Fascism 13, 26, 116
feminism 18n.10, 96
Filles D'Amsterdam, Les 107
Film Fables 78
Filmkritic (magazine) 67
Fisher, Mark 17
Flying Komarov, The 69
Foster, Hal 10, 12, 102
Foucault, Michel 14, 15, 27–9, 36–9, 43–4, 47–8, 135, 141
From the Travel of Jonathan Harker 31
Fukuyama, Francis 13

Gamer 153
Gehr, Ernie 39, 132
gentrification 90, 94
Geocities 128–31, 133–5, 154n.2
geodesic dome 45–5
Ghostgames 57
Godard, Jean-Luc 30, 33, 62
Godfrey, Mark 10, 12
Greene, Rachel 126
Guattari, Félix 14, 145, 148–52, 163
Gunning, Tom 39, 132

Haacke, Hans 94, 119n.15
hacker 123, 134–5, 144; *see also* counterculture
Happiest Man in the World, The 54, 68–77
Harrison, Rachel 16, 87–90, 98–106, 115–17, 162
Hell's Angels 146
heritage film 5
heterotopia 15, 27–9, 36, 37, 43–4, 48, 51n.53; *see also* Foucault, Michel
Hight, Craig 56
hippies 36, 45, 125; Danish community 31, 40
histories 30
Hitler Asleep in His Mercedes 3
Hofer, Johannes 2–3
Hollywood 31, 39, 73, 74, 96, 99, 100, 129, 146–7, 150–1
Horizon 136
Hotel Palenque 35, 36
How To / Internet 123
Hughes, Howard 146
Hutcheon, Linda 1, 18n.10
Huxley, Aldous 13, 26
Huyssen, Andreas 9, 35n.20

I'm a Juvenile Delinquent, Jail Me! 153
individualism 11, 17, 48, 73, 77, 97, 105, 116, 125, 128, 134–6, 143–4
In Free Fall 145, 147–53, 160n.84
Internet: aesthetics of 17, 136, 142; art of 126, 129; creation of/development of 123–4, 128–9, 133, 142–3, 154n.5; obsolescence 132; post-Internet 16, 123–153; regulation of 137; romanticism of 17, 144
Intervista 54, 57–62, 68

Jacobs, Ken 39, 132
Jameson, Frederic 4–12, 17, 44, 47, 89, 116, 147–8, 153, 163
Jay, Martin 28
Jenson, Kevan 146, 147, 150
Jobs, Steve 134, 143; *see also* Internet

Journal No.1. An Artist's Impression 54, 63–6, 68
Journiac, Michel 107

Kabakov, Emilia and Ilya 15, 16, 54–8, 68–81, 84n.n.44,46
Kant Walks, The 31
Kelsey, John 98, 112
Kiefer, Anselm 1
kitsch 87, 94, 97, 129; commodity 99; propaganda 71, 77
Koester, Joachim 2, 15, 29–37, 40–2, 45–7, 162
Koons, Jeff 97, 119n.23
Kosic, Vuk 124
Kracauer, Siegfried 7, 67
Kuban Cossacks, The 68–9, 71, 76
Kubrick, Stanley 4
Kusturica, Emir 66–7

Lak-Kat 57
Left 3, 13, 14, 42, 111, 116
Leonard, Zoe 16, 87–100, 106, 115–17, 119n.14, 158n.59, 162
Le Prince, August 38–9
LES 91–2, 94–5
Levine, Sherrie 3, 30
Levitas, Ruth 10, 12, 80, 163
Lialina, Olia 131–2, 135, 145
Licklider, Joseph 142
Lieux de Mémoire, Les 4–6
lipogram 140–1
Little History of Photography 132
Live Portrait of Tim Berners-Lee (An Early Warning System), A 137–9
London Wall 136
Long Sorrow 57
Lovely Andrea 62
Lowenthal, David 6, 53
Lower East Side of Manhattan 90; *see* LES
Lukács, Georg 7
Lunacharskii, Anatolii 72–3
Lyotard, Jean-François 26, 163

Maier, Charles 9

Man Who Flew in Space from His Apartment, The 69
Marin, Louis 51n.53, 162–3
Marker, Chris 55, 62, 78
Marxism/Marxist 4, 6, 12, 16, 58, 79–81, 95, 99, 115, 117, 118n.5
Marx, Karl 8, 27, 80, 88, 95, 115
mass culture 10, 12, 79, 115, 116, 147, 164
mass media 15, 83n.20, 88
McDonough, Tom 61, 94–6, 119n.19
memory 3–17; collective 2, 16, 64–7, 135; crisis of 7, 8; cultural 2, 5, 9, 35n.20; end-of-memory 5, 6, 7; historical 58, 67; hypertrophy of 4, 9; *lieux de mémoire* 4, 6; politics of 7; popular 135, second-grade 4
Message from Andrée 30
mise-en-scène 73, 75, 150
Mixed Behaviour 57
Modernism 6, 7, 8, 11
MOMA Tank, from Life 124
More, Thomas 25–6, 40, 162; and Utopia 161
Morin, Edgar 61
Morning of the Magicians 31–6
Moulène, Jean-Luc 16, 87–90, 106–16, 121n.44
multiculturalism 3, 65
Murakami, Takeshi 97
My_Contacts 136
My Frontier Is An Endless Wall of Point 30
myth/mythical 17, 34, 35, 36, 44, 53, 79, 125, 129, 134–5, 141, 143–4, 149; see also hacker

Nauman, Bruce 139
Nazism 26, 79
Negri, Toni 14
Negroponte, Nicholas 125–6
neoliberalism/neoliberal 3, 17, 123, 125, 128, 134; and capitalism 116, 143, 145, 153
Net art/artist 123–31, 136, 144, 154n.6; see also Internet
Net.art per se 124

New, The 97
new media 125–7, 137, 139, 141–3
Nights of Labor 113
nihilism 77, 98, 153
Nora, Pierre 3–8, 62
nostalgia 1–18, 20n.35, 26, 30, 53, 70, 98, 123, 128, 131, 133, 137, 163; accusation of 10; characteristic of 8, 10; claims of 8; contemporary 11, 17, 136; critical 8; current 11; definition of 7; denigration of 8; discussion of 5; dismissal of 9; emergence of 9; evaluations of 3; exercise in 7; idea of 4; indictment of 3, 6; image of 1, 2, 3; models of 29; pathologisation of 2; phenomenon of 2; reduction of 7; theory of 5; politics of 30; reactionary 9; undercurrent of 54, 136; utopia and 10, 55, 57, 79
Notes from the Underground 13; see also anti-utopia
November 62
Now I See 57

Occupied Plot 30
October (journal) 132, 136, 156n.36
One Plus One 33
One + One + One 31, 33, 36
One Side of Broadway 37–9
Operation Thunderbolt 146, 147
Oulipo 140–1

Palace of Project, The 69
Palast 25
Pallasvuo, Jaakko 123
Perec, George 43, 140–1
photography: analogue photography 90, 92–3; digital 100; essays 30, 43; kitsch 87; photoconceptualism 30, 94
poor image 144; see also YouTube
populism 116–17; global 97; romantic 116
postmodernism/postmodern 2, 3, 4, 5, 6, 7, 8, 15, 30, 44–5, 56, 57, 89, 104, 116, 147, 153, 163

Produits 111
propaganda: films 15, 53–81 kitsch 71, 77; political 6
Pyriev, Ivan 68, 70–1, 73–4, 76–7

Rabelais, François 31–2, 104
Rancière, Jacques 14, 78, 113–14, 122n.73
Reagan, Ronald 6, 7, 143, 152; *see also* neoliberalism/neoliberal
Related and Different 99
Rhizome (magazine) 128
Richter, Gerard 87–9, 101–2
Right 3, 4, 13, 14, 17, 54
Roelstraete, Dieter 2, 8–9
Roscoe, Janet 56
Ross, Christine 10–12
Rouch, Jean 55, 60–2
Row Housing 30
ruins 15, 26–31, 43–7, 51n.50; aesthetics of 25–6, 44–5, 47; architectural 31; film 45; modern 26; nostalgia for 29; photography 45; porn 45; in reverse 46; romantic 46
Ruscha, Ed 30, 100

Sala, Anri 15, 16, 54–62, 68, 77–81, 83n.21
Sandra of the Tulip House or How to Live in a Free State 40–3
Sarajevo 63, 66–7, 81
schizophrenia 147–9, 151, 152, 148
Schmidt, Michael 101
Scott, Ridley 26, 44
Sekula, Allan 88–9
Several Interruptions 136
Shapolsky et al. Manhattan Real Estate Holdings, a Real Time Social System, as of May 1, 1971 94
Short Films about Flying 138
Short Film about War, A 136
Situation Leading to a Story 37–8
Six Years of Monday 136
Snake in the Grass 99
Snow, Michael 132
Smithson, Robert 25, 35–6, 46, 139

socialism 9, 14, 75, 76, 80, 113; and Socialist Realism 72–3, 75–6; and utopia 113
Sound Mirrors 25
Soviet Union 9, 13, 25, 70–1, 75, 81; post-Soviet 77, propaganda 77, 81; *see also* socialism
Speed 146, 147
split-screen 64–6, 83n.32, 136
Stalinism 26, 27, 69; cinema 75; era 77; ideologies of 13; musicals 71–2, 74, 77; spectacle 68
Steinbach, Haim 97–9
Steyerl, Hito 15–17, 54–7, 62–8, 72, 77–81, 84n.39, 128, 144–53, 158n.65, 159n.81
Stewart, Brand 134, 142
Stewart, Susan 1–2
Stiegler, Bernard 5
Strange Fruit 96
Streeter, Thomas 17, 127, 128, 142–3

Tale of the Siberian Land, A 68–9
Teignmouth Electron 25
Ten Characters 69
Thatcher, Margaret 6, 7, 116, 143, 152; and post-Thatcherism 17; *see also* neoliberalism/neoliberal
Thelema 31, 32, 35–7, 47; frescoes of 33, 37, 47
Thompson, E.P. 12, 143
Thomson, Jon 16–17, 107, 128, 136–42, 144
Tom Tom the Piper's Son 39
totalitarism 23, 26, 48, 53
Touraine, Alain 139–40
Tranberg Hansen, Karen 96–7
Tretyakov, Sergei 145–6
24 Hours in the Life of an Ordinary Woman see *Vingt-quatre Heures dans La Vie d'un Femme Ordinaire*

Ulysse 59
U-ni-ty see *Ein-heit*
utopia: anti-utopia 8, 12, 13–15; utopianism/anti-utopianism 9, 10–15, 29, 53, 57, 77, 81, 112, 115, 128, 134, 135

Uomoduomo 57

Vaisseuax Verseurs, 5 février 1992, Les 111
Valdet 58–62, 68; and deaf people 58–9
Varda, Agnès 58–9
Vattimo, Gianni 26, 44
Vijgen, Richard 16, 17, 128–36, 144–5
Vingt-quatre Heures dans La Vie d'un Femme Ordinaire 107
Vingt-quatre Objets de Grève 87, 106–7, 110–14
visual culture 39, 45, 56, 66, 127
Voyage of the Beagle 87, 89, 99–106, 120n.30

Walter Defends Sarajevo 66
Weather Gauge 136
Weekend 30
Weightless 136
Wired (magazine) 125, 156n.39
working-class 3, 38; and LES 92–95
World War I 102, 146
World War II 13, 27, 58, 63, 66, 71; and post-World War II 142

YouTube 123, 144
Yugoslavia 15, 54–6, 58, 59, 63, 65–6, 81, 83n.33; disintegration of 83n.33; post-war cinema 72

Zuckerberg, Mark 143

GPSR Authorized Representative: Easy Access System Europe, Mustamäe tee
50, 10621 Tallinn, Estonia, gpsr.requests@easproject.com

www.ingramcontent.com/pod-product-compliance
Lightning Source LLC
Chambersburg PA
CBHW021949290426
44108CB00012B/1006